THE BIBLE & THE TAROT

THE BIBLE & THE TAROT

a PERSONAL PILGRIMAGE of DISCOVERY

GIL STAFFORD

Monkfish Book Publishing Company
Rhinebeck, New York

Translations from the Bible are taken from the New Revised Standard Version (NRSV), King James Version (KJV), Jerusalem Bible, or the Tanakh, and sometimes with slight modifications by the author.

Paperback ISBN 978-1-958972-45-8
eBook ISBN 978-1-958972-46-5

Library of Congress Cataloging-in-Publication Data

Names: Stafford, Gil W., 1953- author.
Title: The Bible & the tarot : a personal pilgrimage of discovery / Gil Stafford.
Other titles: Bible and the tarot
Description: Rhinebeck, New York : Monkfish Book Publishing Company, [2024] | Includes bibliographical references.
Identifiers: LCCN 2024017106 (print) | LCCN 2024017107 (ebook) | ISBN 9781958972458 (paperback) | ISBN 9781958972465 (eBook)
Subjects: LCSH: Tarot. | Occultism--Religious aspects--Christianity. | Bible--Criticism, interpretation, etc.
Classification: LCC BF1879.T2 S729 2024 (print) | LCC BF1879.T2 (ebook) | DDC 133.3/2424--dc23/eng/20240606
LC record available at https://lccn.loc.gov/2024017106
LC ebook record available at https://lccn.loc.gov/2024017107

Book and cover design by Colin Rolfe

Monkfish Book Publishing Company
22 East Market Street, Suite 304
Rhinebeck, New York 12572
(845) 876-4861
monkfishpublishing.com

For Catherine

"Isaac embraced faith, seeing Wisdom Sophia dwelling in his wife."

(adapted from the Zohar)

CONTENTS

— CHAPTER 1 —
THE HABITATION OF DRAGONS

The wilderness and the solitary place
Shall be glad for them
And the desert shall rejoice
And blossom as a rose,
In the habitation of dragons.
And there shall be a highway
Named the Sacred Way
Isaiah 35

My colleague said, "Tarot is bad business, my friend."

As an Episcopal priest, I had experienced life as a series of one-on-one conversations. Parishioners dropping by to chat that turned into pastoral counseling. Or, visiting the lonely, the sick, and those in prison. Premarital, marital, and post-marital counseling. Entertaining the questions of the spiritually curious but not religious, or my bishop. Each conversation partner had their own reasonably well-defined boundaries.

The trickiest of all conversations were with my colleagues, other clergy. Vagaries are harbored in the very nature of being an Episcopalian, those who ascribe to the *via media*, "the middle way," some indeterminate position between Roman Catholicism and Protestant-Evangelicalism. Most Episcopal priests cling to the ambiguous middle with all their might—for them, it is the only safe ground. But in truth, there is no single set of dogmas to which all must commit. One's beliefs sort of depend on what congregation you grew up in and what seminary you attended. Even the Nicene Creed is vague enough to leave room through which anyone could maneuver a double-wide house trailer. Episcopalians have the Book of Common Prayer, which has little or nothing to do with dogma. It is what it says it is, a book of prayers that have been collected over the history of Christianity, mostly derived from biblical texts. Catholics have the pope. Lutherans have Martin Luther. Presbyterians have John Calvin. Methodists have John (and Charles) Wesley.

Having lunch with a colleague is only enjoyable if you're talking about the two agreed upon subjects: increasing attendance and raising money. Any other topic and you'll find yourself on the other side of the coin, or roasting over a fire.

"How's things at church?" my colleague asked.

"Okay, I think. Normal stuff, you know. Not enough people and too little money. You?"

"Oh, we had one of our largest Sundays last week. Things are just wonderful. New people almost every week. Seems like every one of them wants to be baptized. We might have forty people for the bishop to confirm at his next visitation."

"When's that?"

"Two weeks. Our congregation is so excited. I'm not sure where we'll put all the people. Great problem, huh?"

"Yeah. I doubt if we'll have that problem at the bishop's next visit."

"When's that?"

"Next year."

"What's wrong? Isn't your church growing? Are you having problems with your vestry?"

"Not that I know of."

"Well, you know, a few couples have left your church and showed up at our ten o'clock service. They were pretty open about why they left?"

"And?"

"You really want to know?"

"You brought it up."

"It's your sermons. They're too liberal."

"Meaning what?"

"One of them said it was, and I quote, 'the whole package.'"

"I don't know what that means."

"Your long hair, your tattoos, you don't wear shoes at the altar."

"That doesn't have anything to do with my sermons."

"They said you mentioned something about going on a pilgrimage. Which they said you talk about too much. Aside from that, they told me you said something about being a fool, and then something about Tarot."

"Do you want to know the context of what I said?"

"No. Tarot is bad business, my friend. Better stick to Jesus loves me. You'll be better off. And you had better hope the bishop doesn't hear about this."

"*This*, meaning, Tarot?" I asked.

"What are you, insane? Of course, Tarot."

I did indeed use Tarot as metaphor in a sermon. And yes, it was in the context of going on a pilgrimage. The Fool in the Tarot deck is headed off to find the True Self. Just like when Abram (Abraham) left home, which was the scripture of the day (Genesis 12:1-4).

God pointed out to Abram that some people would curse him. Why? Because, at the age of seventy-five, he was going to take his family on a pilgrimage to nowhere. Easy to imagine that more than one person called him a fool. My point in the sermon was that maybe God was calling our congregation—and the Episcopal church at large—to leave behind our security and venture out into the unknown. What if we replaced some of the liturgy from the prayer book with contemporary language and imaginative theology? I imagine this is where the two couples who were visiting my colleague's church stopped listening. Or maybe it was simply at the mention of the Tarot. I don't know. When I called them later to see if we could meet, they declined.

Was my using Tarot as a metaphor, a mistake? Was I equally mistaken to suggest replacing some of the prayer book liturgy with twenty-first century language? People had already left the congregation because I'd preached against the war in Iraq, against racism, for gun control, for women's rights regarding their bodies, and in support of immigration and the Dreamer's Act. We were a university congregation. But we were also in the divided state of Arizona. A divided congregation—on all the above topics.

Not sure about the Tarot. I didn't take a poll on that one.

After my colleague told me that "Tarot is bad business," I decided to let the topic drop. We ordered lunch, and as I put the first bite of salad in my mouth, my colleague asked a rhetorical question.

"So, please tell me you don't actually use Tarot cards. Honestly, I can't believe you'd be that unorthodox."

I was chewing, and judiciously decided not to defend myself by mentioning the names of two other clergy I knew who owned and used Tarot cards. I also thought it would be best not to say that I had several Tarot decks and used them daily in my journaling practice. I could honestly say "no" to the question of whether I "use" Tarot cards. I don't. I read the Tarot like a book. But my colleague didn't ask me that question.

Sometimes, silence is best. Don't lie, but don't confess. Confession would be an admission of sin. I haven't sinned. Besides, maybe I don't read Tarot—the Tarot reads me. Yes, that's better. But that would take too much explanation.

"I read Tarot," I said.

"Holy Jesus," my lunch mate said.

I put more salad in my mouth.

"Well, for your sake, I hope the bishop will ignore the rumors that are circling about."

The server came by, and while filling our glasses of water, asked if I wanted more coffee. If my mouth wasn't full, I would have ordered something stronger. Instead, I smiled and nodded yes.

My colleague went on, "Gil, when I was a kid, a friend gave me a deck of Tarot cards. My friend went through the cards and showed me how to do a three-card draw."

In the middle of a sip, I had to choke the coffee back to keep from spewing it across the table.

My colleague seemed not to notice. "That night, I hid in the closet in my room," they went on. "I had a tiny flashlight. I was in there in case my mom burst in unannounced. She had the bad habit of never knocking. I was so afraid she'd find out. You know, lose her shit."

"Anyway. I shuffled the deck and drew three cards, exactly like my friend had instructed. And do you know what I drew?" They paused.

I thought, *The Devil, The Hanged Man, and Death.*

My colleague leaned over the table and mouthed barely audibly, "The Devil, The Hanged Man, and Death." Leaning back, they said, "When I saw the cards, I put my hand over my mouth to keep from screaming. And, do you know what I thought?"

I tried to give a quizzical look. But, instead, must have thrown off my weirdness vibe.

"You know, don't you? I know you know what that means."

"It's more important what you think it means."

"This isn't therapy. I know you know what those cards mean. What they were forecasting."

"There are as many meanings for those three cards as there are for every person who draws them. It's like the Bible, a hidden text that requires a polyvalent interpretation."

"No wonder the people that left your church think you're a heretic."

"I was quoting Walter Brueggemann. Sorry. Back to your story," I said.

"Never mind. I took a risk telling you this. You can't repeat this to anyone."

"Held in priestly confidentiality."

"No one abides by that."

"Okay. Well, I do," I said.

The server came by again. "Would you folks need anything else? Dessert maybe?" We demurred and the server set the check on the table. "No hurry." I set down my credit card.

"You don't have to buy my lunch."

"I'm afraid I've caused you undue stress."

My companion sighed. We sat in silence until I signed the bill, and then walked together to our cars. "I am sorry if I've upset you," I said.

"Just remember not to tell anyone," my colleague implored. Then we shook hands and drove away in opposite directions.

We would meet again, but the topic of Tarot never came up. I hoped it would. But I also wouldn't push my experience of the beauty of the Bible and the Tarot working in tandem upon another person. I wanted our exploration of the two to be an invitation, as in "come and see" from Psalms 46:8 and John 1:39. And I definitely did not want this to be a conversation we had while hiding in a closet.

The Bible and the Tarot is for those who might read the Bible daily as well as those who know very little about it but are not averse to it. As well as those who are curious about the Tarot and those who read the Tarot daily. You don't need a background in either Bible or Tarot to gain insights from what you find here. I do, however, suggest that you have a Bible and a deck of Tarot cards close at hand as you make your pilgrimage.

You might be curious about the Tarot because your teenager has picked up a deck. Possibly you've met a new friend or an old acquaintance who talked about Tarot with glowing reviews. Or someone in your community condemned the use of these cards as the work of the devil, but you want to find out for yourself. *The Bible and the Tarot* is an easy to understand, non-confrontational presentation of the material.

This is a personal pilgrimage of discovery, a bridge between the Bible and the narrative of the Tarot. At times my book will read like a novel. At other times it's a commentary on the Bible and the Tarot, both material manifestations of archetypal ideas. The biblical mythos with its complex characters, actors, symbols, stories, and parables are the backstory of the magnificent creatures of the Tarot's inner psychic world—a place where Tarot images function as portable stained-glass windows for the Bible's beguiling story. Together, Bible and Tarot portrait the journey of the universal human narrative with personal application. To understand both and their effect on our lives we must open our imagination. For, to know one's self depends on a willingness to ask soul-shaking questions about our assumptions.

The first two chapters provide the needed background to place these two mystical texts in correspondence. Then, *The Bible and the Tarot* maps the ancient story of the androgynous Fool on their soul pilgrimage through the other twenty-one Major Arcana of the Tarot. The subsequent two chapters on the House of Tarot explore the Minor Arcana and their numerology in relationship to the Bible.

Finally, we investigate how to read the Tarot and Bible in tandem. Both can provoke the unconscious, the dream world, waking visions as well as provide wise instruction on how to live a healthy life. In a final chapter I have provided easy to follow, practical methods of connecting the mysteries of the biblical story with the archetypal images of the Tarot. Reading the two together can expand our imagination and understanding of the complex world we live in. And *The Bible and the Tarot* is a tool that can help you articulate the story of your pilgrimage through life.

— CHAPTER 2 —

THE BIBLE

The devoted seek out
The Wisdom of all the ancients,
Penetrates the hidden meanings of proverbs,
And are at home with the obscurities of parables.
Listen to me my faithful children and blossom
Like a rose growing by a stream of water.
Ecclesiasticus 39

Thomas Cranmer wrote my favorite prayer in the Book of Common Prayer in 1549. Cranmer (1489-1556) was the chief compiler and author of the first prayer book of the Church of England. He borrowed many of the prayers and most of the liturgy from ancient Roman Catholic books that were steeped in scripture. What made the first Anglican prayer book so valuable was its accessibility to those who read English (which was way more people than those who could read the Latin of Roman Catholic books).

In the most recent version of the Book of Common Prayer (1979), Proper 28 is to be prayed on the Sunday closest to November 16:

> Blessed Lord, who cause all holy scriptures to be written for our learning: Grant us so to hear them, read, mark, learn, and inwardly digest them, that we may embrace and ever hold fast the blessed hope of everlasting life, which you have given us in our Savior Jesus Christ; who lives and reigns with you and the Holy Spirit, one God, for ever and ever. Amen.

This mirrors the prophet Ezekiel's vision. The Lord said, "mark well, look closely, and listen attentively," and then "Open your mouth, and eat this scroll. Then I ate it; and in my mouth it was as sweet as honey." Written on the scroll were words of "lamentations, mourning, and woe," for Ezekiel was being sent to a rebellious people who were living among scorpions (Ezekiel 2 and 3).

To take seriously the admonition of inwardly digesting the scroll of shadows (scorpions) means to inquire deeply of the text. To search between the words and lines for a dialogue with the Divine. To have ears to hear requires an imagination that is willing to experience the nuances and sublime subtlety of what is not written on the page, but on the heart. The Bible is a living document as long as the reader will "read, mark, learn, and inwardly digest" the whole of the text. I've also found that it's good to have an antacid close at hand.

As soon as I could read, my parents bought me a Bible for Christmas. I still have it. I've worn out dozens of Bibles—reading, marking, learning, and inwardly digesting every one of them. Long before considering a life of work in the church, I read countless books on biblical history, commentaries, and theology. To the first Episcopal service I attended, I carried my Bible. The priest politely and gently suggested I drop by the church bookstore and pick up a Book of Common Prayer, which I came to realize was the book to carry there. But no one ever suggested I eat the BCP. It was the Bible that remained the daily source of nourishment.

My parents were dedicated Southern Baptists. They took my sister and me to church twice on Sunday and every Wednesday night. Oddly enough, Mom never said much to me about leaving her church. It wasn't until I was on the track toward ordination that the questions arose. I invited her and Dad to attend a service with us. At lunch afterwards, she said that many of her friends told her that Episcopalians aren't Christians. These friends told her that Episcopalians didn't believe in the Bible. Some of the folks who had known me as a child were wondering aloud to my mom if I ever was really a Christian.

After a bit of silence, Mom followed that last sentence with, "Well, I heard more scripture read this morning than I ever have at a service in my own church. You read the Old Testament, an Epistle, a Psalm, and the New Testament. Good Lord, if you all aren't Christians...well...you can't read that much Bible and not be Christians." Little wonder I had dreams about tearing pages out of the Bible and eating them.

The Episcopal Church has a beautiful interactive technique for teaching children the Bible stories. Jerome Berryman wrote the stories and the curriculum, which is called *Godly Play.* The stories come complete with "holy toys," manipulatives to be used in bringing the ancient tales to life. The action takes place with everyone sitting on the floor in a circle. After the storyteller finishes, children are invited to join in the play by making the story their own. They can use the holy toys and tell the story to one another. They can act out the story. Or they can use art supplies to create their own version of what they heard. The best part for me is when the children arrive early for Sunday school, asking if they can be the morning's storyteller. The stories have become a part of their daily diet.

I have come to see the Tarot as an adult version of godly play. A small box of holy toys that asks me questions about how I'm digesting the scroll I have just consumed.

Images on Tarot cards all have biblical references and carry with them backstories from both the Hebrew Bible and the New Testament: Abraham, Sarah, the Pharoah, the Queen of Sheba, Joseph, Isaac, Rebecca, Jacob, Rachel, Leah, David, Solomon, the stories of Exodus and exile, the Tree of Life, The Tree of the Knowledge of Good and Evil, Lucifer, Jesus, birth, death, pilgrimage, the sun, the moon, the planets, the stars, Wisdom Sophia, Judgment Day, Ezekiel's chariot, temperance, strength, love, justice, and choice. Each like a little portable holy toy.

But there is so much fear. One Christian website states, "To receive a Tarot reading is to attempt to find out things about one's life or future through the occult.... Obviously, reading Tarot cards places a heavy emphasis on fate, 'hidden knowledge,' and superstition." I have to wonder if whoever wrote that realizes how much the Bible places a heavy emphasis on fate, hidden knowledge, and superstition? The most cited texts from the Bible used as an admonition against Tarot are these:

◊ Leviticus 19:26 "You shall eat not anything with its blood. You shall not practice augury or witchcraft."

◊ Deuteronomy 18:10 "No one shall be found among you who makes a son or daughter pass through fire, or who practices divination, or is a soothsayer, or an augur, or a sorcerer, or one who casts spells, or who consults ghosts or spirits, or who seeks oracles from the dead."

◊ Acts 16:16-18 "One day, as we were going to the place of prayer, we met a slave-girl who had a spirit of divination and brought her owners a great deal of money by fortune-telling. While she followed Paul and us, she would cry out, 'These men are slaves of the Most High God, who proclaim to you a way of salvation.' She kept doing this for many days. But Paul, very much annoyed, turned and said to the spirit, 'I order you in the name of Jesus Christ to come out of her.' And it came out that very hour."

Ezekiel, in the biblical book named for him, offers two exceptions for the use of divination. The first being, that divination is fine as long as it's not a "lying divination" (Ezekiel 13:7). Nobody wants a Tarot reader to lie to them. So, absolutely, ban those lying Tarot readers. Second, divination seems to be perfectly okay as long as it benefits God's purpose. With Ezekiel at his side as interpreter, King Nebuchadnezzar stood at a crossroads. He used several divinatory techniques to decide which road to travel. God had some stake in the path Nebuchadnezzar would choose. The king would shake arrows, which sounds similar to the *I-Ching*. He also consulted the teraphim, which were amulets or images of gods, kind of like Tarot. And he used Hepatoscopy, interpreting the markings across a liver. I guess that's okay unless it was your liver the king wanted to use for divination.

Here are a few things to remember when it comes to Tarot and divination:

◊ Most people who own and use Tarot decks do not read Tarot for other people. The cards are for their personal use and practice.

◊ Most Tarot readers—those who read for themselves as well as those who read for other people—are not fortune-tellers. Tarot reading is a form of personality typing, like the Myers-Briggs Type Indicator or the Enneagram. The cards are used to tell the story of our personal journey through life. Readers use Tarot cards as a mirror for them to see what's happening. And to sort out sticky situations and relationships. They can also use the cards for dream interpretation.

◊ Tarot can help us see our blind spots and deal with our shadows.
◊ I use Tarot in my spiritual companion (direction) practice to help people sort out all of the above.

The Bible, as you probably already know, is full of restrictions and long lists of "thou shalt nots" that are ignored by most Christians today. All for good and valid reasons. Keeping that in mind, let me respond quickly to those three oft-cited passages.

Regarding the Leviticus text, if you chose to follow the second sentence, be sure to follow the first and only eat your steak and hamburger very well done—no pink centers for you.

The Deuteronomy text is straightforward, so if you want to adhere to it, don't use Tarot for future-telling. Also, don't talk to your dead uncle Bob and Aunt Louise. And make sure you also follow all the other 613 Levitical laws listed in Deuteronomy and Leviticus, like not wearing clothes made of mixed fabrics. And be sure to discipline your children in ways that will eventually find you in prison.

The sixteenth chapter of Acts is an interesting expose on the personality of Paul, as well as a curious insight into divination. Paul was the first missionary of Christianity. In this story, Paul and some of his followers had serious disagreements (Acts 15-16). Their differences were so severe that they parted company with the apostle. Typical church politics. At that point, Paul had a series of visions and heard voices of the spirit and Jesus. Oops, he violated the admonition we just read in Deuteronomy.

Anyway, Paul, now with new followers, told them that the visions, voices, and dreams he experienced had instructed him (and therefore, them as well) to take a long journey by land and sea to the Roman colony of Philippi. There he goes again, violating the scriptural law. Before they got on the ship, however, all of his male followers had to be circumcised. Well, isn't that a quaint story? But it gets better. Upon their arrival in Philippi, a "slave-girl" followed them throughout the city, repeatedly crying out, "These men are slaves of the Most High God, who proclaim to you a way of salvation." I sometimes wonder if Paul paid her to be a walking vocal billboard.

In fact, Paul thought she was terribly annoying. Was he offended by slavery? Obviously not hers. Was he afraid that others would know that he and his disciples were slaves to the Most High God? Paul called himself a "slave of Jesus Christ." Maybe Paul didn't like being shown up by a woman? This story makes little sense. Regardless, these three verses have been used by Christians as a deterrent against Tarot cards. The story could, however, be used to teach us about the immorality of enslaving people—but fortune-telling and the use of Tarot, evidently, are greater sins. Hmm, I wonder.

"Can we talk about the Bible?" I asked my Baptist pastor years ago. Our relationship was more friend to friend than pastor to parishioner. But I deeply respected his knowledge, and we often had sweeping theological discussions. His office was only large enough for his small metal desk and the two chairs that sat across from him. Well, his office was actually larger, except that it was overpowered by the double-layered bookshelves that nearly swallowed his desk and two chairs. I once asked him how many books he had and he simply waved his hand around the room and laughingly said, "that many."

"Okay," he said. "We can talk about the Bible but with one condition. We stick to the canon."

"What do you mean?"

"This canon." He pointed to the Bible sitting open on his desk.

"The Protestant version of the Bible?"

"The Bible with sixty-six books. That canonical Bible," he said.

"What about the Apocrypha?"

"That's my point. That opens the conversation to a debatable number of additional books that have not all been recognized as scripture."

"By whom?"

"I already told you. Protestants."

"What about Episcopalians? They consider themselves to be Protestants. It even says so in the official name: The Protestant Episcopal Church of the United States. And they include the Apocrypha in their Bible."

"Good for them. Then, I'll rephrase my answer. Protestant Evangelicals. How's that? Good enough for you?"

"Well, what about the Dead Sea Scrolls?"

"If you want to talk about the Bible, then we stick to the canon with sixty-six books. If you want to talk about the Apocrypha, then we can talk about the Apocrypha. If you want to talk about the Dead Sea Scrolls, then that's another conversation. To include all three in one conversation can only lead to a migraine, mine not yours." At that point, he pulled his well-worn book with the black leather cover in front of him. Tapping his fingers on the cover, he said, "So, if you want to talk about the Bible, then we will stick to this Bible."

"That feels, so...so...what's the word I'm looking for?"

"Doable."

"Restrictive?"

"Possible."

"Confining?"

"Productive."

"Claustrophobic. That's it. Yes. Claustrophobic. Being confined to the biblical canon as my spiritual inspiration and resource feels claustrophobic. You know my doctor wanted me to take an MRI," I said. "I told her I couldn't do that. I'm claustrophobic. But she encouraged me, saying it would be an excellent opportunity to practice my meditation technique."

"Are you sick?"

"I don't think so."

"Did you get the results from the MRI?"

"No. There weren't any results. I only lasted eleven minutes in that tomb. Then I had a panic attack. That was two weeks ago, and I still have a high level of anxiety and nightmares."

"Is that why you want to talk about God?" he asked, shifting into pastor mode.

"I wanted to talk about the Bible. Not God. But if you want to talk about God, then I have one condition."

"I think I know where this is going," he said.

"We have to stick to the Rose Bible."

"Okay, I'll fall for it. What is the Rose Bible?"

"The word of the mystics in pictorial form."

"Is this something you made up?"

"Not really. Well, I kind of borrowed the idea from another book."

He chuckled, sort of, as he looked at his watch. "Ah, I hate to do this, but I have to make a hospital visit and I promised the family I'd be there before the end of visiting hours."

"Do you have time for me to tell you a dream?" I asked.

"If you can tell it to me on the way to my car." He pulled on his coat, put his phone and keys in his pocket, and picked up his Bible. "Ready," he said. And we walked out the door.

"I was walking down a long pathway into a cave. The further I went the narrower the shaft became. Eventually the light from the entrance faded. The air was stifling and began to close in on my throat. A daimon fetched me further into darkness. I broke into a cold sweat as panic clutched my heart. I could have stopped, turned back, but the blackness had plummeted me into confusion. I was lost and then the silence was broken."

My pastor opened his car door and slid into the driver's seat. Before closing the door, he asked, "Was this dream before or after your failed attempt at an MRI?"

"I had this dream months ago. And there's more."

"I don't believe in what I'm about to say—but if I did believe in such stuff—maybe you had a prophetic dream."

"What do you mean?"

"Oh, come on. It's obvious," he laughed with pleasure. "Think about it. I'll see you Sunday."

He closed the door, started the engine, and backed out of the parking lot, leaving me standing there as the desert sun slid down into a rose-colored sky. Souls who had died that day were gathering in Ezekiel's chariot to make their journey across eternity's panorama. Maybe the sunset was forecasting my endings with one tradition and a venture into another?

An ancient mystic wrote the first words of the mythical "Rose Bible" eons ago when they carved a spiral into a stone. Petals of the rose form a deep spiral and may have inspired those magical etchings. From the beginning of time, artists have tried to capture the imagination of our relationship with these heavenly flowers. Entwined, the rose, the spiral, and the stone have long been symbols in the archetypal book of Tarot.

The beauty and mystery of the Rosey Tarot attracts the full complement of our six senses: sight, smell, touch, taste, sound, and our Spidey sense. In contemplation of the mystical spiraled rose, we experience a bouquet of multi-colored flowers, collectively containing the wisdom of the ages. A spectrum of divine colors spans the rainbow. Red and white are the soul of love and remembrance. Red of love and sacrifice. White of holiness. Pink, gratitude. Purple, awe and wonder. And the yellow is the rose of wisdom. The intoxicating emblem of love is associated with the aroma of the angels, the incense rising into heaven (Revelation 8:3), pleasing the nostrils of God (Philippians 4:18).

For those who love to bake, the use of rose water and rose extract can excite our taste buds with a spiritual delight as well as provide a medicinal effect. Roses can have anywhere from thirty to forty petals of velvet to touch. Each represents a knot of wisdom along the flower's spiral of prayer beads.

The poetic metaphor of the singular rose is a reminder of their collective irascibility—such beauty, so much pain. How ironic if the Romans had twisted the spiraled crown of thorns from a rosebush. "I am the rose of Sharon," would take on its paradoxical intent. Enticing beyond imagination, but oh so dangerous. The Three of Swords in the *Hidden Realms Tarot* pictures a woman wearing a crown of pink roses while she clutches three large, open red roses by the stems. Blood is streaming between her fingers onto her pale pink chiffon dress. Easy to imagine that she is the broken-hearted Mary Magdalene.

A rose has symbolic importance in many mystical traditions, and deeply so in the Abrahamic trio. Kabbalists of Judaism picture the rose as the Divine opening into the revelation of Its Presence. For the Sufi of Islam, the rose and its long stem unfold the eternal mystical and spiritual journey toward the manifestation, grace, and Love of the Divine. Christian mystics have entwined the rose within their Marian devotion. Gnostics and alchemists wrote of the *Rosa Mystica*—the mystical rose—Wisdom Sophia, as the feminine of the Divine. Rosicrucian's Chartres labyrinth is known as the Sacred Way of the Rose. There are many traditions that reflect the poetic mystery of the scriptural epigraphs that opened the first two chapters of this book. By picturing the Bible as a spiraled rose, the work of soul-making has "plunged me into the darkness of absolute light"[1] There, in the luminous light, we experience the capaciousness of a relationship with the Divine, the Bible, and the Tarot, which knows no limits.

Second century Christian scholar Origen considered the Gospel of John to be the "first" word, meaning that John's allegorical writings should be considered the primary document when interpreting Jesus as the Christ. 1,900 years later, Anglican Bishop and theologian, John A.T. Robinson, would make a similar case in his book, *The Priority of John.* From its beginning, John's gospel has been considered the bible of Christian mystics and the lens through which Jesus is best understood.

There are at least three techniques of reading the Bible, or any sacred text, for that matter.

1. Read for instruction on how to live an ethical and moral life.
2. Read for wisdom on how to live a life with purpose and meaning.
3. Read for enlightenment and how to be at one with the Divine.

I've incorporated these into how I read the Book of Tarot, as well. On this pilgrimage, we will follow The Fool on the path of instruction, the path of wisdom, and the path of enlightenment. Each path incorporates seven of the twenty-one Major Arcana. (More on this in chapter 3.)

The Bible is a collection of narrative nonfiction that includes instructions for living, wisdom teaching, and guides us on how to reach enlightenment. The prophets, apostles, and Jesus incorporated parables, metaphors, allegories, and poetry to pass along these pearls that are often hidden in the fields. All stories are true, just some had eyewitnesses. At the same time, some stories are false because they need to be. And yet, in a weird way, every story is simultaneously true and false because there are always two sides to every coin. The purpose of every scripture is simple—so simple it's unbelievable: to nurture the polyvalent, complex, and ineffable stream of experiences that manifest themselves between the Lover and the Beloved.

As much as any religion might want to warn their believers against the evils of the Tarot, it's the Bible that encourages us to embrace the mystical experiences of life. And that's what Tarot is: a pictorial expression of the experiences of life. From the first page of the Bible to the last, almost everyone had heard the voice of the Lord, whom they couldn't see, and yet they responded with their entire being. Some did what they were told while others, understandably, ran away. Others had visions. Some heard voices of angels. God and the angels spoke to some in dreams and others in person. Prophets prophesied warnings about the future. Some talked to the dead, including Jesus, who spoke with Elijah and Moses. And the disciples and Mary Magdalene all talked to Jesus after he had been in the tomb for three days. Resurrected or apparition, they talked to someone who had been dead. They all believed in what they saw so much so that they staked their lives on it. The disciples even drew lots to choose the thirteenth disciple.

So, why are we expected to accept voices, visions, dreams, the dead talking, and blind luck that's in the Bible but are then supposed to dismiss the Tarot? All the spiritual experiences recorded in the Bible, the Apocrypha, the Dead Sea Scrolls—and in the stories of mystics who we don't find in the Bible like Hildegard of Bingen, Saint Teresa of Avila, Saint John of the Cross, Julian of Norwich, Marguerite Porette, Ibn al-Arabi, Rumi, and Ba'al Shem Tov—are human experiences. Humans having spiritual experiences—making humans spiritual beings. Human and spiritual beings, the living and the dead, all exist together in a cosmic soup—the milieu of the material and the spiritual, the living and the dead, the good and the evil, God and all the rest of it—one ineffable cauldron of eternal Divinity.

The Bible and the Tarot presents the stories found in the Bible, and occasionally readings that appear outside the canon, in their relationship with Tarot. Our work is to imagine how those human experiences are reflected in the Tarot, a universal story for all ages, past, present, and those to come. The beauty of Tarot is its ability to incorporate the story of any religion without taking on its religious content—and not just the religions founded under the eye of Abraham. Tarot reflects the human quest to find one's True Self, to discover one's interior divine, a mystical journey into the blinding light.

> Only when you have come to know
> Your true Self will you be fully known—
> Realizing at last that you
> Are a child of the Living One. (Gospel of Thomas, Logion 3)

Both Bible and Tarot are filled with events, dreams, visions, and imaginations about the evolving relationship between the pilgrim child and the Living One, the Beloved and the Lover. Such a book is never finished, always evolving.

> There are so many other things that Jesus [and other mystics] did, [that] if every one of them were written down, I suppose that the world itself could not contain the books that would be written. (John 21:25)

Our work is to hear what the Spirit has to say in order to hear, read, mark, learn, and inwardly digest the mystic's book of the rose. To do so, we must be willing to walk the sacred path in the desert where the roses grow by the water and the dragons inhabit (Isaiah 35).

My inspirations are many and varied. Benedictine abbess, writer, composer, theologian, herbalist, and mystic Hildegard of Bingen (1098-1179) and her "The Man in Sapphire Blue," continually draw me into its center. Anchorite and first English woman author, Julian of Norwich (1343-1146?), in *Showings of Love* repeatedly refers to Jesus Christ in feminine terms. Sufi mystic and author, Llewellyn Vaughn-Lee with *The Lover and the Serpent* has deeply influenced my understanding of spirituality and living life in the dream of the Divine. Sufi, professor, and director of the UC Berkeley Medical Anthropology Program, Stephania Pandolfo, has enlightened how I interpret the life of the mystic, art, and mental illness. And descendent of the founder of Hasidic Judaism, Pearl Epstein, has provided me an opening into the mystical world with her *Kabbalah: The Way of the Jewish Mystic.* In the chapters ahead you will find traces of all of their work.

I confess, as did the alchemist and physician, Paracelsus (1493-1541), "I may write as a pagan, but I am a Christian." With that in mind, the two people who have most influenced my connections between the Bible and the Tarot are Episcopal priest and mystic Cynthia Bourgeault, and psychiatrist Carl Jung (1875-1961). Both have written extensively on the Bible, and its intersection with the mystical realm and the story of the Tarot. Interestingly, Bourgeault rarely mentions Jung in any of her books. She relies heavily on Jacob Boehme and George Gurdjieff as her spiritual guides, which also work well with Jungian philosophy. Bourgeault, Jung, and the many others you will read about in this book have written their script into my personal Rose Bible.

Our goal is to build a practice that will enlighten our way and strengthen our soul. As my friend Gaymon Bennett says, "Our craftwork is the foundation of our soulwork." Tarot compliments the craftwork of soul-making. What we work on works on us.

We walk the desert's sacred path under The Moon in the cool of night. On the way we encounter the characters of the Bible reflected in the Tarot. And as pilgrims, we're attentive to those who manifest in our dreams with something to teach us.

— CHAPTER 3 —
THE BOOK OF TAROT

And I looked, and behold
A whirlwind came out of the north,
A great cloud,
And a fire enfolding itself...
Thereof came four living creatures...
And they had hands under their wings...
They had four faces,
Of a man, of a lion, of an ox, of an eagle.
Ezekiel 1

The Tarot is a book, and each card is its own chapter. As Carl Jung pointed out, the collective of our dreams can only be understood as a singular narrative; likewise, the Tarot cards can only be understood within the context of the entirety of its book.[2] He also wrote in the *Red Book* that "There are not many truths, there are only a few. Their meaning is too deep to grasp other than in symbols."[3] The Tarot is a book of symbols; one intended to assist us in unpacking those hidden truths.

The word *tarot* is a French derivative of the Italian *tarocchi,* which was the fifteenth century name for the twenty-two picture cards that set the deck apart from standard playing cards. Those twenty-two picture cards are known as the Major Arcana or the "Greater Secrets." *Arcana* is a Latin word meaning mysterious or secret knowledge.[4]

The remaining fifty-six cards in the deck are known as the Minor Arcana, the "Lesser Secrets." The Minors resemble regular playing cards, except that it contains four more cards than a traditional deck. The fifty-six cards constitute four suits, Swords, Wands, Cups, and Pentacles.

Each suit has a court of King, Queen, Knight, and Page and the Ace to Ten cards, referred to as pips. The Major cards are often considered the fifth suit, or the quintessence.[5] Each Major card, or asset, can be an ally to any card of the Minors. The sixteenth-century tarotists considered this arrangement of the court cards and the pips to be the standard for the Minor Arcana. And most contemporary Tarot readers follow this bipartite organization of the deck.

The Major cards will be covered in chapters 4-25. I will discuss the pips, or numbered cards, in chapter 26, and the court cards in chapter 27. Following are the cards of the Major Arcana.

0 The Fool
1 The Magician
2 The High Priestess
3 The Empress
4 The Emperor
5 The Hierophant
6 The Lovers
7 The Chariot
8 Strength
9 The Hermit
10 The Wheel of Fortune
11 Justice
12 The Hanged Man
13 Death
14 Temperance
15 The Devil
16 The Tower
17 The Star
18 The Moon
19 The Sun
20 Judgment
21 The World

We get a more complete picture of life when we relate to the archetypal images of the Major Arcana as pieces of the larger puzzle. Every card is a component of a much more complex narrative. The images of the primordial archetypes reflect instinctive behavioral patterns found in the psyche. They rise from the unconscious and make themselves present in our visible world as symbols. For example, we see the sun in our everyday life. As an archetype, it is a symbol of the light of a human's developed consciousness. The Major Arcana are symbols of the complex process of human maturation. They contain a limitless resource for what Carl Jung termed as individuation. The Minor Arcana are reflections of how this undertaking plays itself out in our everyday life.

I read Tarot for myself and others as meditation, contemplation, personality typing, dream interpretation, and the imaginal, or as Jung put it, "active imagination." I incorporate the Tarot into my spiritual companioning sessions. There's nothing in the Bible against any of those practices. I like to think of Tarot cards as stained-glass windows. We can envision what the art is telling us, but we can also see through the window in a new imaginative way. Using the Tarot for divination, or cartomancy, is another matter.

Divination is used to decide which road to take. As we saw in the previous chapter, King Nebuchadnezzar was standing at a crossroads. He "threw the arrows" to help discern the path to travel, not to see what was waiting for him at his destination. Proverbs contains two verses about casting lots. "The lot is cast into the lap but the decision is the Lord's alone" (16:35). And "Casting the lots puts an end to disputes and decides between powerful contenders" (18:18). Jesus's disciples may have had these verses in mind when they chose Judas's replacement (Acts 2:26). By the third century CE, bibliomancy had become a popular technique for making difficult decisions. For example, Saint Augustine of Hippo affirmed his conversion to Christianity when he randomly opened the Bible to Romans 13:13-14. Torn by temptation, Augustine read that he should "make no provisions" to satisfy his fleshly desires. And Saint Francis reportedly used the Roman Missal to answer an inquiring pilgrim's question about the distribution of wealth. Each of the three scripture verses that Francis arbitrarily pointed to espoused the virtues of charity and poverty.[6]

Other important biblical characters, Mordecai (in Esther) and David (in Samuel) had to make tough decisions while at dangerous crossroads, and both mused "who knows" what the outcome will be. Likewise, the Tarot might help you decide which path to travel, but without pointing to one road or the other. "Who knows" is to say that I will take responsibility for my decisions. Much like Dietrich Bonhoeffer weighing the risks of attempting to assassinate Adolf Hitler. His "responsibility ethics" buoyed his resolve.

The Tarot will point out your internal and external strengths and weaknesses that you must consider in discerning your path toward selfhood. If the Tarot, or God, or your mom, decides for you, then you could blame them for the outcome. But no one or thing can excuse us from the responsibility for our decisions. Our task is to consider all the options and then make the best choice we can. Reading Tarot is an experience of reading life in the present. "All will be well," Julian of Norwich said in the face of her own decisions about the unknown.

For that reason, the popularity of Tarot has increased significantly. Tarot cards and Tarot readings are big business. Nearly $2 billion annually. There are at least 2,000 unique decks on the market. Plenty of spiritual but not religious folk—and probably more religious people than we know—have embraced this spirituality. I've used it in my daily life for over twenty years, which includes the nearly fifteen years I spent working as an Episcopal priest. While I didn't hang out my shingle as a reader on the church's website, I didn't keep it a secret either. Since leaving my work in the Episcopal Church, I've dedicated more time to being a spiritual companion, which includes Tarot. Not everyone who meets with me is interested in the mysteries of the cards, but many are.

A BRIEF HISTORY OF TAROT

Board games have been a part of the human pastime for over 4,000 years. Middle Eastern archeological excavations have uncovered ornate boards and boxes in Palestine and Egypt, which included moveable pieces and ancient forms of dice. While the instructions for these board games were probably passed down as a part of oral history, it's fairly clear that they usually wagered strategy against risk. Little wonder that in the earliest days of Tarot, the Majors were considered trumps over the Minors.

The history of Tarot can be as mystifying as the cards themselves. The debate over its origination continues amongst Tarot historians today. Kabbalist practitioner Dovid Krafchow, in *Kabbalistic Tarot* posits that the earliest Tarot stories were conceived by the Israelites while exiled in Egypt. In order to protect their ancient narratives, Jews passed their religion from generation to generation through the stories of the Tarot. "The configuration of images and symbols embedded in the cards reflect the ancient esoteric knowledge known as the Cabala."[7] Other Tarot historians also insist that it had its beginnings in ancient Egypt, including Aleister Crowley and his *Thoth* deck. While Krafchow is attempting to draw the Tarot closer to the story of Genesis (the first book of the Bible), Crowley's speculations are based on his intention to move the Tarot away from the Judeo-Christian narrative. Both Krafchow and Crowley have developed theories that, while interesting, are impossible to support. To date, no evidence of Tarot cards has been discovered prior to thirteenth century in Egypt or anywhere else. On one hand the history of Tarot is illusive, while on the other it creates an openness that fuels the imaginal.

The Chinese invented paper in 105 CE. We have evidence that at least one Chinese emperor, Mu-tsung, played cards on the night of New Year's Eve.[8] And during the Middle Ages, the Chinese exported paper into Spain, which then spread to Europe and Egypt.

We know that in the thirteenth century the Islamic card game, *Mamluk*, was played in Egypt. The hand-painted cards had four suits, coins, cups, swords, and sticks. There were thirteen cards per suit: One to Ten, plus the King, the Lieutenant, and the Second Lieutenant. Across the top of each card was printed an aphorism, including these:

> "O thou who hast possessions, remain happy and thou shalt have a pleasant life."

> "I am as a garden, the like of which will never exist."
>
> "With the sword of happiness I shall redeem a beloved who afterwards takes my life."[9]

Journalist and teacher of Sufi mysticism, Ayeda Husain, says in *The Sufi Tarot* that the Tarot can be traced back to the Mamluk Sultanate of ancient Egypt, whose cards are still on display at the Topkapi Palace Museum in Istanbul.[10] Husain's cards are a delight to behold as they enrich the mystical story found within Sufism, much of which applies to the Abrahamic mystical tradition at large.

If nothing else, it is intriguing that a Kabbalist and a Sufi both point to Egypt as the geographical root of Tarot. We must keep in mind, though, that while Krafchow and Husain suggest Tarot was initiated in Egypt, neither has stated that the more ancient Egyptian religion was the Tarot's creator nor had any influence on the Kabbalah or Sufi traditions. Theories of Egypt's religion as the precursor to Tarot arose among practitioners of Hermetical Christianity in Europe during the fourteenth and fifteenth centuries. And that circles us back to gaming.

In 1367, the city of Bern, Switzerland banned card playing because the Christian pastors of the town associated the games with gambling. The earliest European deck known to exist is the *Karnoffel Tarot*, which dates to 1426. Meissner mentioned this Bavarian deck in a poem prior to 1450.

There is often a debate over which came first, the Tarot or the standard fifty-two-card deck plus jokers. Some historians insist the Tarot came first but theorize that because the Major Arcana made games of gambling difficult, they were eliminated. The Fool was the only Major Arcana to survive this paring down of the deck, becoming the "wild card" Joker. Other historians lean more toward the idea that the standard playing cards existed first, and that later someone added the twenty-two pictures plus four additional court cards. A small group of researchers have posited that a deck of only twenty-two Majors existed at the same time as the standard playing deck and then someone combined the two.

The Major Arcana (known in some decks as the trumps, and in some

French decks as assets) were first published without numbers. During the late fifteenth century, the numbers one through twenty-one were added, beginning with The Magician. Originally, The Fool did not have a number. The fifteenth century *Sola Busca*–the earliest extant 78-card deck—assigned the zero to The Fool. A few Tarot creators numbered the Fool, XXII. It was the *Rider-Waite-Smith Tarot* developers who began the contemporary trend of attributing the zero to the Fool; who is the center and the circumference, both the beginning and the end. The ultimate wild card who is the most valuable asset.

Who wrote the first Tarot story behind the deck? History only leaves us with speculations. There are, however, plausible theories. Italian poet, Petrarch (1304-1374), is considered the father of humanism. He was close friends with Milan's Visconti family, who, in the fifteenth century, commissioned several decks. Some Tarot historians point to Petrarch's poem, "Triumphs" as an inspiration for those cards.

Paul Huson, author of *Mystical Origins of the Tarot,* makes a strong case that the cards of the Major Arcana were the results of medieval Roman Catholic "mystery, miracle, and morality plays." He points out that the twenty-two cards mirror our "soul's journey through life into the afterlife, an archetypal and perennial story recounted in Christian imagery typical of the late medieval period."[11] Huson is convinced that not only were the early Major's based on the Church's sanctioned plays, but that they also printed cards to teach people the biblical story.

Spanish philosopher and artist Ramon Llull (1232-1315/16), is also mentioned among the likely candidates for having developed the Tarot's narrative. Llull was a self-educated man, brilliant, well-versed in languages and philosophy. He was also a mystic, having had a paranormal experience prior to his thirtieth birthday. While on Mount Randa, along the eastern coast of Spain, he saw a vision of the nine attributes of God: goodness, greatness, purity, power, wisdom, free will, strength, truth, and glory. Llull spent the remainder of his life translating his vision into "The Great Art," *Ars Magna,* the art of memory. He became known as Doctor Illuminatus, illuminator of the Christian story through the power of memory. His model for memorizing large blocks of material became a pictorial reference point for generations. Those who make long speeches without notes or teleprompters still use his mental structures for memory today.

Llull envisioned the nine attributes of God as a tripling of the Trinity. He said that these characteristics of the Divine reflected the three levels of the human soul, similar to Augustine's intellect, will, and memory. Llull described the three levels of the soul as:

- ◊ the soul of the Father, the realm of intellect and Divine reflection;
- ◊ the soul of the Son, Divine love;
- ◊ and the soul of the Holy Spirit, memory.[12]

He also wrote a novel—an allegory about the spiritual quest of its main character, Blanquerna. The story has all the components of Joseph Campbell's hero's journey and reads a bit like the Holy Grail legend. Llull divided the novel into five parts, each representing one of Christ's five wounds. According to Tarot expert Robert Place, it's easy to see the three levels of the soul in Llull's novel. The tiers create a map for the septenary path that The Fool must travel.

Blanquerna[13] is a near complete model for the storyline of the Tarot. It's also a book within a book. His fascination with the Sufi poet Hafiz inspired his "Book of the Lover and the Beloved." Llull's prayer poems for each day of the year are included at the end of the novel. They were intended to be used as a source of meditation on God's attributes.

Llull's writings about the convergence of the three mystical philosophies of the Abrahamic tradition had a significant influence on the great minds of the Renaissance. It doesn't take much imagination to see how someone could have taken his ideas about the art of memory and combined it with his adventures of Blanquerna. The purpose being to create the Major Arcana of the Tarot as a mnemonic devise for retelling the thirteenth-century version of the biblical story.

The fifteenth century *Tarocchi* cards may have also been one of the early precursors of the modern Tarot. This 50-card deck was based on the characters of that era: beggar, emperor, and pope, among others. The cards included topics of philosophy, poetry, theology, and the seven planets, which reflected the Renaissance cosmos. Today's Tarot readers would find some of the pictures bearing a significant similarity to ones they use regularly.

The oldest known Major Arcana style Tarot deck we can examine dates between 1412 and 1425. In Milan, Italy, Marziano da Tortona conceived the images, which were painted by Michelino da Besozzo. The original paintings are no longer extant, but contemporary cards have been recreated based upon a 1449 letter by Jacopo Antonio Marcello to Queen Isabelle of Lorraine. The *Visconti-Sforza* cards created in the mid-fifteenth century are the oldest surviving deck. Shortly thereafter, *The Tarot of Marseille* was developed in Italy and introduced into France. This deck became the standard design for future Tarot cards. It's also the deck Carl Jung favored.

With the availability of the printing press, the Tarot became more accessible. At the same time, the Christian Reformation was emerging. Puritans in particular took exception to any imagery associated with the Christian story. They condemned gambling and its associated use of the Tarot as the work of the devil. In contradiction, the Renaissance brought with it humanism. By 1548, religious plays, like the medieval ones Huson pointed to, were banned in Paris. Within a decade, the connection between the Christian story and the Tarot disappeared.

About 150 years later, French occultist Jean-Baptiste Alleitte (1738-1791), known as Ettellia, wrote *Livre de Tarot*, the first book interpreting the cards. His popular work integrated Tarot and astrology as a divinatory tool. He based his theory on what he considered to be ancient Egyptian magic. Eliphas Levi (1810-1875) and Gerard Encausse (1865-1910), better known as Papus, followed with their own esoteric works on the subject. By the nineteenth century, the concepts of Tarot began appearing regularly in literature, making the story of the cards more recognizable. At the beginning of the twentieth century, the *Rider-Waite* deck appeared, eventually becoming history's most popular Tarot cards.

MODERN TAROT

Today, the Aeclectic Tarot website "lists over 2,000 different Tarot, Oracle and Lenormand decks." It would be an understatement to say that the Tarot industry is booming in today's world. Why? Heaven may seem like a nice place to spend eternity, but people are looking for answers about life on earth. Especially when the answers they're hearing feel like answers to questions they're not asking. Besides, the questions are changing faster than we can answer them. Even those folks who want things to return to the "good old days" have given up the notion that anything will ever return to "normal." And now these same people, maybe secretly, are considering what might be the new normal of the next iteration of human existence.

Today's Tarot decks mirror our changing world. We're seeing contemporary Tarot books written and cards designed by women, people of color, LGBTQ+, and the different-abled. We can find decks that reflect almost every worldview imaginable, from the traditional to the alternative to the obscure. The attractiveness of Tarot, unlike most traditional religions, is that the story in the cards is universal and applicable to everyone.

There are contemporary decks related to Kabbalah and Sufism, as mentioned above. Eugene Vinitski's *Kabbalistic Tarot* and Heather Mendel's *The Parallax Oracle* are excellent resources for using and understanding the Tarot regarding Jewish Kabbalah. And author and teacher Ayeda Husain's *Sufi Tarot*, is one of a kind. Her deck is beautiful, imaginative, and bears the Tarot story in the images of the mystics of her tradition's poets.

Prior to the nineteenth century, Tarot creators only illustrated the Major Arcana cards. The pip, or numbered cards, were absent artwork, similar to the common playing cards today. The Renaissance *Sola-Busca* deck was the only set of Tarot cards with a complete illustration of the pips prior to the twentieth century.[14] But in 1909, A.E. Waite and Pamela Colman Smith brought the fully illustrated deck to life. Theirs was originally known as the *Rider* deck, named for publisher William Rider.

Later, Waite's name was added due to his accompanying book, *The Key to the Tarot: Fragments of a Secret Tradition Under the Veil of Divination.* That deck became the most popular of all, and remains so today. With the insistence of Tarot author and publisher, Stuart Kaplan, it has become more appropriately known as the *Rider-Waite-Smith* deck.

The aforementioned Arthur Edward Waite (1857–1942) was an occultist. A member of a "secret order" that searched for hidden mystery found in sacred knowledge. They then enacted this gnosis through ritual. Waite did not support the use of Tarot for divination. He wrote in *The Pictorial Key to the Tarot* that "These cards belong in themselves to another realm [other than fortune telling], for they contain a very high symbolism, which is interpreted according to the Laws of Grace rather than by the pretexts and intuitions of that which passes for divination."[15] Instead of the cards being a devise for fortune telling, they became prompts within theurgical techniques.

PAMELA COLMAN SMITH

Corinne Pamela Colman Smith (1878–1951) was an artist, poet, author, editor, publisher, set designer, and mystic. (Her first name was her mother's and rarely appears in publications.)[16] She once described herself as the "goddaughter of a witch and the sister to a fairy." Little wonder her nickname was "Pixie." Some found it difficult to describe her appearance and more than one writer suggested she was biracial. Her biographers seem at a loss to find any evidence of her being such, but on more than one occasion, she drew pictures of herself as a person of color.[17] She was an independent woman who was involved in the English Suffrage movement.[18] She never married nor had children.

Smith's parents were Americans from Brooklyn Heights. Her mother's family were followers of the Swedish scientist, philosopher, and Christian mystic, Emanuel Swedenborg (1668–1772). Her grandfather, Samuel Colman, was a well-known bookseller and publisher in New York, and his store was a common gathering place for Swedenborgians. Christine Payne-Towler, in *Foundations of the Esoteric Tradition,* provides evidence that Swedenborg had more than passing knowledge of the Tarot and the Freemasons.[19] Whether Smith's family discussed the Tarot in relationship to Swedenborg is unknown, but it seems plausible, making her artistry on the deck even more intriguing.

Pamela was born in London, the place she would always consider home. But at the age of ten, her father took a job in Jamaica and the family moved there for four years. It was in Jamaica where her talents as an artist blossomed. At fifteen, Smith left Jamaica and went to New York to further her art education. By nineteen, she had established herself as an artist and author. In the early 1900s, Smith returned to London where she was introduced to W. B. Yeats and to Waite. Joining them, she was initiated into the Order of the Golden Dawn. She was an artist for *The Illustrated Verses of William Butler Yeats* and a set and costume designer for people like Bram Stoker (1847–1912), author of *Dracula.* Smith was known for her interest in the late nineteenth-century French Symbolist movement, which attempted to discover truth through metaphorical images. Some considered her to have the neurological condition of synesthesia—when one sense is activated, it stimulates the others. Smith would listen to music, enter a light trance, and paint.

It was about this time she also became interested in Catholicism, though it wasn't until 1911 that she entered the Roman Church.[20]

Her eclectic mystical background is often evidenced in her art and particularly in the *Rider-Waite-Smith Tarot.* In 1909, the first set of cards was created and published, and while Waite took most of the credit for design, it has become apparent that Smith was not only the artist of the pictures but the genius behind the world's, still, top-selling Tarot deck.

Most contemporary decks find their roots in Smith's paintings. She took her story line from the Grail legend and medieval Christianity. The art is straightforward making her Tarot easy to read. You only need to add your imagination to gather meaning from the images as presented on the cards.

Still, contemporary criticism of this deck is universal—all the characters, for instance, are white. This was most likely Waite's influence. Smith's art collection, however, is filled with paintings of Black Jamaicans and other people of color. I have to wonder if the deck would not have been so monotone if Smith had had complete control of the faces. Another criticism is that while some characters appear to be androgynous, the figures are mostly binary: masculine and feminine. Given Smith's feminist perspective, again, I believe Waite's influence on the outcome is clear, and unfortunately so.

ALEISTER CROWLEY

The second most popular deck also emerged from the Order of the Golden Dawn, although not out of friendly relationships. Aleister Crowley (1875–1947) was an occultist, artist, poet, and magician. After only two years in the Order, he orchestrated the strife that led to the dismantling of the organization. Soon thereafter, he founded his own esoteric movement.

During the next thirty years, Crowley gathered ideas for the design of a deck based on an Egyptian story. In 1937, he was introduced to the London painter, Lady Frieda Harris (1877-1962). Harris had studied Goethe's theories of geometry, as interpreted by the founder of anthroposophy, Rudolph Steiner (1861-1925). Through this influence, her work took on the vision of the Art Deco movement. Crowley subsequently wrote *The Book of Thoth*, which accompanied Harris's paintings. The deck, however, wasn't published until 1969, after both Crowley and Harris had died. Harris wrote these instructions for Crowley's *Thoth Tarot* deck:

> The Tarot could be described as God's Picture Book or it could be likened to a celestial game of chess, the Trumps being the pieces to be moved according to the law of their own order over a checkered board of the four elements.[21]

Finally, let me mention Angeles Arrien's *The Tarot Handbook*—one of the most accessible guides for the *Thoth Tarot*. Arrien (1940–2014) was a cultural anthropologist who brought her academic knowledge to the Tarot, and particularly the *Thoth* deck. This deck is more reflective of a diverse culture. Arrien wrote that she was initially attracted to the deck because, "It was cross-cultural in its symbolism as well as multi-disciplinary."[22] It contains symbolism from Egyptian, Greek, Eastern, medieval Christian mysticism. Both the *Rider-Waite-Smith* and *Thoth* decks heavily depend on mystical religious stories as seen through the eyes of women artists. And both will be extremely useful in our exploration of the Tarot.

HOW TO CHOOSE YOUR TAROT DECK

You can choose from over 2,000 decks. I have forty-plus in my collection. All the people I know who are interested in Tarot have a significant collection of their own.

I've given some decks away. Despite that, others appear. Some as gifts. But truthfully, I'm always discovering new, irresistible decks. Not that I go looking for them, they just seem to find me. My wife has Tarot decks she shares with me and our son and daughter have recommended cards to us. Friends are always texting, "Have you seen this?" An interesting deck pops up on Facebook and I can't help myself but to check it out. I'm a member of a Tarot Association and they're always displaying new decks. And then someone asks me for a reading and wants me to use their deck, one I've never seen before but find intriguing. And yes, I read Tarot from decks I've never seen before. How? While the unique pictures may inspire a distinctive vision or interpretation, the story is pretty much universal.

Any of the decks introduced above would be good to have in a collection because of their historic value. And any of them would be a reasonable place to begin your work with Tarot. But there are hundreds of other decks that might work just as well. To help you eliminate some of the overwhelming number of options, let's first begin with a few questions.

> Do you want a deck that reflects diversity?
> Do you prefer a more gender-neutral presentation?
> Are you offended by nudity?
> Will you be put off by pictures that seem negative—like a devil, or a man hanging upside down, or three swords piercing through a heart (typically how the Three of Swords is depicted)?

Another good question to ask is, "What are my triggers?" and "What am I not ready to deal with?" These are all good questions and they need to be addressed. You don't want your Tarot deck to freak you out every time you pick it up, because if it does, you'll put it down and you might never reach for it again—and that's not helpful.

One of the best resources I use before buying a deck is YouTube. I type in the deck's name followed by "flip through." I use this phrase as a designator because it usually only takes the person showing the deck less than ten minutes. I don't want to listen to someone spending forty-five minutes telling me why they love or hate the deck. I want to decide that on my own. But that's just me. You might enjoy several opinions. I want the person to slowly flip through the cards so I can decide if the deck is worth my money and if there's anything in it that might trigger me. I'm not easily offended, but there are a few images that can set my psyche ablaze. When that image confronts my personal hot spot, I'll buy the deck with trepidation, knowing that it's time for me to take on that shadow dragon. But that's a decision you'll have to make for yourself.

Unless it is a collector's item, typically a deck costs less than forty dollars, and that usually includes a guidebook. The more colorful and in-depth the book, the higher the price. Sometimes a deck is sold without the book, either because of expense or because some Tarot readers don't want the book and are unwilling to pay for something they won't use. I've gotten to the place that when I buy a new deck, I rarely look at the accompanying material. The only time I refer to it, is when a particular picture the artist has used is vastly different from the traditional Tarot and I can't make the connection. The other times I have relied on the guidebook is while working with a deck from another tradition, like the Sufi and Kabbalah deck I mentioned previously. I'm learning their system and I need to know about their perspective.

Once you've selected a deck and have it in your possession, do your own flip-through. Become familiar with the layout and art. Look for common themes, colors, symbols, and pictures among the Major Arcana, the court cards, and the pips. Are there subtleties in the pictures that make connections between the cards? When I get a new deck, I work my way through it one or two cards a day, keeping notes in my Tarot journal.

Again, let me encourage you to refrain from immediately going to the guidebook. Instead, create your own Tarot notebook. Record what you sense, intuit, think, and feel. I leave space in my journal to add information that I might find later. Over time, as I have added to my collection of Tarot decks and books and taken classes on the subject, I have built my own Book of Tarot. I've been on this pilgrimage long enough now that I have two dedicated journals. One is an easy to carry (and pack) journal with quick reference notes, and the other is a larger three-ring notebook. I am continually adding notes, pictures, and articles about cards, decks, reading spreads, and techniques.

Finally, you may want to draw your own set of cards. For example, to become an adept in the Order of the Golden Dawn, members were required to design their own deck. Yeats' notebook lives in the family museum in Sligo, Ireland. It's a lovely journal with images of the cards he designed.

Whether you create your own deck or cherish the one you bought, working with Tarot can become a spiritual practice. For me, engaging the Tarot and the Bible has become a lifelong pilgrimage; one that continues to instruct, provide wisdom, and enlighten my path.

— CHAPTER 4 —

THE FOOL'S SACRED PATH

And a highway shall be there, and a way, and it shall be called
The way of holiness:
The wayfaring men, though fools, shall not err therein.
Isaiah 35:8

If you think you are wise in this age,
you should become fools,
so that you may become wise.
1 Corinthians 3:18

The Fool is going to guide us through the paths of instruction, wisdom, and enlightenment toward the individuation of the self—the maturation and integration of our mind-body-soul. In the following chapters, we're going to accompany The Fool on his/her/their pilgrimage through the serpentine path of the Major Arcana from The Magician to The World. The value of the Tarot is that it provides us with a visual tool of our inner experience. At the same time, it creates a map for our journey with the biblical characters who mirror our life's pilgrimage.

In my experience, walking the hundred miles of the Wicklow Way is a serpentine path through seven strenuous days of mountains. The cumulative gain from Dublin to Clonegal is roughly 10,000 feet, making a day's hike include the ascent and descent of three peaks totaling 2,220 feet. The Fool's great work of pilgrimage matches the journey through the Wicklows. Each mountain represents one of the Major Arcana, beginning with The Magician and finishing with The World. We may not be walking the Wicklow Mountains every day, but we are living a life with greater demands and challenges.

In the words of Hermes Trismegistus, "What is above is below, and what is below is above." Each card is a journey within itself, within the narrative of the entire Tarot story.

The Fool makes their way through the twenty-one cards of the Major Arcana, following the ancient ascent and descent of the three tiers of the seven-fold pilgrimage. This would be like walking the seven days of the Wicklow Way three times. Each stretch of seven days represents a progression of mind-body-soul development: the path of instruction, the path of wisdom, and the path of enlightenment. I use the mind-body-soul as an indication of the lifelong process of the integration of the self. We are nondual beings who experience ourselves through dualistic constructs, as in masculine/feminine. Our goal is to re-integrate the opposites within, returning our reality to one of being nondualistic. This idea follows the model of Carl Jung both in personality typing and his application of psychological alchemy. For example, recognizing we are both an introvert and an extrovert, working to bring them together in the sense of our total self. The same applies to the other personality pairs, sensing/intuition, and thinking/feeling. Jung, and the alchemist, considered all opposites (including masculine/feminine) as being in the process of returning to their original state of nonduality. (His theories and their psychological practice appear throughout this book and will be discussed later in more detail.)

The path of instruction starts our pilgrimage and follows the seven cards of The Magician through The Chariot. On this path, The Fool walks the first half of life gaining instruction and guidance. In the early years of life, or when we start a new job, open a business, or have our first child, we need to the know the rules of survival. The ancient ones of this path will point us in the right direction. But they won't hand us a manual, only their experience.

The path of wisdom initiates the beginning of our second half of life. We've been to school, now we're living in the real world. Many of our lessons will be learned by experimenting with what we learned on the first path. We'll gain Strength in our weakness. Justice will be acquired by the sharp blade of injustice. And we'll begin to understand Death when we acknowledge its ever-growing presence in our life. Every card has its opposite and with it comes wisdom.

The path of enlightenment takes us toward an expanded consciousness. Traveling with The Devil through The World, we will ask the big questions about the meaning and purpose of life. Enlightenment is the product of doubt and it only comes in drops, spurts, and momentary flashes. But one experience is enough to transmute a lifetime.

Students of the book of Isaiah consider the text to be a compilation of at least three authors. Whoever wrote the thirty-fifth chapter was probably among the Jewish community in exile. These people were living in a spiritual desert on their way to what they believed would be the New Jerusalem. They were experiencing the three-phase pilgrimage as pictured in the Tarot. It was a physical journey with a spiritually mystical outcome. It is our model to walk the desert's sacred way. Following is Isaiah 35 with each path indicated.

> *The path of instruction:*
> The arid desert shall be glad,
> The wilderness shall rejoice,
> And blossom like a rose.
> Strengthen the hands that are slack;
> Make firm the tottering knees!
> Say to the anxious of heart,
> Be strong, fear not;
> Behold your God!
> *The path of wisdom:*
> Though the desert is inhabited by dragons,
> The eyes of the blind shall be opened,
> And the ears of the deaf shall be unstopped.
> Then the lame shall leap like a deer,
> And the tongue of the dumb shall shout aloud.
> *The path of enlightenment*
> And a highway shall appear there, which shall be called the Sacred Way.

> No traveler, not even fools, shall go astray.
> They shall attain joy and gladness.

Walking with The Fool, we will learn to live wise as a dragon and gentle as a dove (Matthew 10:16). The thing I have experienced about walking this path is that every pilgrimage is taken through a desert of challenges, shadows, and dragons. And each journey began when I faced what frightened me the most. But whether we finish or not, the end result brings a satisfying joy, an enlightened wisdom, and oneness with The Tree of Life (Ezekiel 31).

We can never learn enough, have enough wisdom, or be completely enlightened. One day we might draw The Wheel of Fortune and win the lottery. And then the next day, pull the Ten of Swords and lose it all. Both experiences are the journey. Tarot and the Bible each have something to teach us about the ascent and descent on our wheel of life.

As we move through each of the Major Arcana in the following chapters, I have placed five markers at the beginning of the material that will offer you a glimpse into the narrative of the card.

1. We begin with a Quick Read where I offer a few words that describe the meaning behind the card.
2. Artistic Inspiration is the image of the card from a particular deck that I am drawing upon as a model. I have used decks that are easily accessible and whose artist have stayed reasonably aligned with the traditional names and format of the Tarot. (I'm not a Tarot purist. I use decks that don't follow the traditional storyline. However, for those just getting started, I believe it's best to learn the basic pattern and then deviate.)
3. An Illumination is a quote from a non-biblical text that might shine a bit of light on the meaning of the card. These quotes come from a variety of sources, including fiction and non-fiction.
4. For biblical character(s), typically, I have chosen only one person

or image from the Bible as a representation of the card. However, there are a few times when I have suggested two examples. That said, there are, in most cases, other characters in the Bible who could also be identified as reflections of that card.

5. The Scripture Text is one or two Bible verses that relate to the Tarot card being described.

These are only samples. You might disagree and that is perfectly okay. As you make your own pilgrimage through the Tarot's 78-facets of the soul, I strongly suggest you make your own list in these categories. At the end of each chapter on the Major Arcana, I will also ask questions to assist in your reflection on the Tarot and the Bible. Let's get started. And remember, this is supposed to be fun.

THE FOOL

Quick Read: The pilgrim, the beginning and the end. The Fool is androgynous, adventurous, and fun loving.

Artistic Inspiration: *Rider-Waite-Smith Tarot,* Pamela Colman Smith. A rather androgynous figure wearing a brightly adorned tunic. They have a traditional pilgrim's bag and hiking stick slung over their shoulder and carrying a white rose in their left hand. Their companion dog is warning them as they are about to step off a high cliff

Illumination: "The deepest form of wandering requires that we are lost—because when we are lost we can find something; that something is our self." Bill Plotkin[23]

Biblical Characters: Abraham and Sarah

Text: "Ask and it shall be given to you; seek and ye shall find, knock and the door shall be opened." (Matthew 7:7)

Who is The Fool? This interesting character is the entanglement of opposites: foolishness and divinity. In mystical language: divine madness. With few exceptions, prior to the *Rider-Waite-Smith* deck, The Fool was unnumbered and not considered as one of the Major Arcana. Instead, The Fool was the precursor to the Joker, the juggler, the court jester. While these cards often depict the character as a male, Sallie Nichols points to a fifteenth-century Austrian deck with a female joker.[24] In Aleister Crowley's *Book of Thoth*, he tells us that The Fool traveled with his sister, the *Soror Mystica,* the mystical sister. In his version of the Tarot, Crowley was borrowing from the story of Abram and Sarai.

The biblical story of God's people begins with a pilgrimage. Abram was seventy-five when God told him to leave his home and go into the wilderness. The old man gathered up his wife Sarai, who was also his sister, their brother Lot, and all they owned. They began walking in an unfamiliar desert (Genesis 12:1, 20:12). The symbolism is rich. Abram's father must have thought his son was a fool to take everything, including his daughter and younger son, to Egypt. The journey alone could have brought death. Much less the risk of walking into the hands of the feared Pharaoh. But Abram was intent on his mission, so he "journeyed by stages." The mere idea that Sarai was both Abram's wife and sister are a perfect metaphor for the creators of the Tarot's Fool, and the inspiration of Pamela Colman Smith's drawing. The Fool carries in their backpack every facet of the personality and all the pronouns of the human condition onto life's pilgrimage path.

While some decks depict The Fool as male (*Marseille*), and others as female (*Tarot of the Sevenfold Mysteries*), there are those that depict this figure as androgynous (*Rider-Waite-Smith*). I'm following Smith and her image of The Fool as nonbinary. The Fool is me. The Fool is you. The Fool is a pilgrim on the way to instruction, wisdom, and enlightenment. The Fool is each of us individually and all of us collectively.

The Fool is also the embodiment of each of the Major Arcana. For The Fool symbolizes that we are inseparable from all the multiple aspects of our personae. Just as in the Myers-Briggs Type Indicator (MBTI), we are not a singular type, but all sixteen types. The same is said about the personality typing tool, the Enneagram. We are not only one type, but the summation of all nine. Jung said that we have multiple personalities (not psychotic disassociation). And these multiple types are displays of our many opposites. Simply stated, we are incomplete if we only live in a singular type, the one that would represent our conscious ego. We can only become individuated, mature, and complete, when we embrace the opposites of who we perceive ourselves to be—the other fifteen aspects of the MBTI and the other eight types of the Enneagram, plus every other binary imaginable. Thomas Merton[25] and Richard Rohr[26] described this integration of types as the process of evolving from the False Self into the True Self.

The Fool invites us to join them in the process of transformation, one that moves us away from the control of the ego toward a spiritual consciousness of the true self. This is the path of holiness, the sacred way as described in Isaiah 35. Carl Jung, in the opening lines of his *Red Book*, quotes this text from the Bible as the means of warning us that we are about to join him on an exploration into the unconscious:

> Listen and write: All is dark wherever you grope in the depths. I am also dark myself and I can only break loose pieces, fractions of complete entities...because nothing is solid and everything is possible.[27]

The Fool wants us to follow them into the desert of the unconscious, where our dragons (our shadows) will confront us. For Jung, the work of individuation is an experiment intended to bring about the union of the unconscious with the conscious. By standing eye to eye with those shadows, blind spots, and things we've denied and hidden in the darkness, we can bring them into the light of consciousness. There in the glow of The Sun, the dragons of our shadows can be healed as we walk the pilgrim's way. And now that they have been restored, they can travel along our side as an ally, a companion, of support.

Such was the work of the physician and alchemist Paracelsus (d. 1541), a man who traveled the world serving those who suffered pain and illness. He was an early day scientist who had a significant influence on modern-day chemistry, medicine, and psychology. This man was a devoted Christian. Today we would call him spiritual but not religious. Paracelsus took seriously his study of scripture as he applied it to his daily life and science. He worked with archetypal symbolism similar to the ones we find in the Tarot and related this to his efforts as a healer. His enigmatic writing can be difficult to navigate, but he provides clues to the correspondences between the Bible and the Tarot. Paracelsus insisted that every mountain, every stone, every herb would reveal signs and symbols for use in healing the mind, the body, and the soul. But to discover these secrets, we must take the risk to travel with those like Paracelsus who embodied The Fool.

Paracelsus' work would influence that of the spiritual alchemist Jacob Boehme (1575-1624), author of *The Way of Christ*. There, he writes about the pilgrimage process that creates not only a healing tincture for his personal benefit but also for the sake of the world.[28] Our journey through the desert has a grander scheme than simply improving the quality of our life. We travel to understand our true self in relationship with the world in which we live. As we heal ourselves, we heal others.

THE FOOL'S PILGRIMAGE ON THE PATH OF INSTRUCTION

My family lives in the Southwest desert just outside of Phoenix, Arizona. There are several trails in the Estrella Mountains, near our house. We prefer to hike them between October and April. Even then, in midday, the sun can drive the best of hikers off the trail. And hiking desert trails in the summer, well, is just plain foolish. For me, the best time to hike is early in the morning, long for before the sun rises, meaning that some of the hike is in the dark before the aurora when the full moon fills the night sky.

On those wondrous morning hikes, just after the sun has risen in the east and the shadow of the mountains has disappeared, it's best to take a break. In the Estrella Mountains, I have found that the only shade and cool space is in the pockets that were dug by the Maricopa and Pima peoples in the 1500s. The small eye-shaped openings are big enough for two people to sit side-by-side. First, before entering, it's prudent to check for rattlesnakes. They can be pretty territorial. In these caves of the living and tombs of the dead, we can experience The Fool's pilgrimage described in Isaiah. Protected from the day's sun, we can hear the lament of the dead along with The Fool's advice for journeying the desert's sacred way under the midnight sun, the full moon. The Fool is taking us on the path of instruction so that we might begin to write our own book of the mystics, our personal Rose Bible.

The ancient story of the Tarot is an alchemical one, similar to contemporary culinary infusion. Often the most unexpected combinations can deliver delicious flavors served on a platter of aromatic and visual magic. But these mystical delights come at the expense of experimental failure. I've watched more than a few chefs toss their imaginal meal in the garbage after one taste, only to begin again. Such is the alchemical process of transmutation.

The alchemist's end goal is to create their philosopher's stone, which is their soul. An alchemist's craftwork is soul-making. They read Saint James' words in the Bible, "faith without works is dead," as a call to their purpose in life. And they continually put into practice the Apostle Paul's admonition to "work out your own salvation," as the directive to create their own true self. Whether you believe you're born with a soul, or you have to construct your own, the maturation of the soul is never complete. Not in this lifetime, anyway.

I have found that spiritual alchemy (sometimes known as psychological alchemy) is an insightful process for integrating the material (the body) and the spiritual (the mind/soul or psyche). One day, I might pull The Hanged Man and the next The High Priestess. Without the alchemical stages, I could feel that every day is a life lived as a series of random choices of unrelated events. The process of alchemy is an intentional move away from this kind of dualistic thinking and toward holism. Every day and each action are stirred into the cauldron of our mind-body-soul. Each moment contributes to our experience of the past, our knowledge of the present, and our hope for the future. Nothing is lost. It's all melded into a delicious cosmic soup.

Tarot affords me a toolkit of visual symbols I can use to articulate my inner experience that is taking place in my outer world. The Hanged Man points out that, while I might get lost on the way, I can experience the mystical path of The High Priestess. The value of feeling lost creates chaos in the soul. (The first phase of alchemy.) Finding calm in that moment of panic will elicit a glimpse of the feeling of not being alone, but a part of something larger than myself. (The second phase of alchemy.) The uncertainty of being lost evolves into a way of finding the path. (The third phase of alchemy.) Every experience is a combination of the physical (The Hanged Man) and the spiritual (The High Priestess). Our body, our senses, are always at work, for our body is as much our soul is our soul is our body.

My therapist of twelve years taught me the process of spiritual alchemical according to Jung's model of four alchemical phases. As a means of easier identification, I have changed their traditional names. Still, these images are in line with how Jung described each stage of the process:

1. Chaos—the dark night of the soul.
2. Cracking the egg—thankfully, the sun will rise again.
3. The raven with a peacock's tail—sometimes everything feels weird.
4. The phoenix rises from the ashes—we must learn how to lean into our new normal.

My experience is that some understanding of the alchemical process has been helpful to my spiritual companions as they make meaning of life's swinging pendulum. Being that the alchemists built their models relying on the biblical stories and primordial archetypes, I have included some simple basics that can assist our journey forward with The Fool.

Chaos. The process of every pilgrimage begins long before we start walking. The first moment we ponder the idea of going on pilgrimage, the journey has begun. Our pilgrimage requires the preparation of the material and the spiritual. The material includes physical training, planning the trip, purchasing the right equipment, and often buying an airline ticket. The spiritual, however, encompasses the less obvious and more often ignored. Getting one's psyche prepared to embrace the yet to be imagined is accomplished by listening to the silence of the soul. While it is necessary to simultaneously prepare the material and the spiritual, this work can often spawn the feelings of chaos, dis-ease, doubt, and anxiety. Should I spend this much money to go on a long walk? Can I finish? What happens if I get sick or hurt?

Many of us will never walk the Wicklow Way or the Camino de Santiago, or even go on a long stroll through our neighborhood; we will however, "walk" many pilgrimages in our life: some intentional and others that have been forced upon us. Life is a pilgrimage: leaving home, going to college, starting a new career, beginning a family, moving to another city, changing diets, training for a marathon. And then there's the unintentional ones: losing a job, divorce, cancer, loss of a loved one. Every one of these experiences, the intentional and the unintentional, begins with chaos. The storms of confusion—fear, uncertainty, anxiety, loss, illness, grief, disappointment, frustration, betrayal, abandonment—all caused by externals through no fault of our own.

There are other moments of our pilgrimage through life when chaos arises out of our blind spots, the denials that been hiding in the underbelly of our secrets. In two of my previous books, *Wisdom Walking* and *Meditations on Blue Jesus,* I told stories of my blind spots having been exposed in the most awkward of circumstances. The revelations of my hidden and unprocessed shadows hurt someone else and rightfully humbled me. What appeared so innocent on the surface was laced with the smell of unconscious death. One blind spot was pointed out by a person I had never met before. The other was made graphic in a dream. Both were issues I thought I had thoroughly processed in my life, yet the blind spot drove me into oncoming psychic traffic. I was led to amends, which made possible a phase of transmutation. The alchemists say that the aroma of the rose and the stench of death complement one another, creating a poisonous homeopathic tincture for the sake of healing of oneself, and for the health of the other person. One without the other is incomplete.

Each singular card of the Major and Minor Arcana and the court cards will reveal an opposite within the psyche of The Fool, and subsequently within us. Being confronted with our doppelgänger can create a deep sense of psychic chaos. The mystics refer to our opposites as our twin. Not me, but me. The mirror of the other, but not. The Fool's journey is a series of encounters that expose our opposites that are found in the Tarot.

We can only see these archetypes in relationships of spiritual transparency. The experience is akin to French-kissing our dream dragons (Isaiah 35). Not pleasant and extremely dangerous. No wonder we avoid our shadows. But it's the only way on the sacred path. As Jung writes in the *Red Book*, "In the whirl of chaos dwells eternal wonder."[29] We see similar stories played out in the Bible. And The Hanged Man, Death, The Tower, and The Devil are common cards that will show up during our time of chaos. Not so much as forecasting, but more affirmations that our blind spots are on fire and we need to give them some serious attention.

Jesus reminded us that if we sweep out (avoid/deny) one demon (our shadow dragon), seven others are likely to appear:

> When the unclean spirit has gone out of a person, it wanders through waterless regions looking for a resting place, but it finds none. Then it says, "I will return to my house from which I came." When it comes, it finds it empty, swept, and put in order. Then it goes and brings along seven other spirits more evil than itself, and they enter and live there; and the last state is worse than the first. (Matthew 12:43-45)

Jung adds an interesting reflection on such mysterious teachings: "Meaning is a moment and a transition from absurdity to absurdity, and absurdity only a moment and a transition from meaning to meaning."[30] It is better to make friends with our dragons and give them a seat in our psychic circle than try to banish them, for who knows what will emerge at the gate of our soul.

Cracking the Egg. The second step in the pilgrimage process is what the alchemists refer to as purification. Simply put, we're turning up the heat in order to break through the egg of chaos. The two biggest provocations of dis-ease I have witnessed in pilgrims were their lack of physical preparation and their heavy ladened backpacks. The process of purification forces us to be honest with ourselves. Translated into alchemical language: Face yourself in the mirror and you will see your dragons starring back. What's behind the reality that we didn't train our bodies? And what is at the root of our decision to bring too much stuff? Often The Chariot and Temperance will show up to remind us that we're on our way to another adventure, breaking through into new territory both physically and spiritually. This is the biblical language of rebirth and baptism.

A masterful example of the renewal ritual of water—one that includes Tarot archetypes—can be found in Acts of the New Testament (8:26-40). According to the Jerusalem Bible, a man from Ethiopia had been on pilgrimage to Jerusalem and was now on his way home. He was sitting in his chariot reading from the book of Isaiah (chapter 53). The author of Acts described the man as a eunuch and the treasurer for the queen of his land. The Apostle Philip, sent by the Spirit, asked the Ethiopian, "Do you understand what you are reading?" Because he did not, the eunuch sought Philip's guidance. As they traveled together in the chariot, Philip connected the words of the prophet Isaiah to the life of Jesus. As they approached a body of water, the Ethiopian asked Philip to baptize him. As the man came up out of the water, the text says that "the Spirit of the Lord snatched Philip away." (This little sentence is so tantalizingly weird; whatever really happened fuels the imagination of the paranormal.) The Ethiopian never saw Philip again, but "he went on his way rejoicing."

This intriguing story is rich with Tarot images as well as references that reflect psychological alchemy. The Chariot symbolizes movement from one place to another, or from one way of thinking to another. It's also the final Major Arcana on the path of instruction, transitioning onto the path of wisdom. That symbolism fits well with this story in Acts. The eunuch was searching for meaning in the prophecy he had found in Isaiah. Philip provided a Christian interpretation of the text that the Ethiopian found instructive. To ritualize and mark his new way of thinking, he asked the Apostle to baptize him. The water (Cups) represents the Ethiopian having set down the heavy weight of being an outsider. And now he was happy and celebrating his anticipated new life. Little wonder he was rejoicing. Philip had embodied the teachings of Jesus found in Matthew 25:35-40. "I was a stranger and you made me welcome." The Ethiopian was a stranger in many ways. Not only was he like Moses in that he had been traveling in a foreign land (Exodus 2:22), but according to Deuteronomy 23:1, he was considered an outsider because he was sexually different. The baptism did not change this man's circumstances, but it represents that his ways of thinking about himself had now been transformed by his inclusion into the Spirit's community. With Philip's instructive teaching, the Ethiopian had cracked through the barrier of difference that had been placed onto him by others. And now he was on his way into a new world of acceptance.

Whether we are doing our personal work of embracing the dragons—our shadows and our blind spots—or struggling with the weight that others have burdened onto our shoulders, rebirth is possible. Like the unborn chick, we begin to break out of the egg of our chaos. The defenseless bird typically needs its parents, or someone like Philip, to help it peck through a blockade of barbed wire. Once on the other side, the infants need someone to feed them. On observation, we can see the chicks constantly making noises with their mouths wide open.

One of the most difficult lessons to learn when we are coming out of chaos is that it's okay to ask for what we need. We've been taught to go it alone, keep our troubles to ourselves, never show weakness. But as a young bird has just made its way out of the egg of chaos, we need nourishment that we can rarely find on our own. In my life, I've relied on therapists, spiritual companions, and life coaches, all of whom have held up the mirror so that I could see my shadows. They have offered advice that helped me see the edge of the cliff before I would have tumbled down the mountainside. In other words, they helped me peck my way out of the egg.

As a young boy, I dreamt of becoming a professional baseball player. For my tenth birthday, Dad bought me a transistor radio with an earpiece, so I could listen to the Dodger games as I laid in bed at night. At twelve, he took me to a spring training game between the Dodgers and the Giants. I could imagine myself on the field catching the future Hall of Fame lefthander, Sandy Koufax. At fifteen, some friends of my parents were visiting. One of them asked me what I wanted to do after high school.

"I want to play pro baseball."

"You better get over that fantasy," he said.

At seventeen, the Houston Astros offered me a minor league contract, and I never hesitated. I played in the minor leagues for five years. The paradox of a dream come true collided with the cold reality that professional sports is a big business. The end of my playing career felt like a failure. Enmeshed in my story were the archetypes of the son, the brother of a neurodivergent sister, the husband, and the father. Now what? Second best career choice, coach baseball. Coaching three-years at the high school level somehow turned into twenty years at a small college. There, I led two lives: one on the field, the other in the office as an administrator. Choices, some call them opportunities, others, misfortunes, appeared along the way. At mid-life, I chose the path of a second life: university president. Failure. What's next? Episcopal priest. Athlete, coach, president, priest, sounds like a bad novel. At the beginning of each path, I named it a "calling," a vocation, not an occupation. Misnaming anything carries with it the risk of walking down the wrong path. With each vocation of a perceived "higher calling" came a uniform, a job description, a code of conduct, and a paycheck: perform, win, raise money, grow the church. Those expectations were designed by whoever signed the paycheck. I allowed my ego to be identified by the calling, the uniform, the expectations, and the amount of money I was paid. The child who had a baseball fantasy was now buried under the depression and self-destructive behavior of his own making. Now what? My therapist told me if I wasn't living my own life, I was living someone else's. Whose life was I living? And what was the narrative of that story? Better question: who wrote that story? I spent twelve years working with a Jungian analyst, French-kissing my dragons, seeking liberation from past dogmas, and writing my ever-evolving personal narrative. I came to realize that—while the people I worked for wanted me to do a job outlined by a list of duties—the only way I could perform well was to be myself. My therapist told me they didn't hire me to do a job, they were hiring me to be me. My employers might not have known that, and for most of my life, neither did I.

What I came to understand was that before I could be me, I had to know who I was and who I was potentially emerging to be. Carl Jung wrote in *Symbols of Transformation* that no person can change themselves into something they are not, but only into what they already are.[31] Such is a lifetime's work of forming the possibility of latent potential. And that only happens when we get rid of the unwanted weight we're carrying around and do the work to crack out of the egg into a new life.

The Raven with the Peacock's Tail. When we've broken through the eggshell and taken on nourishment, we will soon be ready to leave the nest. What we discover is that the world beyond our safety net is strange and unfamiliar. And sometimes, just plain weird. Although we are excited to have broken free, we have a lot of new learning to take on. Now we are beginning the creative work of the third phase of The Fool's process.

When we walk the pilgrimage, we must be in a constant state of reflection. As Jung advised, we must write in our journal to see where we have been. After walking for five days, we might feel like we can fly high like the raven, but the reality is that we're still on the ground like the peacock. We're beautiful, yet unequipped to soar. We're traveling the process of integrating the mind, the body, and the soul, but we haven't finished our journey. As Jung said, if there's "no inner adventure, [there's] no outer adventure." We are learning how to integrate all things mind and all things body by ascending and descending every mountain we encounter. This is the true landscape of The Fool. It's also the territory of The Magician, The Lovers, Death, and The World. To be The Fool, the Bible advises that we take on the mind of Christ (Philippians 2:4-12). This Christ-like higher consciousness is one grounded in the humility and sacrifice required "to work out your own salvation." A pilgrimage is a process of walking "through the narrow gate" (Matthew 7:13). Or, as Scott Peck aptly put it, traveling the "road less traveled."

This is also the very painful alchemical process of recognizing our true self as nondual and nonbinary. Creativity is stressful work. To live in a world where there is "no longer Jew or Greek, there is no longer slave or free, there is no longer male or female; for all of you are one" in this Christ-like higher consciousness (Galatians 3). This is the challenge of the individuated life. In the Gospel of Mary Magdalene, one of the non-canonical Gnostic gospels, she recounts to the disciples her vision of the risen Christ. "He [Christ] is calling us to become fully human (*Anthropos*)."[32] To engage in the process of becoming fully human requires us to embrace our dragons of the desert. By confronting whatever drove us into the desert in the first place, the work of integrating our shadows into the soul begins to take place. This is never easy. A pilgrimage can be arduous, even treacherous. It may appear as though it's filled with good versus evil, light's battle against the darkness; a series of dual constructs that stand to oppose one another. But The Fool's pilgrimage is one of remembering our nonduality by being one with each of the other Major Arcana, even those that frighten us the most. This type of remembering is known as *anamnesis*: to recall the way we were before we had memory. To remember who we were intended to be, the good and the not so good. A remembering that our potential is more than we ever could have imagined. To accept these images as the reality of our true self can liberate us from the narrative of the false self. The experience of remembering these images will feel weird, like seeing a raven with a peacock's tail. It will also feel exhilarating.

This spiritual idea of the weird has material origins in the second chapter of Genesis. Adam was the *Anthropos*, the original human, the androgynous one. But then the dual construct of the human as male and female—separate from one another—emerged. "And the Lord took one of Adam's ribs...and made a woman." Then Adam said, "This is now bone of my bone, and flesh of my flesh, she shall be called Woman, because she was taken out of Man." The two appear as opposites, but they are from the original One. The alchemical work of The Fool's pilgrimage is for us to remember that we were, and still are, one. We each contain all the opposites in our oneness, even though those memories are often difficult to sustain. We need to be continually reminded of who we have always been. As humans, we must embrace our blind spots when they come into full view. For our dragons are as much of us as is the sweet dove of goodness.

As stated before, in *The Book of Thoth*, Aleister Crowley suggested the Tarot can be understood through the alchemist's image of the *Soror Mystica*, the mystical twin, the one with whom we have always been in union. Emanating from the Father (The Emperor) and the Mother (The Empress), twins (a son and a daughter) are born (The Lovers). The symbol of the androgynous, where the feminine is the progenitor of the union of opposites, the binary becomes nonbinary. He explains: "It is necessary, in order to understand the Tarot, to look back in history to the Matriarchal Age (exogamic age), to the time when succession was not through the first-born son of the King, but through his daughter," the daughter of the Queen—the inheritance of blood.[33]

This story is told also through the Hebrews' first transitions of king, from Saul to David. Jonathan, Saul's eldest son, angered his father by his relationship with the renegade David. And through a dramatic twist, Saul's daughter, the Queen Ahinoam's daughter Michel, would marry David and he would become King (1 Samuel 14:50, 18:17-27). Sounds like a simple story, but the entangled tragic drama of Saul, Jonathan, David, Michel, Bathsheba, and Solomon encompass nine books of Bible. Every character has its own twin. One within itself, and one within another. The poetry of Solomon's Song of Songs opens our soul to the imagination of our opposite. "You are my beloved and my friend (my soul)…fair as the sun, bright as the moon…you have wounded my heart, my sister, my bride" (Song of Solomon 3-4). The Fool is the twin of each of the Major Arcana. Our twin of our self and our opposite united into one: no longer binary. This is the way of the mystic rose, where even the fools on quest will not err but become wise. And it's weird.

The phoenix rises from the ashes. The final stage of The Fool's process of pilgrimage through alchemy is the creation of the philosopher's stone, enlightenment, the expansion of consciousness, soul-making. On the Judgment card, Archangel Gabriel awakens the sleeping with his mighty horn. "Arise from the ashes of darkness," he commands. Awaken and be enlightened. We will be able to engage our creativity for the sake of healing the world and all that inhabit it. The final product is pictured on The World card. There we see a woman stepping through a portal, moving from one level of consciousness into another. At times, we walk through these altered states during our pilgrimage, often from exhaustion, deep dreams, and imaginative images. Alchemists understood these experiences as the transmutation of themselves into a living stone. They were to be a tincture of wisdom for the sake of repairing and restoring the world. They found this idea in the creation story of Kabbalistic mysticism. The holy vessels shattered into millions of shards. And the purpose of human pilgrimage is to restore these pieces of light to the Divine, making the One whole again. Scientist and theologian Pierre Teilhard de Chardin (1881-1955), who often used alchemical metaphors, understood the ritual of the Holy Thanksgiving, the Mass, as being said for the "*divinizing* of the entire universe...the consecration of the cosmos."[34] Teilhard wrote that we labor "to build the Pleroma," that which is the cosmic whole containing all things, living and dead. We endeavor to restore the Omega point, the universal cosmic center.[35] "Each of our works, by its more or less remote or direct effect upon the spiritual world, helps to make perfect Christ in his mystical totality."[36] The alchemist's great work is the restoration of the center and the soul of the cosmos and her Creator.

This fourth phase of the alchemical process is the most arduous. Some never reach this level. Yet, their wisdom will always be enhanced. "Wisdom is the reflection of eternal light, a spotless mirror of the working of God" (Wisdom of Solomon 7:26). We've been through the dark night of the soul (chaos), several times; we did more than survive; we evolved. As Valentin Tomberg wrote in *Meditations on the Tarot*, we have been "plunged into the darkness of absolute light" and now can see with the eyes of wisdom.[37] This fourth phase is a pilgrimage within itself. A pilgrimage of many pilgrimages dancing with one another. Exploring the intimacy of meaning within the complexity of differing experiences held together with a thin red thread.

Enmeshed within the Acts of John, another early Christian Gnostic text, is a dance and hymn that Jesus taught his disciples. He told them to stand in a circle and hold hands. "Dance everyone.... The whole universe is dancing."[38] This hymn is a recitation of the Passion of Christ, reminiscent of Palm Sunday with liturgical dance. We shouldn't be surprised that Jesus danced. He attended a wedding and provided the best wine ever. Who wouldn't celebrate with a dance?

British poet, theologian, novelist, and member of the Inklings, Charles Williams (1886-1945), wrote about the dance of the Major Arcana in his book, *The Greater Trumps*, which is an excellent example of the Christian use of Tarot to enhance spiritual imagination. Williams wrote:

> Imagine that everything which exists takes part in the movement of a great dance—everything, the electrons, all growing and decaying things, all that seems alive and all that doesn't seem alive, men and beasts, trees and stones...there is nothing anywhere but the dance.[39]

Everything, the sacred and the mundane, was and is swirling in the dervish dance. And like every dance in life, it is "a harmony that might at any moment have become a chaos."[40] For without the potential chaos, there is no magic in the rhythmic harmony of souls in motion.

All of creation joins in the celebration: the earth spins, the trees sway, the birds spread their wings, and the essence of creation dances to the heartbeat of the Divine. Returning to King David in the Bible, it says that he "and all the House of Israel danced before the Lord to (the sounds of) all kinds of cypress wood (instruments), with lyres, harps, timbrels, sistrums, and cymbals" (2 Samuel 6:14).

The dance of the four alchemical phases always begins with The Fool experiencing the spiral of chaos. We, like The Fool, will have to dance our way through these phases several times in our life. Each encounter with another character of our persona will be a pilgrimage of all four of the alchemical phases while we journey through Major Arcana. We are ready now to have the experienced Fool as our leader. Wisdom has bestowed her enlightenment upon The Fool. "The light that shineth in the darkness," as it says in the Gospel of John (1:5). The Fool will introduce us to each of the Major Arcana along the paths of instruction, wisdom, and enlightenment. I hope you have some comfy dancing shoes on hand.

REFLECT ON THE FOOL AND THE PATH OF INSTRUCTION

◊ How do you see yourself in The Fool?

◊ What was the most meaningful pilgrimage that you never intended to walk? What did you learn?

◊ What has been the weirdest, but most instructive moment you've experienced?

◊ When did you feel you had risen from the ashes? How did that feel?

— *CHAPTER 5* —

THE MAGICIAN

Quick Read: Practices their craft to perfection, concentrates without effort, skilled at changing someone's perspective, the person of spirit both above and below. When you pull The Magician you are being asked to become a student and to take up years of training. Or, you're being encouraged to be the master teacher.

Artistic Inspiration: *The Sufi Deck,* "The Alchemist," Ayeda Husain. A bearded man wearing a Turban is pouring over his books and scrolls by candlelight. Above him, loose papers swirl in the breeze. In the background are several astral planets of blues and oranges.

Illumination: "'You are a magician,' Brother James remarked. Brother Paul replied. 'I envy you your proficiency with mechanical things. I only wish the spiritual were as easy to attain.'" Piers Anthony[41]

Biblical Characters: Moses and Jesus

Biblical Text: The Lord said to Moses, "What is that in your hand?" And he said, "A staff." And the Lord said, "Throw it on the ground." So Moses threw it on the ground and it became a snake. (Exodus 4:2)

My wife and I love to go to the Cirque du Soleil. Artistry, acrobatics, strength, and magic. A friend of mine was the headmaster of an art academy for high school students. The school has dedicated significant resources to their dance studio. Hanging above the floor were four large rings draped in brightly colored scarves. The rings, my friend told me, were for those who wanted to master the techniques of the Cirque du

Soleil performers. I asked him about their teacher. "Performers from the Cirque," he told me.

Most people go to the circus and magic shows to watch the performance. But there are some, like my friend's students, who attend the show to learn how the magician enchants the space. The Magician is not Santa Claus. Instead, we are enquiring of the master to teach us the secret tricks of the trade. Our desire is to become the magician's apprentice in order to become The Magician ourselves. The Fool is there to learn from the artisan about the mystery, experience, and magic of being a pilgrim.

Carl Jung had a rule of thumb about the first and second half of a human life. He said he wouldn't take on clients who weren't at least forty years old, because they weren't ready for the individuation process. His idea came from his own experience. At forty, Jung had an affair, after which his wife insisted he leave his successful hospital career, move to another city, build a new house, and start a private practice. That qualifies as chaos at mid-life and the first phase of the alchemical process. Shortly thereafter, Jung started his two-year experiment with the unconscious—an experience that produced his *Red Book* and the book that shaped the next forty years of his psychiatric practice, *Psychological Types.* At forty, Carl Jung was on the first leg of the path of instruction. His guides were Elijah, Salome, and the serpent—all personas of his soul.

The Fool's masters will be Moses and Jesus. Moses was The Magician for the Hebrew people. In the Torah we hear his story of abandonment at birth. Secretly, he was raised by his mother, who was disguised as a nursemaid. He spent his childhood and youth in the Pharoah's palace. As a young man, in anger, he protected a Jewish slave by killing the Egyptian who was beating him. Fearing for his life, Moses fled. He found refuge in another land where he was mentored by his father-in-law, the priest of Midian. Years later, through a paranormal experience, a voice spoke from a burning bush to Moses. The Lord wanted him to go back to Egypt in order to free the Jewish people from their enslavement, but Moses was reluctant to return from the land he had fled. He told the Lord he felt inadequate as a speaker. God wouldn't accept his excuses pointing out that Moses's brother, Aaron, would become his consultant and mouthpiece.

Returning to Egypt, Moses became an adept magician. He turned a rod into a serpent and back again, struck a stone for water, healed his sister, caused plagues, and parted the Red Sea. While in the desert, God gave Moses the Ten Commandments. He taught his people the very basics of living a moral life and building a cohesive community. Through all this, Moses was an influential mentor, preparing Joshua to lead the Israelites into the Promised Land. Magicians need teachers, mentors, guides, and counselors—and in turn, Magicians teach others the way of the pilgrim.

It is no accident that Jesus has, for millennia now, often been called a "new Moses." After walking countless miles with Jesus, his disciples asked him, "Master, teach us how to pray" (Luke 11:1). They knew the technique of prayer; what they longed for was Jesus's intimate relationship with God. They wanted to experience the master's movement of life as being in perpetual communication with the One he knew like none other. To the disciples, his prayer life appeared so natural and effortless. But Jesus had learned how to pray from years of practice.

At twelve, he went to the Temple to hear what the teachers had to say. Joseph taught him how to listen to his dreams as well as how to be a master carpenter. And Mary taught him the ways of the angels. He also received transfigurative counsel from Elijah and Moses, according to the Gospel accounts. The living and the dead in deep conversation witnessed by bystanders (Matthew 17). Jesus may have been born with the magical gift of Divine communication, but the relationship that sustained him in the garden was built upon a lifetime of preparation.

The chief among his disciples, Mary Magdalene, and the apostles, would take what Jesus had taught them and share it with others. They had learned the Master's lessons so well that they would do even greater things than he (John 14:12).

There are many contemporary examples of this mentoring that one might offer. The Reverend Teresa Blythe is one of the foremost spiritual directors in the United States, and longtime director of the Hesychia School of Spiritual Direction. After years of discernment, she created an apprentice program for others to become directors. Some came to her with little or no theological, psychological, or spiritual education. Others came with years of experience but wanting to learn a deeper wisdom from Teresa. Her method is simple. She provides a one-on-one mentoring setting with materials she designed and wrote. When a student is ready, she sends them out to practice what they've learned. Then they return to discuss their experience. This process is repeated until a student is ready to practice without Teresa as their safety net. Her plan is to develop greater spiritual directors than she is.

Every great athlete or performer has a master coach. I coached college baseball for twenty years. It took me way too long and too many failures to realize that the best way for me to coach was in one-on-one sessions. In a group, the players' attention spans were less than three minutes and it was easy for some to hide behind others. The same strategy applied to my work as pastor in an Episcopal church. Preachers have perhaps ten minutes to deliver a sermon. Most parishioners can listen for about ninety seconds at a stretch, then their minds wander for another ninety seconds before they return to what you're saying. I learned over time that people only listen to well-told stories because they are the magic that transmutes. All else is excess and considered, at the best, to be mildly interesting and at the worst irrelevant. But a one-on-one conversation can be extremely fruitful, lasting an hour and only feeling like minutes have passed. Over several sessions, both the storyteller and listener become deeply invested in the dialogue. Mutually, they grow from a relationship that shapes them both. This is the ideal of spiritual companionship.

In this process, The Fool has become a magician and the two companions are better for having known each other. Throughout their lives, they will share their secrets and little tricks for success. Eventually, ready to reveal their magic with other pilgrims who will walk the way of the desert.

REFLECT ON THE MAGICIAN AND THE PATH OF INSTRUCTION

◊ How do you see yourself in The Magician?

◊ Who's been your best mentor? Why? How?

◊ Whose mentor have you been? How did that relationship make you feel?

◊ At what point did you need a mentor and no one showed up for you?

— CHAPTER 6 —

THE HIGH PRIESTESS

Quick Read: Counterpart to The Magician. When you draw The High Priestess, you are being challenged to see yourself as the magic. You are the presence that is a generative force of creation. You are intuitive and sensitive to the needs of those around you, and you carry the knowledge of Divine love into the world.

Artistic Inspiration: *The Alchemical Tarot*, Robert Place. A woman wearing a purple cloak is standing in a moon-shaped boat that is floating on the waters of the unconscious. Her head is adorned with the crown of the moon. She's holding the alchemist's green book of secrets in her right hand. The index finger of her left hand is pressed to her lips, signifying she is keeping the secrets of the arcanum to herself. The full moon shines over her right shoulder.

Illumination: "She is the symbol of the Great Secret, the Hidden Feminine...the Book of Wisdom...God consciousness...the Glory of Shekinah...the manifested Presence of God." Corinne Heline[42]

Biblical Characters: Miriam and Mary Magdalene

Biblical Text: "Do not forsake wisdom, and she will protect you; love her and she will watch over you." (Proverbs 4:6)

The High Priestess and The Magician are companions and she holds the keys to the gate that guards the path to the wisdom of instruction.

> Wisdom is radiant and unfading
> And she is easily discerned by those who love her

> And is found by those who seek her.
> She hastens to make herself known to those who desire her.
> Those who rise early to seek her will have no difficulty
> For the pilgrim will find her sitting at the gate. (Wisdom of Solomon, 6)

Now, she will be The Fool's teacher on this next stretch of the pilgrimage.

While walking the Wicklow Way, it was common for locals to join us for the day. One day, three sisters caught up as we were just leaving our hostel. They had that distinctive accent of the Wicklow Irish. "No boter," and "we're tree sisters," rolled smoothly off the tongue. And their gait up the hill was effortless. At first glance they were difficult to tell apart. Maybe it was their jet-black hair with a natural highlight of red—cut the same length—that made them hard to distinguish one from the other. And while they weren't dressed the same, their well-worn hiking boots were identical. They had a symbiotic relationship. They could finish one another's sentences, but they also were very willing to correct each other of any deviance from a tale they must have told a hundred times. I wondered if we were interrupting their weekly ritual. But they were very open to sharing their knowledge of the terrain, as well as what to expect in the next village. And if asked, they shared the secrets of the ancient lore of the Wicklow Mountains: the political fugitives, the bandits, the hunters, and the ghosts. I felt like I was walking with "tree" High Priestesses.

Miriam, the sister of Moses and Aaron, is the biblical equivalent of The High Priestess. She was Moses's magical counterpart. Pharoah, fearful that his Israelite slaves were overpopulating the land, ordered all male Hebrew babies to be killed. Moses's mother, instead, put her child in a basket, and floated him down the Nile. Pharoah's daughter, feeling pity on the child, rescued Moses from the water. It was Moses's sister Miriam who would connect Pharoah's daughter to the baby's mother, subsequently becoming the baby's nurse.

We meet Miriam, again near the water, as the Israelites crossed the Red Sea, escaping from the Egyptians. In celebration of their survival, she taught her people the Dance of the Arcanum:

> Then the prophet Miriam, took a tambourine in her hand, while all the women went out after her with tambourines, dancing; and she responded to them: Sing to the Lord, for he is gloriously triumphant; horse and chariot he has cast into the sea. (Exodus 15:20)

Miriam never took a husband or had a child. She and her brother Aaron worked by Moses's side during their forty-year sojourn in the desert. At one point, however, Miriam complained that Moses had not recognized her place as a prophet. She spoke up for the equality of women in leadership roles. As has been the case with patriarchal systems, Miriam suffered from speaking out. Her legacy as The High Priestess would extend for eons into the lives of the Israelite women, and her energy would migrate into the New Testament's story of the three Marys.

Mary Magdalene was Jesus's companion. Non-canonical gospels describe them as much more than simply good friends. In the biblical account, Jesus's mother Mary, Mary of Cleophas (her sister-in-law), and Mary Magdalene were all present at Jesus's crucifixion. The esoteric tradition of these three holy women being maid-mother-crone plays out in the Tarot. (Which will be discussed in the next chapter.)

Magdalene, as The High Priestess, was the feminine manifestation of The Magician, the rose of Wisdom Sophia.[43] After Jesus's death, she encountered his spirit just outside his tomb. He spoke, and she recognized his voice. "Teacher," she called him. Later, recounting her experience, she said, "Lord, I saw you today in a vision." Jesus responded, "Blessings on you since you did not waver at the sight of me. Where the mind is, there is the treasure.... A person sees neither through the soul nor the spirit. The mind, which lies between the two, sees the vision" (Gospel of Mary).[44] In a manner that is baffling, the mind coalesces what it sees with our experiences. Then it translates the vision into an art that tells a story which others can relate to.

In 2015, I was privileged to see and touch the original manuscript of *The Saint John's Illuminated Bible*. It's the first handwritten and illuminated Bible to be made in the last 500 years. The artwork is intended to shine a light on the words, not depict a historical event. The artists used a unique nineteenth century Chinese ink for the calligraphy, and the artwork includes combinations of vibrant colored ink and 24-karat gold. The calligraphers and artists scribed the book on three hundred pieces of vellum because much of the Dead Sea Scrolls were written on the same materials. The pages of the vellum are two feet high and three feet wide. With writing on both sides, each weighs approximately two pounds. The book has not been bound. If it were, it would easily take four very strong people to lift it. The size of the book is intended to emphasize that the Bible was originally meant for the entire community and not for private use.

There are two illuminations in the *Saint John's Bible: Gospels and Acts* that provide a symbolic representation of the central images of Christianity—the Crucifixion and the Resurrection. We find the illumination of the Crucifixion in the Gospel of Luke and the Resurrection in the Gospel of John. Set against one another, these pieces of art disrupt our commonly held views of the events of Holy Week. Typically, Christians think of the Crucifixion as the darkest moment in the Christian story. Artists often depict this scene in the dark hues at the apex of a terrible storm. From the Cross, Jesus cries out, "My God, my God, why have you abandoned me?" A portrait of chaos, abandonment, and death.

The Resurrection, however, has been portrayed as Christ bursting forth into a victorious light over death. To symbolize the event, Christian clergy often wear Easter vestments that are covered with gold.

As with The Hanged Man, the illuminators of the *Saint John's Bible* did their best to flip the perspective of these two events on their head. Instead of being dark and foreboding, the Saint John's artist depicted Jesus hanging on the Cross in the brilliant light of pure gold. The gold is thick, raised off the page, bringing the crucified Christ into three dimensions. This scene is the most striking of any within this *Bible*.

In contrast to the blinding light of the Crucifixion scene, they painted the Resurrection in dark blues. Here, we only see the shrouded hood of the Christ figure from the back. We do, however, see the face of Mary Magdalene, who is clad in a deep red robe. The only gold in this scene is on the hands of Jesus' companion. The priesthood of the Christ figure has now been transmigrated into Mary. "I have seen the Lord and he has spoken to me" (John 20:18). When we view this in conjunction with the Tarot, we understand that she has been transmuted into The High Priestess.

In her book, *Mary Magdalene,* Cynthia Bourgeault suggests that while the Bible displayed the historical Jesus as male, he was only his complete archetypal self in the union of ChristoSophia.[45] In other words, to become who he was intended to be, Jesus had to complete the union of all opposites and become the androgynous One. He had to find The High Priestess within himself. A union only satisfied in both the material and spiritual states—and a oneness that all humans must discover within their own self.

In the Wisdom traditions, Sophia has been depicted as the androgynous One. She has many names and has appeared in multiple forms, through which she has spoken her truth to the ages. She is the co-creator: "Before the beginning of the earth…I was there when Yahweh drew a circle on the face of the deep" (Proverbs 8:23, 27). She is the teacher: "Now my children, listen to me; happy are those who keep my ways" (Proverbs 8:32). She is the mystic: "For it is in the silence that the Teacher spoke to her" (The Gospel of Mary 17:8). She is the great high priestess: "Come, eat of my bread and drink of the wine I have mixed. Lay aside immaturity, and live, and walk in the way of insight" (Proverbs 9:5). She is the revolutionary: "The Divine has brought down the powerful from their thrones and lifted up the lowly; the Divine has filled the hungry with good things and sent the rich away empty" (Luke 1:52-53). She is the eternal Queen: "A woman clothed in the sun, with the moon under her feet, and on her head a crown of twelve stars" (Revelation 12:1). She is worthy of praise and worship: "Nothing you desire can compare with Her…She is a Tree of Life to those who lay hold of Her" (Proverbs 3:15, 18).

To become one with the Divine starts with meditation upon *their* attributes. To envision the very essence of our being slipping into the mystic's vision of oneness. Imaging that we are becoming androgynous; the union of The Magician and The High Priestess that resides within every one of us.

The Fool sits at the feet of The High Priestess. She shares the secret lessons of the desert's sacred way. "The nature of matter…the good, came to be with you, to enter the essence of each nature, and to restore it to its root…Whoever has ears to hear, should hear," as it says in The Gospel of Mary. And we shall hear and heed the words of The High Priestess, for she has placed some gold on The Fool's hands.

REFLECT ON THE HIGH PRIESTESS AND THE PATH OF INSTRUCTION

◊ Where do you see yourself in The High Priestess?
◊ Have you been unappreciated, like Miriam? What inspired you to continue on?
◊ Who is Mary Magdalene to you?
◊ Have you had a mystical experience(s)? How have they instructed your spirituality?

— *CHAPTER 7* —

THE EMPRESS

Quick Read: She is Mother Earth, the Great Mother: maid, mother, and crone. She will open the door to the new heaven, and her feet rest on the moon. The Empress is vigilant, persistent, and faithful to her children. She is the Celts Green Woman. When you pull this card, you are being asked to nourish creation as if its ambilocal cord were connected to you.

Artistic Inspiration: *The Light Seers Tarot,* by Chris-Anne. This contemporary deck is one of the most ethnically inclusive on the market. The Empress is a woman who may or may not be pregnant with child but is ready to birth the world.

Illumination: "It is she who carries the seed from which ultimately will spring a new transcendental awareness in which mysticism and science, and spirit and flesh, inner and outer, can be experienced as one world." Sallie Nichols[46]

Biblical Characters: Rachel and Naomi

Biblical Text: "A great and wondrous sign appeared in heaven, a woman clothed with the sun, with the moon under her feet and a crown of twelve stars on her head. She was pregnant and cried out in pain as she was about to give birth." (Revelation 12:2)

The Empress is the Great Mother, the Mother Queen, and first in the lineage of the wise women of the land. She is the secret rose who binds all of nature together. She is the chalice and the basin of the bowl from which flow blood and water. The Empress is the vessel of transmutation. She was present before the beginning of the earth. "When

God established the heavens, I was there, when God drew a circle on the face of the deep…when God marked out the foundations of the earth, I was beside him, like a master worker" (Proverbs 8:23). (You will notice some overlap between the archetypes of the Tarot as there are in human personalities. That's why this same verse was cited for The High Priestess.) These verses point back to creation, when God said, "Let *us* make humankind in *our* image" (Genesis 1:26).

The Empress has always been present, never to be considered anything other than an equal image of the Divine. In the Kabbalah, the masculine is represented by Hokhmah as wisdom, and the feminine Binah as understanding, each are equal aspects of God. All other facets of creation emanate from these two. The Tarot places The Empress before The Emperor stressing that life emerges from water. The child begins life in the mother's womb, birthed by her. Drawing their first nourishment, the child looks into its mother's eyes before any other's. Creation has worshipped the Great Mother first.

In the Bible, Rachel is the embodiment of The Empress—maid, mother and crone. Born of Adinah and Laban, Rachel seemed destined for a life of tears. When she met Jacob—her cousin and future husband—he kissed her, and he wept (Genesis 29:11). Some might say Jacob's tears were shed from the heart of romantic love, and maybe so. But for the Kabbalist, his tears symbolized an awakening from spiritual slumber into a life of oneness with the Divine. These were tears of Jacob's vision; one of Rachel weeping. Her long journey of barrenness ending in grief. A birth into death and a lonely grave. Her tears spilt, envisioning the shards of hundreds of soul's lights living in exile.[47]

Rachel lived in constant conflict with her sister Leah (Genesis 30:1). Both were married to Jacob through the trickery of their father. Jacob loved Rachel, but Leah was the eldest, and by custom, would be the first to marry.

Leah gave birth to six sons of the tribes of Israel and one daughter, Dinah. After years of barrenness, Rachel gave birth to two sons, Joseph and Benjamin. She died giving birth to the latter and was buried beside the road on the way to Bethlehem. Her two sons would become clan chiefs of the tribes of Israel. Zilpah and Bilah, handmaids to Leah and Rachel respectfully, each gave birth to two of the four remaining tribesmen.

Rachel is known as the great mother of Israel because of her long forbearance, devotion to prayer, difficult labor, and subsequent death in childbirth. The prophet Jeremiah enshrined her role with his reference to her weeping from the grave for the exiled and enslaved children of Jerusalem (Jeremiah 31:15). But the Lord said, "I will turn their mourning into joy" (31:13). Rachel, the maid who won Jacob's heart. Rachel, the mother of Israel. And Rachel, the crone who weeps from the tomb, consoling a nation.

We cannot expect any human being to live up to the model of The Empress. My mother was a saint. Against all odds, she and my father not only kept my sister, who suffered from Prader-Willi syndrome, alive, but now Dinah is the oldest known living person with PWS. Average life expectancy for people like my sister is mid-thirties. As I write this, she is sixty-nine. But our mother had her faults and fragilities. The cost of raising Dinah was monumental. Near the end of her life, our mom journaled that she felt her soul had been sacrificed in order to become Dinah's mother. The weight was heavy, the physical issues traumatic, and the chronic depression darkened her days until the moment she died. Empress, she was, shadows and all.

The mother-in-law is equally The Empress. Naomi, found in the Bible's book of Ruth, is an excellent archetypal model. Naomi's husband, as well as her two adult sons, had died. She decided that the best thing to do was return to her homeland, where she hoped some distant relatives would care for her. Naomi implored her two daughters-in-laws, Ruth and Orpah, to remain in Moab and return to their fathers. Orpah kissed Naomi and followed her rational advice. Ruth, however, clung to Naomi, begging not to be sent away. The mother-in-law acquiesced, and the two made the long journey to Bethlehem. Ruth eventually married Boaz and they had a child named Obed, who would become the grandfather of King David.

Naomi's character is strong, kind, attentive, and resourceful—all characteristics of the biblical eagle: "An eagle stirreth up her nest, fluttering over her young, spreadeth abroad her wings, taketh them, beareth them on her wings" (Deuteronomy 32:11). The Tarot Empress is often depicted as accompanied by an eagle representing strength and creativity in establishing the new heaven and new earth. She is the mystical union of head and heart. And she teaches her children the ways of birth, life, and death.

The archetype of The Empress is a complex of layers, both mother and mother-in-law. Rachel and Naomi, lives filled with joy and grief, plenty and scarcity, death and rebirth. These traits also found their way into Ireland's Patron Saint Brigid. She became The Empress, entwined into the legends of her namesake goddess. Saint Brigid's hagiographers drew upon the heroic stories of their own mothers to fashion the greatest of Ireland's saints, who was both Druidess and Christian. She was the firekeeper, the mother of Gaul, the midwife of Jesus, the maiden warrior, the protector of the poor, the abbess of a male and female monastery, herbalist, healer of the human and animal alike, and the crone of wisdom. And her daughter, Darlughdach, Black Brigid, became the last of the ancient firekeepers. Brigid was goddess, saint, and mother. But she wasn't perfect. Every saint has a shadow.

When we place the archetype of The Empress, or any of the other Tarot characters, on an elevated pedestal we distance ourselves from the possibility of an intimate relationship with the shadows of life. The person who we wish would have been our empress, or emperor, or hierophant, or lover, will never live up to our hopes or even the least of normal expectations. And for that loss, we grieve. Still, in the greatest paradox of life, we come to recognize that the most sacred of all will be found in the most obscure and unexpected places. Every archetype, even the Great Mother, must have the courage to embrace the worst of themselves. And when she does, she will be present to mentor us so that we may take on our important roles, and in turn, sharing with the next generation.

A note to men. While you will never give birth to a child, you have the psychic capacity to mother a child. But unless you embrace your inner empress, those opportunities will pass you by. Men who are open about their inner feminine are not weak, they are wise.

REFLECT ON THE EMPRESS AND THE PATH OF INSTRUCTION

◊ Where do you see yourself in The Empress?
◊ Who's been The Empress in your life? What are the traits that make them so?
◊ Where have you unexpectedly been Empress?
◊ Can you see The Empress in someone who doesn't exhibit the Maid, Mother, Crone?

— CHAPTER 8 —
THE EMPEROR

Quick Read: Father Sky, architect, builder, companion to The Empress, provider and protector of children, the Celts Green Man. Spending time with this card will challenge you to be a people-centric leader, one who sees a leader in every chair within the circle. You will have to be strong enough to defend the weak without anyone every knowing you're in charge.

Artistic Inspiration: *Tarot of the Hidden Realms*, Julia Jeffrey. Her deck is filled with faery and imagination of the fey. Her Emperor is shrouded in shadows and ravens. He wears the emblem of the dragon. The picture expresses his willingness to engage the personal shadows of life.

Illumination: "The feminine power of love and the male force of life-giving potency is balanced in The Emperor's hands as orb and scepter." Stephen Hoeller[48]

Biblical Character: David

Biblical Text: "The Lord has sought out a man after his own heart; and the Lord had appointed him to be ruler over his people." (I Samuel 13:14)

The Bible's most conflicted characters are its emperors and kings. Their stories are filled with both the brightness of the midday sun and the dark moonless night: bold confidence and uncertainty, success and failure, the good and bad. We could say this about every character in the Tarot story, except that The Emperor's actions are always on full display in some of the Bible's most gruesome scenes. The easiest example to choose would be King Saul. But no one likes him. So, let's pick on King David. Everyone loves him, everyone except Saul, perhaps Michel, and Absalom, and...maybe we should say everyone simultaneously loves him and hates him.

Historically, it's difficult to make any definitive statements about the man known as King David. Most Bible scholars today accept the stories of the books of Samuel and Kings as being written generations after David. As best as anyone can surmise, David lived somewhere around 1000 BCE. More recent archeological evidence seems to affirm this. Without regard to such vague details, David was a musician, poet, lover, rebel, renegade, warrior, and king. Given the biblical mythos, he could have been bi-sexual, was an adulterer, and without question, was complicit in murder. Still, we are told that he was a man after God's own heart (Acts 13:22, 1 Samuel 13:14). Metaphorically, King David has been the paradoxical emblematic totem of the messy union between the material kingdom of humanity and the spiritual relationship with the Divine—complete with a complex of shadows. Of course, one man's shadow might be another man's moment of selfhood.

The point here is not to be an observer of the obvious. Our project is to look between the lines and search for thin places between the opposites that live within every person's masculinity, without regard to their sexuality or born identity. Love is no respecter of cultural norms.

Love is a matter of the soul. "The soul of Jonathan was bound to the soul of David, and Jonathan loved him as his own soul.... And Jonathan made David swear again by his love for him; for he loved him as he loved his own life" (1 Samuel 18:1, 20:17). As Jesus wept at the tomb of his friend Lazarus, so David cried tears of grief at Jonathan's death. "I am distressed for you, my brother Jonathan; greatly beloved were you to me; your love to me was wonderful, passing the love of a woman" (2 Samuel 1:26). The best part of the story of David and Jonathan is that they pledged their love for one another and were not afraid to sing it out loud. Whether they were lovers or not, they expressed their feelings for one another freely. A good model for today's men regardless of sexuality.

The dark side of The Emperor card is not that love is a matter of the soul, but that he is typically unwilling or uncomfortable to express love to another male, whether it be his father, son, grandson, friend, or lover. The Emperor might believe that their father, son, grandson, friend, or lover "knows" they love them without telling them. But we all realize that this type of head knowledge is never felt in the heart. Words have souls and speak soul to soul in matters of love—heart to heart. It's the soul of words that have the potential to transmute The Emperor's heart and his beloved, be they male, female, binary, or LGBTQ+.

King David had many sons, three in particular, each who attempted their own coup. Absalom, the most charismatic of the three, drew significant biblical attention. While the Bible never implicitly says the King loved Absalom, when his son died trying to overthrow the throne, David wailed. His grief was so profound that the King's general, Joab, reprimanded him. "Today you have covered with shame the face of all your officers who have saved your life...for love of those who hate you and for hatred of those who love" (2 Samuel 19:5-6). Joab believed David's love was misplaced.

As David approached his own death, Queen Bathsheba, the prophet Nathan, and the seer Zadok influenced the King to choose Bathsheba's son, Solomon, as successor and heir. At Solomon's birth, the prophet Nathan told David that "The Lord loved" his new-born son (2 Samuel 12:27). God's love for any individual is rarely mentioned in the Bible, but the interplay of Logos and Eros was repeatedly played out in dramatic fashion over David's life.

Solomon's mother was the woman David seduced, got pregnant, and then killed her husband to cover up his indiscretion. Bathsheba's first child died seven days after its birth. Who was responsible for the baby's death? "The Lord struck the child," forgiving David, but causing the child to die. This action was nothing new from God. The Lord tells Moses:

> God [is] merciful and gracious, slow to anger, and abounding in steadfast love and faithfulness keeping steadfast love for the thousandth generation, forgiving iniquity and transgression and sin, yet by no

> means clearing the guilty, but visiting the iniquity of the parents upon the children and the children's children to the third and fourth generation. (Exodus 34:6-7)

There is more than a bit of contradiction here from father God. Which is it, steadfast love or punishment of innocent children? Evidently, the key to any love or forgiveness from The Emperor seems dependent upon their subjects keeping the law. Love here is definitely conditional.

Not to complicate the story of this archetype, but evidently God wasn't above changing God's mind. Job (in the biblical book that carries his name) "was blameless and upright, one who feared God and turned away from evil." Yet, by virtue of a wager between God and Lucifer, Job's children were killed, and he was stripped of his health and wealth. God never even had the graciousness to say, "I'm sorry." It was Job who had to repent, and for what? Job's brothers and sisters eventually arrived on the scene to show their sibling "sympathy and comforted him for all the evil that the Lord had brought upon him" (42:11). They even took up a collection and gave their brother money to start up his business again. The Bible says that God gave Job another family and restored his health and wealth fourfold. Yet, we are never told what Job thought about the trauma exacted upon him. Surely, he suffered from PTSD. But I guess the author of Job thought that some things are better left to the imagination.

The acclaimed Old Testament scholar Walter Brueggemann wrote in his *Theology of the Old Testament* that Christians believe in an irascible God who is found in elusive texts that require polyphonic interpretations.[49] Little wonder the emperors (or want to be emperors) of "God fearing nations" want a reciprocal relationship with conditions. "If you love me, I'll give you a treat. If not, well…there's hell to pay for generations to come."

In order to evolve beyond the all too familiar destructive behavior of patriarchal misogyny, The Emperor must repent, acknowledge his shadows, and begin the most arduous work of re-inventing themselves for the sake of creating a new role model for future generations. Significant transmutation requires serious alchemical work: chaos, breaking through the egg, dealing with the weird, and rising from the ashes. From my perspective, the current institutional culture of American emperors has yet to find their way out of the tornado of their own making, and they're running out of time. Hope lies in the upcoming generations. But they will have to choose their role models carefully.

REFLECT ON THE EMPEROR AND THE PATH OF INSTRUCTION

◊ How do you access the role of Emperor in your culture, in the twenty-first century?

◊ How has your view of the Bible influenced your understanding of patriarchy?

◊ If there's one thing you could tell The Emperor in your life, what would that be?

— CHAPTER 9 —

THE HEIROPHANT

Quick Read: The Hierophant is a teacher, sage, mentor, shaman, and priest. And when you draw this card you're being asked to take on at least one of these roles.

Artistic Inspiration: *The Wildwood Tarot,* John Matthews and Mark Ryan. They identified the Hierophant in their deck as "The Ancestor"—a persona wearing a stag head while striking a tri-spiral drum. The Ancestor is standing in a snow filled field surrounded by leafless trees.

Illumination: "We at the Church of the Heavenly Message rest content and secure in our faith...My dearly beloved, the doors of Spiritual Truth are open to all.... Whatever your creed it will serve simply to strengthen it, whether you are accustomed to worship God in meeting house, cathedral, or synagogue." William Lindsay Gresham[50]

Biblical Character: Melchizedek

Biblical Text: "And King Melchizedek of Salem brought out bread and wine; he was priest of God Most High. He blessed him and said, 'Blessed be Abram by God Most High, maker of heaven and earth; and blessed be God Most High, who has delivered your enemies into your hand.'" (Genesis 14:18-20)

The Hierophant might be more misunderstood than The Hanged Man. In the *Marseille* deck, The Hierophant is called The Pope (*Le Pape*). But because of the political sway of the Roman papacy, the Reformation, and Renaissance humanism, Tarot devotees moved away from the use of the papal reference in favor of The Hierophant. The meaning of the character "as one who teaches wisdom," however, did not change.

In the eighteenth century, French Protestant pastor and expert on Tarot, Antoine Court de Gabelin (1725-1784), associated the Pope card with a more pre-Christian ancient esoteric wisdom, thereby being one of the first to identify the card as The Hierophant. Nineteenth-century card creators A.E. Waite and Aleister Crowley were both generally anti-papist, though for different reasons. And with the gaining public popularity of their decks, the name Hierophant still carries forward on most Tarot cards today.

The *Marseille* deck casts some interesting light on the union of opposites and correspondences between the first seven cards. In that deck, The High Priestess is *La Papesse*, the feminine pope. During the thirteenth century, a story appeared that a woman, Pope Joan, sat on the papal throne four centuries earlier. This legend held sway until modern scholars dismissed the story as more wishful thinking than fact.

According to legend, Joan disguised herself as a man. Through her intelligence and wise action, she rose through the ecclesiastical ranks, eventually being elected pope. Two years after her installation, she gave birth to a child while processing down the halls of the Vatican. The story goes she died on the floor while in labor. One version says she died of natural causes; the other said she was murdered as a fraud. Church historians have done their best to blot out the story, but the power of the archetypal image lives on.

Without regard to the historicity of Pope Joan's reign, the weight of the story has continued to provide an intriguing twist in the Tarot's lexicon. To read Tarot is to consider every symbol available on the card. Numbers carry significance in their own right as well as when added or subtracted from another integer. As with the Bible, numerology is vital to having a complete understanding of Tarot. Biblical and Tarot numerology will be explored in more detail in Chapter 26 about the pips. However, the numbers of the Major Arcana are also significant in reading the first seven cards (The Magician through The Chariot).

The earliest teachers of Tarot paired the first six cards so that their numbers would equal seven—completeness—the sacred number of The Chariot, the card of transition, and the last milepost on the path of instruction. Wholeness equals the incorporation of the instruction given by the first six Major Arcana. This is why the paths are septenary in design: path of instruction (one through seven), path of wisdom (eight through fourteen), and path of enlightenment (fifteen through twenty-one). The final card of each path is a derivative of seven; the symbol of transition from one level to the next and the continuum of all Tarot numbers from the One. The numbers of each card have meanings and as well they have correspondent meanings with other cards.

The repetitive nature of the lessons offered by the original Tarot is intentional. Remember, the early Tarot was used as a mnemonic devise to learn about the mysterious things of life, like God, relationships, life, and death. And as the Rule of Seven applied in days past, recent research affirms that someone needs to hear and read new material between six and twenty times to retain it. Hence, seven is a critical number for both the Bible and the Tarot.

In older decks, like the *Marseille*, *La Papesse* (two) was paired with *Le Pope* (five).[51] Two represents duality as well the potential for the union of opposites. Five symbolizes disturbance and contradiction. French physician and author Gerard Anaclet Vincent Encausse (1865-1916), also known as Papus, explained in *The Tarot of the Bohemians* that the original pairings were based on theosophic mathematics. Simply put, the addition of numbers to find the correlational meaning. For example: The Popess is two and The Pope is five, (2+5=7). Here, we have a perfect example of two opposites coming together to form a higher union. The male pope is incomplete without the female pope but together they form a strong union.

Other pairings on this first path of The Fool see The Magician (One) joined with the Lover (Six), (1+6=7). And the Empress and Emperor are three and four, respectively, which equals seven. Seven, for the Tarot, is a sacred number of wholeness (as it is in the Bible), and the spirit of transmission. In reading Tarot, we are asked to pay attention to every piece of information the cards offer: numbers, colors, symbols, nature, sexuality, everything provides clues to the riddles of life. This is particularly important in relationship to reading more than one card in a draw. (Again, more information on numerology will be discussed in chapter 26.) The cards are revealing instructions, wisdom, and enlightenment through a wholistic model.

The idea that completeness equals the transmission of instruction, wisdom, and enlightenment was taken from the Bible's interweaving of Wisdom, or Sophia, as YHVH's partner. "I [Wisdom Sophia] have good advice and sound wisdom; I have insight. I have strength" (Proverbs 8:27). Again, this is another reference to the union of The Popess and The Pope. The ideas, however, are not confined to the Bible.

Christian Hermeticist, Papus, brought together concepts from several mystical traditions including esoteric Christianity, the Kabbalah, and alchemy. As we've already seen, Papus believed that numerology could reveal vital secrets about the Bible. He combined the number three of the Christian Trinity and the number four of the Tetragrammaton as it was understood in Jewish mysticism. The unpronounceable name of God—YHVH—was conceived of in Papus' system as Yod (the Father), He (the Mother), Vau (the Son), and He (the daughter). Three, the Trinity, plus four, the Tetragrammaton equals seven. Wisdom, in Papus's theology, is derived from the unity of all aspects of the Divine.

While the names of the Divine may have gender identity attached to them, the intent is not to see them as separate detached facets, but as the many faces of the Divine One. As in, adding the value of the second card of the Tarot, *La Pappesse* with the fifth, *Le Pape,* in order to experience the sacred marriage of the opposites. For the mystic, this union represents the androgynous figure of the original human, *adam*: to be in a state of complete oneness with one's self. In Genesis 1:26-27, "God said, 'Let us make humankind (*adam*) in our image, according to our likeness.... So God created humankind (*adam*) in his image, in the image of God he created them; male and female he created them." Then *adam*, the man, speaks, saying in Genesis 2:23:

> This one at last

Is bone of my bones
And flesh of my flesh.
This one shall be called Woman,
For from Man was she taken.

And from that moment (psychologically speaking) humans have been at the work of re-uniting their opposites in order to uncover (or re-remember) their true unified self.

One of the more complex and mystical figures in the Bible, Melchizedek, appears in Genesis as spiritually androgynous.[52] A figure of which there is no evidence of this character's birth or death. Melchizedek seems to appear out of nowhere "yet it is testified that he lives" (Hebrews 7:8). In one of the earliest Jewish gnostic texts, it is suggested that this priest of the God Most High, was an angel. With Melchizedek's bread, wine, and a blessing, this mystical priest spanned the long arc of the pre-Abrahamic traditions, to Abraham, to Jesus as the Christ, and the early Christians. And this biblical character may be the best representation of the union of The High Priestess and the Hierophant into the pure potential of unity.

In Genesis 14:18-20 we are introduced to the ancient concept of the royal priesthood. Melchizedek is both king and priest of Salem (Jerusalem) who blessed Abram. This is the only time Salem—Jerusalem—was mentioned in the Torah. The God Most High, *El*, was worshipped in pre- and ancient Israelite times. Melchizedek "was the founder of a royal priesthood" in Jerusalem.[53] "The Lord has sworn and will not change his mind. You are a priest forever according to the order of Melchizedek" (Psalm 110:4). One hundred years before Jesus appeared on the scene, the community at Qumran wrote the hymn, "The Heavenly Prince Melchizedek."[54] The text declares that in the "Year of Grace for Melchizedek," this priest will be the one that "proclaims liberty to the captives," and "judge the holy ones of God" (quoting from Isaiah). Melchizedek will prophesy the day of peace and salvation of God. Then, one hundred years after Jesus, the first century Church tried to bolster the strength of the faithful by declaring in the Letter to the Hebrews that Jesus Christ was of the Order of Melchizedek.

As mentioned in the chapter on The High Priestess, Mary Magdalene's spiritual union with the Christ, The Hierophant, births the ChristoSophia figure, Wisdom. Such a union mirrors the mystical union of Wisdom Sophia with all the aspects of YHVH—Divine Wisdom. "Long ago God spoke to our ancestors in many and various ways" (Hebrews 1:1). Those ancient ways have been taught to us through the words and actions of Melchizedek, The Hierophant. Yet another figure who has taken on the work of becoming at one with their interior opposite. Together, this spiritual androgyne will teach us how to become at one with our own self by walking the path through the desert's Sacred Way, one that is inhabited by our dragons—the opposites.

REFLECT ON THE HIEROPHANT AND THE PATH OF INSTRUCTION

◊ Where do you relate to The Hierophant?
◊ Who has been The Hierophant in your life? What's the most important lesson they have taught you?
◊ Have you encountered Hierophants of different genders? How have they impacted your life?
◊ How might you consider yourself a priest of the Order of Melchizedek?

— *CHAPTER 10* —

THE LOVERS

Quick Read: This is the first card to have an angelic being. Sometimes referred to as "The Twins." Reliant upon the alchemical ideas of analysis and synthesis. The symbol of the caduceus, the union of twin serpents (Moses Numbers 21:9 and Jesus John 3:14). The message of this card is about choices we make in regard to our relationships with those we love. Upon pulling this card from the deck we might be thinking of romantic love, or the lack of it—and that might be the case. However, the card may be speaking to our relationship with the Divine. Or someone else we love: parent, sibling, child. Or, perhaps someone we love that is no longer with us.

Artistic Inspiration: *Guardian of the Night Tarot,* M.J. Cullinane. All the figures in this gorgeous deck are non-human, eliminating, for the most part, gender duality. Cullinane chose the scorpions as her lovers because they are independent, grounded, self-reliant, passionate, and dangerous.

Illumination: "I think that when I grow up," Maggie announced, "I shall go back to Magdala and become a fisherman on the Sea of Galilee." I laughed, "Don't be silly you are a girl. You can't be a fisherman." "Yes, I can." "No, you can't. You have to marry and have sons. Are you betrothed, by the way?" Joshua said: "Come with me, Maggie, and I will make you a fisher of men." "What the hell does that mean?" Maggie asked. Christopher Moore[55]

Biblical Charactesr: Solomon and Pharoah's daughter

Biblical Text: "I am black and beautiful, O daughters of Jerusalem, like the tents of Kedar, like the curtains of Solomon.... Ah, you are beautiful my love, truly lovely." (Song of Solomon 1:5, 16, sometimes known as Song of Songs or Canticles.)

The love poems of Solomon are steeped in erotic magic. The opening line, "Your love is better than wine," is a direct reference to the ecstatic mystical experience within the throes of passionate love. For centuries, professionals sang Solomon's songs as part of marriage ceremonies. Those who witnessed the performances knew precisely that these were expressions of Eros.

Christianity has struggled, however, with the overt sexual content of the Song of Songs. Despite being included in the Bible's canon, theologians have tried to water down the graphic images by postulating that they are a figurative expression of Christ's love for his beloved Church. Such a theology intends to table any notion of sexuality. Say what you will, believe what you want, the Song of Solomon is steamy stuff. Why else do you think Saint Teresa imagined "the ecstasy of devotion," an experience she described as "mystical transverberation"? Sounds rather orgasmic, don't you think? I've seen Bernini's sculpture, "Ecstasy of Saint Teresa," on display at Santa Maria della Vittoria in Rome; though the marble stone is cold, the sculpture itself heats the imagination quite well. Such imagery is in line with the Kabbalists, who consider the Song of Songs a metaphor for being in sublime union with the Divine. And it also pours over into their love relationships with their spouse. Arthur Green writes in *A Guide to the Zohar*, "*Shekhinah* does not dwell where the wholeness of male-female union is lacking."[56] The mystic's spirituality is meant to uncover the sacred in every human experience. And seeing the Divine in one's lover is intended regardless of the sexual identity of those who are in love. As the Apostle wrote, "there is no longer male or female" (Galatians 3:28). We are all spiritually androgynous and love's attraction knows no bounds.

Whether King Solomon wrote the love songs is debatable. His reputation, however, as a poet and a lover would be enough to inspire the love-soaked heart of many a song writer. Solomon's love for Pharoah's daughter is well documented in 1 Kings. (3:1, 9:16, 24, and 11:1) Of course, like Saul and David, the kings before Solomon were polygamous.

The charge against Solomon was not that he had many wives, but that they were foreign.

Maybe the riddle of The Lovers card lies in its relationship to The Magician. Italian priest Marsilio Ficino (1433-1499) wrote that "Love is a Magus." As in, love itself is the magic of enchantment. What makes the riddle of love so maddening is that no one knows the answer to the question, "What is love?" Who to love seems to be easier to negotiate. Solomon loved many. The ancient Rabbis loved God. And Christians speak of loving the Church. But what does it mean to experience love as a mystical transverberation? Solomon, the Rabbis, and the Christians presumedly knew whom they loved. But do they intimately "know," in the biblical sense, the substance of their love? The question posed by The Lover in the Tarot, may not be who to love, but to know love itself.

Once again, we turn to the Song of Solomon. Love itself is the concern—to know love, to love, and to be loved. All something we desire from the heart. More than a feeling, but a longing, the soul's desire, that grows and blossoms. "And God will place these desires in your heart" (Psalm 37:4). The desire of love manifests itself in our heart, for then we will know love. This kind of love.

> Set me a seal upon your heart,
>
> As a seal (tattoo) upon your arm;
>
> Its flashes are flashes of fire,
>
> A raging flame.
>
> Many waters cannot quench love,
>
> Neither can floods drown it.
>
> If one offered for love
>
> All the wealth of one's house,
>
> It would be utterly scorned. (Song of Solomon 8:6-7)

The Lover has spoken love to The Fool. If you can sing Solomon's song and imagine making a sustainable commitment to whoever, or whatever, you're making such a pledge, then love could be at hand. But in the end, you must define love for yourself. That is the ultimate message of

The Lovers. The interchangeability of the relationship between the lover and the beloved.

At one point in our lives, my wife and I accepted the reality that we would not have grandchildren. The reasons were honest and realistic. But the grief of loss of a love hoped for cut deep. A grief that Pauline Boss identifies as ambiguous loss. Nine years later, our first grandchild was born. Friends had told me that grandchildren would change my life. I believed them, but I had no idea what that would be until I held our grandchild for the first time. As much as I know love, I had never felt *that* kind of love staring back at me.

I mentioned British author and Inkling, Charles Williams, in chapter 4. His novel, *The Greater Trumps,* addresses the correspondences between Christianity and the Tarot. One of Williams's more prominent theological ideas is that of "Romantic Love." Simply put, in that first moment of falling in love, the image of the person who is the object of our love represents the Divine Beloved. That's what I felt when I held our grandchild for the first time.

The person we love is not God, but the essence of the Divine within that person. I dedicated this book to my wife, Catherine. And I quoted these words (with adaption) from the *Zohar* that expresses what I can in no other way. "Isaac embraced faith, seeing *Shekinah* dwelling in his wife."[57] Williams tried to explain the thinness between that which is inseparable. "This also is Thou and neither is this thou." The space between the image of our devotion and that of Divine love is no more than the air we share. For Williams, "Romantic Love" replicates the intoxication of this way of being in love.[58] He relied on Dante's unrequited love of Beatrice as an example. There aren't enough idyllic phrases or artistic images that can recount a love we grieve, an ambiguous loss. For Williams, that love and those feelings are tantamount to our daily relationship with God. A love that never tires or becomes mundane or bores us. Romantic Love is a love beyond the intellect, a love that intensifies over a lifetime. Imagine such a powerful love being shared mutually.

To worship God is one thing. To love God is quite another. Psalm 100 outlines the acts of worship, as making a joyful noise, offering thanksgiving, and praising and blessings the Lord God. But the Shema makes it quite clear that loving God requires actions of the soul. "Love the Lord your God with all your heart, and all your soul, and with all your might" (Deuteronomy 6:4-9). In answering the question as to the greatest of the commandments, Jesus cited the Shema and added the admonition "love your neighbor as yourself" (Leviticus 19:8). In Tarot language, Charles Williams was trying to answer the Lover's riddle, "what is love?" His response was the theology of Romantic Love. Where he translated Solomon's feelings of love for the Shulamite and hers for the king into how we are to love God with our entire being and, in turn, receive God's love for us. Love is an act of intimate mutuality that defies definition. You have to see it, feel it, and know it, to experience the transverberation.

REFLECT ON THE LOVERS AND THE PATH OF INSTRUCTION

◊ To which of the figures on The Lovers card do you most relate?
◊ What did a first experience of love feel like for you?
◊ How might you put words to the mutuality of love in your own life?
◊ What are your thoughts about Cullinane's scorpions as The Lovers?

— CHAPTER 11 —

THE CHARIOT

Quick Read: The charioteer is enthroned in the chariot of four pillars, which is drawn by two or four mystical figures. These could be horses, sphinx, or humans with animal faces. These figures are one with the vehicle. Chariots carry the metaphorical sacred Holy Grail. The Chariot is the symbol of transition. When you make a blind draw and pull this card it mirrors transitions in our lives. It also asks two questions: "Who is in control of your chariot?" And "Where are you going?" The answer to that last question can be physical, spiritual, or mystical.

Artistic Inspiration: *Rider-Waite-Smith*, Pamela Colman Smith. The charioteer is at one with the chariot. Two sphinxes pull the throne shaped vehicle away from the city. Neither sphinx is harnessed to the chariot and the charioteer is guiding them with a magical wand.

Illumination: "To the splendor of the chariots and the excellent beauty of the horses, the charioteers added the personality necessary to perfect the display.... Even the horses have a share in the ovation; nor were they less conscious than their masters of the honors." Lew Wallace[59]

Biblical Characters: Ezekiel and Zechariah

Biblical Text: "And again I looked up and saw four chariots coming out of heaven from between two mountains—mountains of bronze. The first chariot had red horses, the second chariot black horses, the third chariot white horses, and the fourth chariot dappled gray horses." (Zechariah 6:1-2)

"The four had the face of a man, and the face of a lion, the face of an ox, and of an eagle. And the four had one likeness. Their appearance and their work as it were a wheel in the middle of a wheel and their rings were full of eyes round about them." (Ezekiel 1)

The Chariot is the last stop on The Fool's path of instruction. Our Chariot weaves together the important lessons of the first six Major Arcana within its own message—a wheel within a wheel. This ancient vessel symbolizes significant transition, both physical and spiritual. Each of the previous six archetypal symbols has at their heart the importance of integrating their opposite. And The Chariot may be the most graphic of the Major Arcana that displays the vital importance of the mystic's way.

Think back to the beginning of the path of instruction. YHVH is immanent—present and active in the people's everyday lives. Moses, the biblical equivalent of The Magician, and Miriam, his sister The High Priestess, call upon and celebrate YHVH's victory in their escape from the oppressor. Moses raised his hand, the Red Sea parted, and with another signal the waters engulfed the pursuing warriors. The tsunami drowned their mighty chariots (Exodus 14). YHVH emerged as the warrior God. His chariots were the clouds and his messenger was the fierce thunder and lightning (Psalm 104). The Tarot's Chariot symbolizes both the presence (immanence) of God on Earth—and the transcendent God of other worldly experiences.

Melchizedek, the biblical Hierophant, represented the ancient worldview of an imminent (present) God, both physical (bread and wine) and spiritual (a blessing). That relationship with God has not evaporated. Yet, the transcendent God—"Our Father who is in heaven"—can feel so very far away. To find our way into the heavenly realm, we are often told that we need someone like Melchizedek, a mediator, a medium, a priest, a pastor, a Bible, a prayer of salvation, a sacrament. But The Chariot offers a mystical experience beyond the world. One that can help us navigate our unmediated way between what is below (Earth) and what is above (God in heaven). An experience of the Divine and a human being who are in complete presence with one another.

The text from Zechariah (6:1-2), with four chariots and the different colored horses, is very similar to the images found in Ezekiel. Their experiences were incorporated into the Kabbalah as *Merkavah mysticism.* These mystics are known as chariot voyagers. Through deep and repeated meditation, they seek visions of God that allow them to travel through the Divine palace. On their chariot journeys, they envision the throne of God and the presence of angels. Often these travelers are invited to join their voices with the angelic choir. In asking a few of these mystics about their meditative experiences, they were without words to describe the ecstasy of such profound presence. Inviting me to sit in circle with them was humbling. While I did not travel on the chariot, I felt as if we were collectively lifted out of our seats. If for just a moment, it felt like the Divine was breathing in rhythm with us.

In the presence of these mystical travelers, I was left wondering if I, too, could have the chariot experience of Ezekiel and Zachariah. My meditation companions offered some sound advice.

Enter into a meditative practice that cultivates your inner space, making your ground fertile and ready to receive God's seed. Sitting in a circle of silence is not for everyone; meditation has many forms, experiment until you find one that nourishes your soul and expands your sense of the presence of the Divine. Then stay with your practice. Be patient. Trust that at some moment, probably when you least expect it, you will experience what you need. That will be your chariot. The Spirit will be your charioteer. Get on it and "I will make you ride the heights of the earth" (Isaiah 58:14).

As with Pamela Colman Smith's Chariot, God is both the charioteer and the chariot. The mystical throne moves through space and time without the need of harness nor reins. As well, the Divine is also those magical animals that give the vehicle its energetic force. God is in all and all is in God. The promise that we can experience the chariot journey through the cosmic palace lies within a deeper secret. On one hand we can get in God's chariot and ride through the great palace. On the other, by being one with the Divine, we too are the chariot and the charioteer. God is in us and we are in God.

The Chariot's story for The Fool is both true and false at the same time, known as dialetheism. For God to be God, the Divine must be everything—the unity of all—fully and absolutely present to all. If God created the cosmos in order to experience Godself as the "endless unity," then according to the seventeenth century mystic Jacob Boehme, God had to become conscious of God's self in creation's diversity. Cynthia Bourgeault in *A Short Course on Wisdom* quotes a teaching from the Sufi tradition: "I [God] was a hidden treasure and longed to be known. And so I created the world."[60] For God to completely experience God's self, then God must invite each of us into The Chariot for an experience of lifetime. In that joyous mystical ride, God will know human ecstasy and God will know Godself as we come to know our true self. This is the experience of being one with the Divine—pure mutual presence. The presence of the lover is inescapable. Whether we are in the palace of The Chariot or cleaning out the horse's stable, the lover is completely present to us simply because that is where we are at that very moment.

The impossible paradox of that idea opens a portal into the reality that we have been created in the image of the Cosmic Holy One. Therefore, God can be pure silence and speak loudly at the same time. God can be absent and present simultaneously. And we can live into our own paradox without fear. We can hunger for wisdom and unity while living life as agnostic atheists and still lean into our unexplainable experiences. We can question the mystically absurd and simultaneously be critical of the literal. We can experience the world both as enchanted and as disenchanted without being contradictory. The Chariot of four gyrating wheels can be pulled by four horses of four different colors going in four mystical directions and driven by the charioteer who is the chariot, the Divine One with four opposing faces. Mysticism is a vision of the drunken dervish of whirling faces flying above the cosmic sea, bringing us into an intimate experience of orgasmic sublimity and absolute presence.

The mystic's way of The Chariot is so spiritually pervasive that it is found in the Kabbalah, Meister Eckhart's Christian mysticism, and Ibn al-Arabi's Sufism. The Divine is the center that is everywhere and the circumference that is nowhere, says Hermes Trismegistus. The Chariot can be here, there, and everywhere at the same time. The Chariot's voyage is carrying its passenger into the spiral of transition that reveals the yes and no of the human mind-body-soul experience. We are one with the Divine, but not Divine. We are the chariot and the charioteer, but we are not. We are present, but also absent. Nothing is left behind in the mutuality of presence. We are living in what contemporary theologian Barbara Brown Taylor beautifully describes as the "luminous web of consciousness."[61] A web that makes space for paradoxes and contradictions, both of which nourish the soul in some strange unexplainable mystifying way of The Chariot. And it's only going to get more intense as we pilgrimage further in our discovery of the self.

REFLECT ON THE CHARIOT AND THE PATH OF INSTRUCTION

◊ What transition experiences in your life have felt Chariot-like?

◊ According to Richard Rohr, we are all mystics. Have you had a mystical experience? What was that like?

◊ How have you experienced Barbara Brown Taylor's "luminous web of consciousness"?

— CHAPTER 12 —
STRENGTH

Quick Read: Strength is depicted as a woman of power. One who will stare down the mightiest and most fearful of terrors. She is the warrior with a spear of the flaming serpent. She and nature work in tandem. When holding this card, we are challenged to summon our inner fortitude and manifest it externally in the world. We are being asked, *What rarely summoned character traits can I call upon for assets in my challenge?* We're also being asked to look around and count our allies. Who or what can support us?

Artistic Inspiration: *Navigator Tarot of the Mystic Sea,* Julia Turk. Strength is a female figure holding a flaming serpent spear above her head. A green serpent connects her to the lion on her left and the wolf to her right. Turk identifies the image as "omnipotence."

Illumination: "[Annie] Sprinkle is a many-gendered mother of the heart. And many-gendered mothers of the heart say: *Just because you have enemies does not mean you have to be paranoid.* They insist, no matter the evidence marshalled against their insistence: *There is nothing you can throw at me that I cannot metabolize, no thing impervious to my alchemy.*" Maggie Nelson[62]

Biblical Characters: Esther and Mary, the mother of Jesus

Biblical Text: "Wisdom herself is clothed with strength and dignity, and she laughs at the time to come. She opens her mouth with wisdom, and the teaching of kindness is on her tongue." (Proverbs 31:25-26)

Our next leg of pilgrimage with the Tarot's Fool is the path of wisdom. The seven Major Acana who guide us, do so more by example than by word. We are no longer initiates but have yet to become adepts. We've walked a long way, but there's much more to breathe into our soul.

On the penultimate day of my 353-mile pilgrimage across Ireland, I walked down into Black Valley. In 1967, this ancient hideaway was the last place in Ireland to be connected to electricity. That night, my wife and I shared a lovely meal and a bottle of wine. We were the only people staying in the B&B and enjoyed the star-filled night and a cool breeze. The plan was that I would walk two more days to Glenbeigh. At dinner, I talked about combining the two days into one twenty-four-mile hike over the Magillicuddy Reeks and Carrauntoohil Mountain, the highest in Ireland. My wife asked me a dozen times, "Are you sure?" The Irish are more straightforward. "Are you daft?" That's a nice way of asking if I'd lost my mind.

As I climbed the last peak, I felt a bit delirious. I came to a sign that pointed in two opposite directions: "The Scenic Path or The Easy Way." And yes, I took the scenic path. I topped the final rise just as the sun was setting. Staring at the darkening gulf of water reflecting the lights of Glenbeigh, I was about to finish a pilgrimage I never thought possible. Twenty-six days of mountains, rain, wind, bog, sheep-shit trails, being lost, falling, all while mesmerized by the mysteries of an ancient world. Down that last mountain, I laughed, cried, stumbled, shouted, and gave thanks to Saint Brigid of Ireland, Sophia Wisdom, and the One Living God each for saving my ass on more than one occasion. As Jung once put it, "My spirit reflected on everything rare and uncommon, it pried its way into unfound possibilities, toward paths that lead into unfound lights that shine in the night."[63]

To pilgrimage, I had to take the risk of beginning, even though I had no idea of the outcome. It was the risk that created the strength I needed to walk the path of wisdom. But this was not the last pilgrimage I would walk. There would be more to come. So equally joyous. Others infused with confusion and pain.

No other character in the Bible more embodies Tarot's Strength than Esther. Barely a teenager, she was swept up in a tale of deceit, betrayal, lust for power, antisemitism, and genocide. The book of Esther is one of only two in the Bible that does not mention the name of God, the other being the Song of Solomon. The Jews created Purim in her memory, making her the only woman in Jewish history for which a holiday was established.

The author of Esther set the novella in Persia under the reign of King Ahasuerus. Written with its Jewish audience in mind, the story is rich with metaphor. Esther and her older cousin, Mordecai, were part of the Jewish Diaspora community living in Susa, the Persian capital. Mordecai had established himself with a position in the royal court. Esther's parents had died and Mordecai adopted her as his own daughter. Mordecai and Esther's lineage was through the tribe of Benjamin, a descendent of King Saul, but Mordecai and Esther kept their Jewish heritage secret. All the while, the story's villain, Haman, who was not Jewish, was a descendent of King Agag the Amalekite, Saul's defeated adversary.

As the story begins, King Ahasuerus of Persia is throwing a seven-day feast for his subjects. Amid a wine-soaked celebration, the king demands that his beautiful wife, Queen Vashti, put on her most lavish garments and play the role of trophy. She refuses. Ahasuerus is enraged. Vashti is exiled.

The search for Queen Vashti's replacement ensues. Hundreds of candidates fail to meet the king's standards. But when he is introduced to Esther, she wins his heart and is made queen.

In the meantime, as if Haman is exacting revenge for his ancient relative, King Agag, he contrives a plot to kill the Jews living in Persian exile. Unknowing of the consequences, the king agrees with Haman's plan of genocide. Mordecai, upon hearing this planned travesty of justice, seeks Esther's assistance. He begs her to plead the Jew's case before the king. Esther reminds Mordecai that the law prevents anyone from approaching the king without being summoned. Her life is in double jeopardy. Mordecai's response is prophetic. "Who knows? Perhaps you have come to royal dignity for such a time as this." She concludes, "After a three-day fast, I will go to the king, though it is against the law; and if I perish, I perish."

Esther prepares herself to carry out the plan, and when the right moment comes, she stands near the king, awaiting his invitation. Enrapt with her beauty, he offers her anything up to half his kingdom. She asks for a banquet with him and Haman.

The next day, the two men arrive at the appointed hour. Esther unravels Haman's plot to kill *her* people. Distraught, Ahasuerus leaves the room. Haman, in a panic, throws himself next to Esther, who is resting on her couch. The king returns and finds Haman in a compromised position. Haman not only wants to kill Esther, Mordecai, and *her* people, but now he has accosted Ahasuerus's queen. The king can take no more and orders his soldiers to hang Haman on the highest gallows—the one he had constructed to execute Mordecai and the Jews.

From orphan to queen to savior of her people, the story of Esther is one of awe-inspiring strength. In my retelling, I've left out several twists in the plot and have not done the story its true justice. But little wonder the Jewish people celebrate reading Esther's story once a year at the Feast of Purim.

Strength can be epigenetic. The courage of our past generations having left a stamp on our resolve. My mother repeatedly told my sister, who has Prader-Willi syndrome, "Your name is 'S.' You are strong." Tough words to speak into the soul of a developmentally disabled child who can't defend herself against what my sister calls the "mean man." Such an admonition had been passed down through the strong women of our mother's ancestors. Women who faced immigration, pandemic, and cancer—and God knows what else—with pure raw Strength. Our mother died years ago from being treated for cancer. Being the messenger of our mother's passing, I thought this would be my sister's undoing. But in her strength, she survived. Now the oldest known living person with Prader-Willi, she frequently reminds me that her name "is S."

Strength can also be an acquired character trait. The courage to face adversity may have been beaten out of our ancient ones, but now the resolve to stand against the oppressor has been remembered, restored, and renewed. Such a force can be ignited when Strength recognizes that she is not alone. When Strength is reborn, she becomes the living embodiment of power. She leads and others follow. From where does such Strength emerge?

> "Do not be afraid, Mary." The angel said.
> And Mary said:
> My soul magnifies the Lord,
>   and my spirit rejoices in God my savior.
> For *she* has looked with favor
>   on the lowliness of *her* servant.
> Surely, from now on all generations will call be blessed;
> For the mighty one has done great things for me,
>   and holy is *her* name.
> *Her* mercy is for those who *revere her*
>   from generation to generation.
> *She* has shown strength with *her* arm;
>   *She* has scattered the proud in the
>   thoughts of their hearts.
> *She* has brought down the powerful
>   from their thrones, and lifted up the lowly.
> *She* has filled the hungry with good things,
>   and sent the rich away empty.
> *She* has helped *her* servant Israel,
>   in remembrance of *her* mercy,
> According to the promises *she* made to our ancestors,
>   to Abraham *and Sarah and their* decedents forever.
> (Luke 1:46-55; italics are mine where I have adapted the words)

Mary's song, "The Magnificat," has reverberated among the oppressed and brought revolution to nations. From her strength, her fearlessness, we are lifted up.

In Laura Saetviet Miles' essay, "Queer Touch Between Holy Women," I was presented with a glimpse into the sacred and brave space created by a circle of women—women who have often been mistreated by men and their patriarchal religions.[64] Miles focused her research on the mystical literature found in women's writings. In this essay, she begins with the intimate conversation between two pregnant women, Mary, the mother of Jesus, and her cousin Elizabeth, the mother of John the Baptizer, a story first told in the Gospel of Luke 1:39-56. Mary, the younger of the cousins, was pregnant "without husband," and Elizabeth, "too old to bear a child," was pregnant with her first. The women spent much of the last trimester of their pregnancies together.

We see Mary enter Elizabeth's home and the women greet each other with a blessing and probably an embrace. Elizabeth offers Mary the words that been repeated countless times by the followers of Jesus and those devoted to Mary. "Blessed are you among women, and blessed is the fruit of your womb." And then we hear Mary's Song, the Magnificat. Borrowing from a late medieval Book of Hours, Miles layers a tender moment between the two as they stare in the face of ridicule and potential death. In these small devotionals that were once common, there is often a painting that depicts Mary and Elizabeth in an affectionate embrace. The visual is palpable because it happens around us every day—in our living rooms, at the coffee shop, in the grocery store—pregnant women's affection for one another seems inherent in their very being. A touching that draws them into a sphere of safety, an opening in time and space that stands outside the "rules of normalcy." They stand together in a space of freedom that is away from the oppression of intrusion, suspicion, and violence. The two have stepped into a time and space where men are rarely invited and typically unwelcome. At this moment, Miles invites Julian of Norwich, Margery Kempe, and Birgitta of Sweden to join Mary and Elizabeth's circle. Miles suggests that "divine prophecy could be read as queer not only because prophecy comes from the margins to challenge dominant authorities but also because it disrupts the present as it looks backward and forward in time."[65]

Miles fetches these women across time to stand as allies with one another. She gathers them into a "visionary" timelessness that is "transgressing multiple realities, obeying no rules of the normative world, a space where dead women can confide in living women and God can reveal his secrets."[66] We know such an experience is possible because we have seen it—not only in the lives of these women—but countless others. An intimacy of Strength. A brave space where all women can say, "My name is Strength."

REFLECTIONS OF STRENGTH AND THE PATH OF WISDOM

- ◊ Where do you see yourself in the Strength card?
- ◊ Where have you witnessed strength laced with wisdom?
- ◊ Why do you think the Tarot has identified the archetype of Strength as feminine?
- ◊ From where does your strength come?

— CHAPTER 13 —
THE HERMIT

Quick Read: The Hermit brings the light so that we may walk the desert's sacred path in the cool of night. The light shines on the dragons and The Hermit opens the secrets of the Orphic egg for all generations to read and follow. When presented with The Hermit card, we are being asked to consider the necessity of time alone for reflection. We are challenged to offer our experience as a light for others who are taking a long walk in the darkness.

Artistic Inspiration: *The Thoth Tarot,* Aleister Crowley and Lady Frida Harris. We view The Hermit from behind. With long white hair wearing a full-length red robe, we cannot tell the character's gender. The Hermit carries a crystal of luminous light bearing the symbol of The Sun. The figure is moving toward the Orphic egg enwrapped with a green serpent, and the three-headed hell hound trails behind The Hermit.

Illumination: "According to wisdom traditions, the most profound fruit of the transformative process is that the individual ceases to be an individual and is transformed into a person…sounded through…illuminated." Cynthia Bourgeault[67]

Biblical Characters: Elijah and Dinah

Biblical Text: "And the word of Lord came to Elijah and said, 'Go from here…and hide yourself.'" (I Kings 17)

"Now Dinah the daughter of Leah, whom she had borne to Jacob, went out to visit the women of the region." (Genesis 34:1)

South of Dublin, Ireland, are the ruins of Saint Kevin's Monastery at Glendalough. Standing amid a lush landscape, it's hard to imagine this as Kevin's Desert, but the Irish insist we can find the *spiritual desert* in any landscape. According to hagiographers, Saint Kevin (498-618) left home after being made a priest in the Catholic Church. His popularity had grown and he wanted to get away from his many followers. In the sixth century, Glendalough—the Valley of Two Lakes—was an isolated, unpopulated hideaway in the Wicklow Mountains. But after living there as a hermit for a few years, Kevin's followers began making pilgrimages to his one-man monastery.

When visiting Glendalough today, we can follow the hermit's progression up the valley of the two lakes in order to escape the encroachment of other would-be monastics. Eventually, Kevin found a small, isolated cave on the face of a hill high above the upper lake. Even for those who took the risk of making the climb, the cave was too small for more than one person.

For thousands of years, hermits have gone into the desert. Holy people craving solitude. They've made personal sacrifices in order to hide away. Yet their devotees continually sought the hermit's wise council concerning the spiritual life. For this reason, few hermits have been successful in their desire to be left alone with God.

If choosing to be a hermit were the point of the Tarot's ninth Arcana, this character would lose its archetypal meaning. While not everyone may at first connect with all universal characters of the Tarot, the potential exists that each and every image on the cards is somewhere in all of our psyches.

In the few Bible stories about hermits, they were either sent by God, like Elijah, or were running from God, like Jonah. However, the Christian legacy of hermits, typically makes the point that the person either felt a call by God, were seeking solitude, or were running away from something (more often, themselves).

In 1 Kings 17 and 19, Elijah was sent into the desert to hide from displeased kings. In the latter chapter we hear that God spoke to the prophet in "a sound of shear silence." In both cases, Elijah would receive a Divine message. It's in solitude and silence that we can best hear the voice of God. Being on a silent retreat does not have to last for a lifetime. However, there are times we may be thrust into circumstances beyond our control; situations where we may have to consider our life as a hermitage. Such is the story of Dinah.

Dinah was the youngest child and only daughter of Jacob and Leah. By the time she was a young adult, the women of the Israelites and the Canaanites were able to travel about freely among each other's tribes. The story begins as Dinah goes out to "visit the women of the region." In the next sentence, violence ensues. Leah's daughter is raped by Shechem, prince of the Hivites. Her brothers seek revenge, killing not only Shechem, but all the males of the city. Dinah's brothers took her "out of Shechem's house and went away." We don't hear of Dinah again until near the end of Genesis when Jacob takes his entire family into Egypt (46:15).

There are two speculative stories that appear in non-biblical sources about Dinah's future. One from Jewish Midrash and the other a modern novel. According to the commentary in *The Anchor Bible,* Job was the grandson of Esau and son-in-law of Jacob. In the Midrash, some Rabbis suggested that Dinah was either the first or second wife of Job. They based their theological extrapolation on Job 2:9-10.

"His wife said to him: 'Do you still maintain your integrity? Curse God and die." Job said to her: "You talk like a foolish woman. Shall we accept good from God, and not accept evil?" After all that had happened to Dinah, it would be easy to speculate that her heart had been hardened against God. But even so, she never left Job's side. And in a way, her counsel came out of her own painful experience. And what of the other source?

Anita Diamant's novel, *The Red Tent*, offers another ending. Dinah still suffers great loss, but in her isolation brings life to others. Dinah tells her story as midwife, one in which the blood of the red tent brings both birth and death. Her wisdom embraces a love that knows no bounds. I tell this story because I see the novelist's image in my sister. You have read about her earlier in this book. Both my mother and sister suffered the pain of loss and loneliness, the life of being an emotional hermit. Yet both of them have been sought out by others for wise counsel. My mother in obvious ways. But Dinah as well. If you have the patience to listen, her advice comes on the back of a life of disability. A hermitage of its own.

Our Fool has sought spiritual advice and companionship from The Hermit. The Celts called this person their *anam cara,* their soul friend. The ancient tradition of spiritual direction is one of companionship—soul friends in an intimate conversation. Brigid of Kildare, patron saint of Ireland, who established the first monastery that included women and men, said that a "person without a soul friend (*anam cara*) is like a body without a head." The Celtic monk Pelagius (354-418), whose progressive views on freewill and universal salvation were at the root of his being declared a heretic, wrote in his letters, "Indeed we each need a special friend who may be called the friend of the soul, hiding nothing and revealing everything." Hildegard of Bingen, Teresa of Avila, and Julian of Norwich were all venerated mystics of wisdom and soul friends to others, and because of their vast spiritual knowledge, mystical experience, and prophetic approach, they were often considered out-of-bounds by the Church of their day.

Julian of Norwich and Margery Kempe met in Norwich, England in 1413. Julian was seventy-one years-old and Margery forty. Both were mystics and outspoken about their visions of Jesus. Neither was a nun, yet both lived under the suspicious eye of the patriarchy of the Roman Church. They met in private for several days in the tiny apartment just off the chancel of the church where Julian lived. What little is known about their conversation was recorded in Kempe's book. Margery whispering her stories while Julian counseled, consoled, and encouraged her "sister."

At thirty, Julian had had a near death experience that resulted in sixteen visions of Jesus. While recovering, she wrote *Showing of Love,* which includes these visions and tender, loving devotional material. There, she repeatedly referred to Jesus as Mother. The unknown causes of her traumatic illness left her with a lifetime of lingering health issues.

Speculations about Julian's life range from being an unmarried woman to having been a widow with child. Because of her mystical experiences, she became an anchoress—a female hermit—living in a cave-like cell off the side of a church. Julian would receive visitors in a tiny stone room. They came seeking spiritual counsel and advice. It seems plausible that she would privately share parts of her then unpublished handwritten book with those who craved her spiritual guidance, including Margery Kempe. Julian's *Showing of Love* was published posthumously and considered the first book written in English by a woman.

Kempe wrote her book in the third person, as if it had been dictated to her priest. This style gave it an appearance of having the imprimatur of the Church. She could only hope that the perceived approval of Rome would protect her from the prying eyes of the Inquisition. *The Book of Margery Kempe* is considered the first autobiography written in English by a woman. In it, she provides us with a detailed look into the life of a unique medieval woman that includes dress, travels, religious ideas, and spiritual practices.

Kempe's book was written after the birth of her first child. The birth was evidently traumatic and caused, what would now be diagnosed as postpartum depression. Some scholars have suggested her depression was so severe that it resulted in psychosis. Without regard to the diagnosis, her experience would initiate Kempe's spiritual pilgrimage of visions, including vivid conversations with the Virgin Mary, Jesus, and the Godhead. Kempe would give birth to thirteen other children and in between each of those deliveries pleaded with her husband to allow her to commit to a life of celibacy. Apparently, her request was denied, but it did not deter her intent to live a uniquely spiritual life as a solitary. Despite having fourteen children, she made pilgrimages to holy sites in Jerusalem, Rome, and Germany.

To become a hermit in the interior desert, she became a vegetarian and abstained from wine, both unusual for her times. She dressed in a unique white garment that drew criticism. Her asceticism and her visions caused many of the male clergy she confided in to question her sanity. Often the charge the religious institution makes of its eccentric hermits.

The Church frequently burned the books of Julian and Margery as heretical. Specifically, because both women insisted Jesus had spoken to them personally. They validated their messages from Jesus by referencing the Bible, and their interpretation of it, as their support. They considered their perspectives of the Bible worthy enough to teach women and men alike. Some Catholic priests considered the fact that these women had the audacity to teach men to be heresy itself. But this was not the first time the institution had faced deeply spiritual women. Centuries before, Hildegard of Bingen wrote of her visions while challenging the patriarchy on several fronts.

There is no evidence that either Julian or Margery was familiar with Hildegard of Bingen's writings, which were scribed 300 years prior. The possibility of Julian and Margery being aware of Hildegard, however, exists given the power of the connection among the international network of women living in churches and convents. The theology of these three women regarding wisdom, nature, and the feminine aspect of God was extra-ordinarily similar. And by their own proclamation, they heard the urging of Wisdom Sophia encouraging them to speak truth found in mystical words that could not be silenced. The words of the divine feminine had been frozen for centuries and were being thawed by the warm companionship of these mystical women.[68]

The history of the *anam cara* is not limited to Christianity. The Sufi mystic Rumi (1207-1273) is one of the most oft quoted poets regarding spiritual friendship. And in Judaism, long before the Rabbinic tradition, people would seek wise counsel from a spiritual friend. Those intimate relationships are found in the biblical stories of David and Jonathan, Mordecai and Esther, Naomi and Ruth, and Elizabeth and Mary. And the long tradition of spiritual companionship is also a significant component in traditions other than the three Abrahamic faiths. Author and spiritual director John Mabry, in his book *Noticing the Divine,* provides an excellent introduction into the vast number of traditions that regard spiritual companionship as vital for the evolution of their religious experience.

Even in The Hermit's longing for solitude, there are always seekers who will go to all ends for their wise counsel. "Ask, and it will be given you; search, and you will find; knock, and the door will be opened for you. For everyone who asks receives, and everyone who searches finds, and for everyone who knocks the door will be opened" (Matthew 7:7-8). This is a good motto for all who are walking the long pilgrimage on the way toward the self.

REFLECTIONS ON THE HERMIT AND THE PATH OF WISDOM

◊ How might you identify with The Hermit?

◊ Who have been your spiritual companions? What has that experience been like for you?

◊ Have you taken time to be alone? Imagine your best experience of being a Hermit, if for only a week.

◊ If you could have dinner with any living person in the world, who would that be? And why?

— CHAPTER 14 —
THE WHEEL OF FORTUNE

Quick Read: The Wheel of Fortune is the ouroboros, life without end, the cycle of life. The Wheel is the experience of ascending and descending the Tree of Life. The Wheel of Fortune asks us to reflect upon life's events: *Is this fate, chance, or synchronicity?*

Artistic Inspiration: *Rider-Waite-Smith* deck, art by Pamela Colman Smith. This card has the mixture of Christian and Egyptian symbolism. I've described the card below in significant detail.

Illumination: "From one change to another I invite you to unite with the wheel of life, accepting changes with patience, docility, and humility until the moment Consciousness is born." Alejandro Jodorowsky[69]

Biblical Character: Joseph the patriarch

Biblical Text: "Removing his signet ring from his hand, Pharaoh put it on Joseph's hand; he arrayed him in garments of fine linen and put a gold chain around his neck. Pharoah had Joseph ride in the chariot of his second-in-command; and they cried out in front of him, 'Bow the knee!' Thus he set Joseph over all of the land of Egypt." (Genesis 41:42-43)

Joseph the patriarch, son of Jacob and Rachel, is the Bible's poster child for The Wheel of Fortune, known in some Tarot traditions as The Wheel of Life. The *Rider-Waite-Smith* deck is the perfect flag-bearer for Joseph. This card is based on the biblical interpretation that the patriarch Joseph was significantly influenced by Egyptian culture and religion. As I've pointed out, there are Tarot traditions that suggest Egypt as the originator of the Major Arcana. The Wheel of Fortune card, as designed and painted by Pamela Colman Smith, is the central focus of such a notion. Whether Tarot was based upon Egyptian mythology is a point of conjecture. The narrative of the cards is never about historicity, it's about the universality of the archetypes. Without regard to the versimilitude of Joseph's story, his character's connection to Egypt is central to the biblical narrative and true to the archetypal symbols it represents.

Before we get to the fascinating story of Joseph, let's inspect Pamela Colman Smith's art and her symbolism for the tenth card of the Majors. Beginning in the center of the card, we'll work outward.

◊ Three concentric circles—the sun is the center of life, the "fire of heaven," a sphere; Ra is patron of the sun, the king of Egyptian deities and father of creation. Hather is Ra's wife and the mother of Pharoah. Heliopolis is the cultic center and Joseph's father-in-law is a priest of Heliopolis.
◊ Eight-pointed star—the intertwining of the mystical tradition of YHVH, the Kabbalah, and the Tarot.
◊ Alchemical symbols for mercury, salt, Sulphur, and water, which is the symbol of Aquarius, representing the twelve signs of Zodiac.
◊ Taro/Rota—short for Tarot and inverse of Rota (the wheel).
◊ YHVH—Hebrew name for the One whose name may not be spoken.
◊ Sphinx—guardians of the mystical secrets.
◊ Serpent—the twisting path of descending The Tree of Life.
◊ Anubis—jackal figure sacred in Egypt, and Thoth's companion dog. The Anubis is also the guardian of the dead, and symbol of enlightenment.
◊ Angel/human—autumn consciousness. The angel of the Lord is a messenger.
◊ Bull—symbolizes winter. The bull is steady. The "Mighty one of Jacob" (Genesis 49:24).
◊ Lion—represents spring and strength, as in "Saul and Jonathan, beloved and lovely! In life and in death, they were not divided;

they were swifter than eagles, they were stronger than lions" (2 Samuel 1:23).

◊ Eagle—embodies summer, elevated vision, and swift in flight.

Simply put, the symbolism of The Wheel is a mirror of the cycle of life. No matter how many seasons of the year we cycle through, our experiences of them are never the same. Change and the alchemical process generate the energy of The Wheel—both the good and bad. Martin Buber wrote, "The world is a spinning die, and everything turns and changes."[70] And no one in the Bible's story was more emblematic of this truth than was Joseph the patriarch.

The story of Joseph and his family takes up a quarter of the book of Genesis. The ebb and flow of every biblical tale can find its roots in this primordial history: the journey of Abraham, the lineage of Jacob, and the ascending and descending nature of Joseph and his brothers. Without Genesis and its cast of characters, the cohesive arc of the remaining biblical mythos would be hollow.

The Genesis saga opens with the creation of life across the chaos of a formless void and ends with Joseph's death in Egypt. So crucial has been the archetypal image of Egypt in the mythic narrative of three Abrahamic traditions that the last word of Genesis is "Egypt." The second book of the Torah builds on the first, unpacking the requisite tale of Israel's Exodus from Pharoah's oppression. In the Bible, Egypt is typically the symbol of darkness and oppression. However, the story of Joseph casts an alternative view to this interpretation.

Joseph's life can best be described as the conundrum of love and hate. The youngest son of Jacob (later renamed, Israel) was in a constant state of flux between being cherished and despised. His life was perpetually spinning on the Wheel of Fortune—descending and ascending, circling and spiraling. Without going into every detail of Joseph's life, here are a few of the highlights from his fortune.

◊ First, we see Joseph when he was seventeen, the youngest son and his father's favorite. Joseph was full of hubris. He had a dream that his brothers would bow down before him. Under such pronouncement, they resented him, as most siblings would. Soon, Joseph has another similar dream and tells his father, who finds it disturbing, but "kept the matter in mind."

- ◊ After another similar dream, his brothers despised Joseph even more. So much so, they threw him down a well intending to leave him for dead. Rethinking their deed, they instead sell Joseph to a caravan of Ishmaelites on their way to Egypt, who, in turn, sell him to Potiphar, the captain of the guard.
- ◊ Joseph worked his way through the wheels of slavery and became the overseer of Potiphar's house.
- ◊ Potiphar's wife spun the wheel and tried to seduce Joseph. He rebuffs her, and she reports to her husband that Joseph tried to entice her into unwanted sex. For his valor, Joseph finds himself in prison.
- ◊ Joseph's gift of dream interpretation helps him this time to find favor in Pharoah's eyes.
- ◊ Pharoah placed Joseph over his house and Egypt. The king changed Joseph's name, gave him a ring that symbolized his authority, and presented him a wife, the daughter of a priest of the sun god. Joseph's power and influence increases over the next fourteen years.
- ◊ During seven years of famine, Joseph's brothers, seeking food, journey to Egypt. After several episodes of intrigue, uncertainty, and fear of retribution they reunite with Joseph, now their savior.

Joseph's story is the alchemical Wheel of Fortune in all its glory. As a teenager, Joseph was full of himself. The ego of a young man is subjected to the cauldron's heat—first at the bottom of a well and then in slavery. But he uses his wit and intellect and makes the best of a chaotic situation and the egg cracks open. Once again, however, fate's Wheel spins down, and unjustly he finds himself in prison. Undeterred, Joseph makes the best of prison and his dream interpretation skills. The raven with the peacock tail emerges and unexpectedly he finds himself as Pharaoh's right-hand man. Synchronicity comes to play again and Joseph and his family reunite with a positive end, forgiving one another. The phoenix has risen from the ashes. But the Wheel never stopped turning, and in the last days, Joseph mourned his father's death. In the end, Joseph lived the remainder of 110 years peacefully in Egypt.

In the Abraham and Moses stories, Egypt was projected as the evil empire. The Joseph narrative, however, presents the Egyptians as an ancient nation not unlike any other.

While our life might not be as tumultuous as Joseph's, we, as The Fool, can easily see ourselves somewhere on this Wheel. Some days, some seasons, descending. At other moments in life, we are ascending. There are instances when we sit at the sphinx's feet. These are those moments when we drink in wisdom from the ancients and their mystical texts. And there are times we'd most like to forget—spinning too much in Alice's tea cup, leaning over the edge, spilling the insides of our soul onto the pavement below. The key is not to be consumed by what's happening in any one moment, for our wheel will spin around once again. The Wheel's ten is the number of completeness; it's also the number of beginning again (1+0=1).

REFLECTIONS OF THE WHEEL OF FORTUNE AND THE PATH OF WISDOM

- ◊ Can you find yourself somewhere in Joseph's story?
- ◊ How have dreams played a factor in your life?
- ◊ Where are you on The Wheel of Life?

— CHAPTER 15 —
JUSTICE

Quick Read: Impartial (blindfolded), speaking truth to power, scales that weigh the record of one's life, service, balance of the opposites (fire and water). This card challenges us to represent those without a voice and to stand against injustice. It is also reminding us that Justice carries a two-edged sword.

Artistic Inspiration: *The Sufi Tarot,* "Adal," Ayeda Husain. An African woman dressed in her cultural attire stands in the grasslands. In the background are great snow peaks. She holds the balance above her head in her right hand and a sword in her left, pointing to the ground. *Adal* is not only the word for justice, but also one of the names of God in Islam.

Illumination: "Black women, who have traditionally been the purveyors of culture and religion in the Black community, have handed down…a 'spirituality of resistance,' [which they] have nurtured and passed on to their sons and daughters." Kelly Brown Douglas[71]

Biblical Character: Deborah

Biblical Text: "Deborah's general, Barak, said to her, 'If you will go with me, I will go; but if you will not go with me, I will not go.' And [Deborah] said, 'I will surely go with you, for the Lord will deliver Sisera into the hand of a woman.'" (Judges 4:8-9)

Most of the woman that made their way into the Bible were bad ass. How else would they have survived and become a huge enough legend to warrant the memory of a biblical storyteller? Deborah might be at the top of the list of warrior women of justice. To capture the complexity of her story, it was told in prose, poetry, and music. The Israelites sang her song to remember and memorialize this powerful woman, passing her legend from generation to generation as a "spirituality of resistance."

Deborah assumed three roles among the Israelites: 1) a judge with legal authority, 2) prophet, and 3) military leader. Given that this story's origin began in the twelfth century BCE, Deborah was a figure larger than life. While the Bible says she was the wife of Lappidoth, some scholars have suggested that the more correct interpretation be that she was a *spirited* woman. (The name Lappidoth does not appear again in the Bible.) Honestly, if a woman living in our day was a judge, prophet, and military leader, she would be a force to reckon with. Think of her as a supreme court judge, who is also a five-star general, and a spiritual guru.

Deborah's story appears in the book of Judges. She developed a plan to lead her army into battle against the much superior Canaanites, led by Sisera. The stakes were extremely high, for whoever won the battle would have control of most of the Holy Land. Deborah informed her general, Barak, of the strategy she wanted him to carry out. But he was not willing to go it alone. His reaction revealed two concerns. One, Deborah's plan required a tremendous amount of risk. And two, Barak knew their army was significantly outnumbered. Subsequently, he believed the soldiers would only follow Deborah into battle. She never hesitated a moment and off they went to war, with her leading the charge.

In the story, it's easy to see that Deborah was in complete control of the situation, directing when and where Barak should attack. He followed her commands to perfection. Even "the stars from heaven," joined in the conflict, it says. Deborah's army subdued their foes, and in defeat, the Canaanite general Sisera abandoned his chariot and fled on foot. Looking for sanctuary, he stood in front of Jael's tent. Her husband, Heber—the clan leader of the Kenites—and Sisera's king, Jabir, were at peace. Jael's invitation to hide Sisera in her tent must have seemed reasonable to him. He asked for a drink and she offered him warm milk. That must have been soothing to the beleaguered warrior. To hide Sisera, Jael covered him with a blanket. Hmm. Rather motherly. Sisera implored Jael to watch guard and deceive his pursuers, sending them away. While

Sisera slept, Jael went and got a tent stake and a hammer, and she drove the stake through his temple.

Why did Jael kill Sisera? We get a hint in Deborah's song. While Sisera's mother anxiously waited for her son to return from battle, her handmaidens offered consolation. "Are they not finding and dividing the spoil? A girl or two for every man." Maybe Jael, a heroic nomadic woman, had experienced enough of the marauding Canaanites who would rape and pillage women of a conquered tribe. Indeed, the Lord delivered Sisera into a woman's hand, full of hammer and stake. Justice was served. Deborah's prophecy had been proven true.

But justice is a subjective matter, even in the face of written laws. Every story of war and violence in the Bible (and history) confronts us with questions that have uncertain, even troubling answers. This is why we rely on judges who will act with blind impartially. The Justice card reveals her sword is two-edged. Meaning sometimes we don't agree with her decision. This is the way of Justice. But sometimes we have witnessed individuals within our legal system who have been persuaded to move out of their seat of impartiality. At that point, what would the "spirituality of resistance" look like?

The Bible is clear. A judge's responsibility is to "Seek justice, rescue the oppressed, defend the orphan, plead for the widow" (Isaiah 1:17). According to the prophet Isaiah, their failure is grounded in evil. These judges did not take up the cause of the oppressed. Instead, they were willing to take bribes to advance their own welfare. For such actions, Isaiah admonished judges: "Wash yourself and make yourself clean." A resounding theme throughout the Bible is the call to the faithful and their responsibility to enact justice on behalf of the voiceless.

The prophet Amos never minced words on this topic. "The Lord roars from Zion…. Hear this word, you cows of Bashan…who oppress the poor, who crush the needy…establish justice at the gate. Let justice roll down like waters, and righteousness like an ever-flowing river" (Amos 4-5). The words of Isaiah and Amos are no less relevant for those of us living in America in the twenty-first century. Martin Luther King, Jr.'s words still resound: "The arc of the moral universe is long, but it bends toward justice." His trumpet calls for social justice is as loud today as it was in 1968. And his message imploring us to live a life of what Kelly Brown Douglas calls a "spirituality of resistance" is no less critical, for the work of Justice is never finished.

REFLECTION ON JUSTICE AND THE PATH OF WISDOM

- ◊ How do you see yourself in the Justice card?
- ◊ Have you acted in a situation with a "spirituality of resistance?" What was that experience like for you?
- ◊ What lack of Justice in your community concerns you the most?

— CHAPTER 16 —
THE HANGED MAN

Quick Read: The Hanged Man experiences chaos that induces a reversal of perspective: an emptying of the ego, self-sacrifice, and expanded consciousness. The heart is above the head, and the feet are grounded in the realm above. The Hanged Man wants us to turn our treasured beliefs upside down and evaluate them with our heart and head looking from different perspectives.

Artistic Inspiration: *Rider-Waite-Smith*, Pamela Colman Smith. A nimbus surrounds the hanging person's head, signifying a saint-like status. The light-headed Hanged Man represents a mystic. This character wears a blue shirt symbolizing spiritual royalty and red leggings of devotion.

Illumination: "He who allows himself to be called a Christian must allow himself to be called a fool and a godless person." Jacob Boehme[72]

Biblical Character: Jonah

Biblical Text: "Jonah said to the sailors, 'Pick me up and throw me into the sea; then the sea will quiet down for you; for I know it is because of me that this great storm has come upon you.'" (Jonah 1:12)

The Hanged Man is one of those "hard problems" of the Tarot. As in, *"What do I do with this card? I'm not sure I want to go there?"* The image is emblematic of the ancient story of Apostle Peter and his desire to be crucified upside down. In the *Acts of Peter*, an apocryphal text that appeared in the second century CE, the Apostle says, "Unless you make the right as the left, and the top as the bottom, and the front as the back, you shall not enter the kingdom."[73] To see the kingdom of God, one must see everything turned on its head. Feed the hungry, give water to the thirsty, clothe the naked, visit the sick and those in prison, embrace the alien in your land, and love your enemy. We are to enact these charities not for any benefit of our own but for the sake of those we serve. I'm pretty sure that's what Peter had in mind. No easy commandments. And it can take us a while to get there. Like the end of the Wicklow Way. There, a celebration can get spun on its head.

Clonegal is a two-pub village at the southern end of Ireland's Wicklow Way. Osbourne's is the traditional pub to stop for a few celebratory pints, and the place to pick up your official certificate of completing the arduous journey. I've been there more than once. And on each occasion, at the perfect moment, with a twinkle in his eye, the bartender will tell whoever is standing nearest the bar that they are leaning on used casket lids. That always gets the unsuspecting celebrant to remove their pint from the bar. Without a smile, the bartender continues his story. Those caskets had been intended for the soul who was hung on the spike just outside the entrance. "You saw it didn't you?" Most nod, no. "Depending on the crime," he says, "the body was placed in the box, then dumped into a shallow grave in the forest. Later, they returned the casket to the pub, awaiting its next victim." Quaint tale to be told after having faced your own demons during the 100-mile trek through the dark forest. Aye, the stories we tell one another to twist our heads upside down.

The tale of Jonah is no less jarring and as equally as short as the Irish bartender's. From a certain point-of-view, it could be the most humorous book in the Bible. The tale is fantastical, Disney-esque. (There is a *VeggieTales* version and an animated musical by *Sight and Sounds Theaters.*) The Bible's version is complete with self-sacrifice, a large fish, fasting animals, the bush, a worm, and a sultry eastern wind. But as I've heard in a hundred sermons, the moral seems somewhat suspect given its vague ending.

I chose Jonah as the biblical character to represent The Hanged Man for three reasons. First, in some older Tarot traditions, this figure is known as The Drowned Man, a direct biblical correspondence to Noah's Ark and all that were drowned to turn humanity's behavior upside down.

And to Jonah, who was swallowed by the Leviathan to flip his path's direction. Hence, the card is identified as a water element with the symbol of Neptune's trident.

At one point in my career, I worked as a pastor and priest in a church whose nave and chancel were designed as the inverted Noah's Ark, with the ceiling being the bottom of the ship. To accentuate the effect, they constructed the ceiling from lumber and it creaked exactly like one would imagine an old wooden ship might. For me, this has been the perfect example of the inverted Hanged Man, whose feet are in "heaven" and whose head is in the sea of the unconscious. The one who sees everything upside down and can hear underwater.

Jonah must have felt like God had hung him upside down. As in, why me? Or maybe, upon hearing the word of the Lord, he was scared to death. Think about it, have you ever heard the verbal voice of God? Wouldn't that scare you enough to start packing your bags for some foreign land? "How far do I have to run to get away from that voice in my head? Besides, if I tell my family, they'll want to have me committed."

Maybe God was The Hanged Man. God did change "his mind about the calamity that he had said he would bring upon [Nineveh]." I really like the King James Version. "And God saw their works, that they turned from their evil way; and God repented of the evil that he had said that he would do unto them; and he did it not" (Jonah 3:10). Maybe Nineveh's king, his kingdom, and God were all looking at the spiritual world from a weird, inverted perspective. But what about Jonah?

God instructed Jonah to go to Nineveh and preach against their wickedness, but he went in the opposite direction. He booked a fare on a ship to Tarshish. Out to sea, Jonah went below to take a nap. A terrible storm arose, so dangerous the captain ordered the men to throw their cargo overboard and to pray to their various gods to save them. In the verse cited above, Jonah had admitted to the sailors that he was the cause of their troubles. To remedy their potential disaster, he implored them to toss him overboard. But the sailors and their various gods believed it would be wrong to kill him, or maybe bad luck, or they feared Jonah's

God. For whatever reason, they rowed harder against the storm, to no avail.

The ship began to break apart. With no other alternative, the innocent sailors threw Jonah overboard and immediately the sea calmed. In a salvific moment, the Lord sent a large fish to swallow Jonah. Like every excellent novel, the story now goes from bad to worse. Jonah spent three days in the belly of Leviathan. Begrudgingly, like a good Hanged Man, Jonah thanks God for saving him from drowning, and like everyone else in their personal moment of hell, pledges to do whatever God wants of him. Sound familiar?

The whale has had enough of bad indigestion and vomits Jonah ashore. A divorce of sorts. Jonah kept his word, and now with a bit of vengeance on his mind, headed to Nineveh to preach hell and brimstone to the citizens. To Jonah's, and God's, surprise the king of the city called upon his people to dress in burlap and cover themselves in ashes. The king then demanded that his people, and their animals, fast from food and water. "Who knows," the king said, "God may relent and change his mind." The phrase, "who knows," appears quite often in the Bible—always in reference to what God might or might not do.

Well, in this situation, God reconsidered, even to the point of repentance. Did Jonah celebrate the success of his Nineveh tent revival? Nope. He pouted. But God, being in a merciful mood, raised up a bush to offer Jonah shade. Does Jonah enjoy the relief from the sun? No. God being God, then sent a worm to eat the bush and ordered up a hot wind to wither Jonah's soul. Then Jonah considered death the better option. But like the shadow of The Emperor, God delivered a speech reminiscent to the one he laid on Job, and the story ends on that sour note.

I'm not convinced the intended moral of this fable was what my Sunday school teacher taught me years ago. "When God calls you to be a missionary, you better go." (Southern Baptists were big on missionaries.)

If there is a point to the story of Jonah, it might be another ending. At the conclusion of chapter 3, Jonah did what God wanted him to do, the Ninevites repented, and God relented. Such an ending would be in sync with the actions of Jonah, the people of Nineveh, and God. All of them saw the world through the eyes of The Hanged Man, from an inverted, upside down, underwater perspective. They all experienced a dramatic change of the collective mind. So why didn't the story end there instead of with God boasting about not destroying the lives of 120,000 people who didn't know their right from left? (Jonah 4:11) Maybe God wasn't familiar with the *Acts of Peter*.

REFLECTION ON THE HANGED MAN AND THE PATH OF WISDOM

- Have you had any Hanged Man experiences?
- What do you think it means that God repented?
- What does the king's response to Jonah's sermon have to say about salvation?

— CHAPTER 17 —
DEATH

Quick Read: Death wears many masks. Death is androgynous and no respector of genders. All who die are incorporated into Nature, for nothing is lost, only transmuted. *Oh no, I've drawn the Death card.* Am I'm going to die? Eventually, yes. The point of the card is to confront us with that reality. In the meantime, live life like you are already dead. In other words, by confronting the fragile nature of life with eyes wide open, our thoughts and actions will be invigorated.

Artistic Inspiration: "Morta," *Tarot of the Sevenfold Mysteries*, Robert M. Place, artist. *Morta* is the Latin word for death. In this card, the artist portrayed Death as a woman. Though she is pale, her face appears gentle and comforting. Supported by the sickle in right hand, Death kneels by a leafless tree. A dove flies under the long silver blade, while a seven-pointed star shines in the night.

Illumination: "In our periods and transitions in this life, are so many passages from death to death…" John Donne "Death's Duel," his final sermon.

Biblical Character: Death. Who else?

Biblical Text: "He that is our God is the God of salvation; and unto God the Lord belong the issues from death." (Psalm 68:20)

The word "death" does not appear on the thirteenth card of the *Marseille* deck. Avoidance of death can become an obsession. Rarely does anyone plan a major event on Friday the thirteenth. No one ever asked me to perform a wedding or conduct a funeral on that day. Athletes avoid wearing the dreaded number as if were the plague itself. Superstitious?

To quote the king of Nineveh, "Who knows?" Still, the king was willing to face death while hoping for the best. That "God may relent and change his mind; he may turn from his fierce anger, so that we do not perish" (Jonah 3:9). Death and God seem to be tightly interlocked in most stories of the Bible. Just read the prophet Ezekiel as case in point. Twenty-two years of God's violent war against the rebellious. For eons, Jewish scholars banned anyone under the age of thirty from reading that book. Too much death.

I've conducted a lot of funerals over the years. Memorial services, celebrations of life, and backyard parties, have replaced funerals. Many families have decided not to have a traditional religious service for all kinds of reasons. But I've only known a few people who preached their own funeral sermon. One person wrote what they wanted to have read at their service. Another made a video and insisted that we showed it as the sermon. On February 25, 1631, John Donne, who I quoted above, crawled from his deathbed and lumbered up the stairs of the pulpit at the old St. Paul's Cathedral in London. There he preached his funeral sermon, delivered before King Charles I, and a crowded church. Donne died a month later.

Our life, Donne wrote, is a pilgrimage of mini-deaths. Daily, we suffer the multiple defeats of our ego. Carl Jung wrote, "Death is as psychologically important as birth and, like it, is an integral part of life."[74] In order to embrace life, one must embrace death, living as if one has already died. The past is irreversible. Our imaginal of the future has scrolled itself backwards into our present time. Realizing that the only time that really exists is the Now. Jung continued:

> As a doctor, I make every effort to strengthen the belief in immortality, especially with older patients when such questions come threateningly close. Seen from a psychological perspective, death is not an end but a goal. For life's inclination towards death begins as soon as the meridian [the second half of life] is passed.

Was Jung suggesting that death is the goal because heaven's gate awaits our arrival? Probably not. What he was saying is that if the heavenly image comforts you, then lean into that belief with all your might.

As a priest, I felt it totally inappropriate to offer anything but hope to the dying, no matter what I might believe about the afterlife. In their last days, no one wants to hear about my theory of transmigration based on John Donne's poem, "The Progress of the Soul." The potential of returning to Earth's life as a worm isn't appealing to most folks. Maybe it could be if you're considering Dante's hell as your only other option. Then being a worm might sound attractive—at least you'd have a second chance at improving your eternal karma. My wife's grandfather said he wanted to come back as an old woman's poodle. That would take some serious good karma, which I'm sure her grandfather had in spades.

Historically, Christians have relied on the hope of streets paved with gold and their loved ones peering down from heaven with delight at the anticipation of their reunion. The stories that have comforted the dying and their grieving families the most have come from loved ones who have gone through similar experiences. A parishioner, for instance, told me he saw a white light approaching him in a near-death-experience. A friend spoke of when he and his brother were visited in the night by their deceased grandmother. And then there was my own mother's experience of her brother showing up at the foot of her bed to say, "I love you," the morning he was killed in a helicopter accident. These stories brought a sigh of relief to many a thirsty soul.

On the other end of the spectrum, I've spent significant time as a priest sitting vigil with families whose loved one died too soon. The questions of "Why?" wrapped in grief's awful shroud often cried out in anger and disbelief. The great horror when a family has lost a child. There is no comfort for the wailing. The shock, the disbelief, can never be silenced in the soul. Being there are no answers, a silent presence seems the clergy's best offering. No one can hear while the deafening sound of death beats its relentless drum. "Silence," Morton Kelsey wrote, "can be a mini experience of death and resurrection."[75] Sometimes only silence can soothe the broken-hearted.

Death is an ever-present character in the Bible. No one is excused.

Well, except for Elijah and Elisha. God's chariot whisked them into heaven before they died. I'm more inclined to entertain that story as a metaphor. Any call upon heaven's chariot to save us from the trials of the process of dying most likely will go unheeded. But no mind. Even Jesus died. But according to the Gospels, he rose again after three days in the tomb and a sojourn into hell. Maybe we are being told that our death will seem like "three days" instead of an eternity. Still, his mother's grief seemed to be everlasting. Grief knows no boundaries and death knows no strangers.

There is another well-known story of death in the Bible: the perplexing Lazarus story in the Gospel of John. I think it provides some insight into Jesus, the human. Jesus loved Lazarus and his sisters, Mary and Martha. Their message to Jesus about Lazarus's illness was touching. Jesus's response to their plea for help is confounding. However, when Jesus stood in front of Lazarus's tomb, we see his humanity in all its reality. The Bible tells us that he wept. Not quietly, not to himself, but for all to see. Jesus was grieving. In his humanity, as in ours, every loss is piled on top of the previous layers of the aching absence that death brings. He was not spared the worse pain of the human experience.

The weight of a lifetime of grief can almost be too much to bear. Even for the most ardent believer in the afterlife, the pain of missing someone in the flesh can drive the strongest person into the shadow of tears. There are no stages of grief. The hollow feeling of grief becomes a companion for the rest of our life. The ache may escape us from time to time, but its after-effects are always lurking nearby. Standing at his friend's tomb, Jesus felt the human sorrow that accompanies death's rattle.

What does it mean when you pull the Death card? Let's be honest, you will probably face some form of death that day, or in the thirteen that follow. (I'm using "thirteen" metaphorically.) Of course, we could say that whether you draw the Death card or not. Jung said that "every gain for the self is accompanied by a defeat for the ego."[76] That's more than a mini-death; that's transmutation. But for every event that reveals our mortality, we can ask, *"How will you bring about dramatic transformation in my life?"*

With the Death card comes awareness, an experience of consciousness, of mindfulness. You have the potential to become awakened to the reality that we live a life of countless paper-cuts of deaths. According to John Donne, you can do nothing to avoid the inevitability that death is a daily process—nor should you. Avoidance is simply postponing life's richest realization. Death carries with it the transmutational power of a destiny no one escapes.

REFLECTION ON DEATH AND THE PATH OF WISDOM

- ◊ What's your experience of Death?
- ◊ How have you worked with grief?
- ◊ What wisdom have you gained from your experiences?

— CHAPTER 18 —
TEMPERANCE

Quick Read: Equilibrium, blending the opposites, the pure essence of fire and water, a combination that has the potential to generate energy. Pulling the Temperance card reminds us that we are alchemists. We are responsible to manage our inner heat when all the world around us is burning to the ground. We can only control one thing in life, and that is how we address our work toward selfhood.

Artistic Inspiration: *The Sufi Tarot,* Ayeda Husain. The Arabic name for Temperance is *Sabr*: the mixing of patience, endurance, perseverance, and persistence. The figure on the card is an angel. Her translucent wings are fully spread. She is facing the horizon of a vast body of water. While standing waist deep in the lapping waves, her feet are firmly planted on the ocean's floor.

Illumination: "Figures are not symbols in the conventional sense.... Their nature is imaginal: a bridge to what they make visible. They have meaning [that] is essential reality in the invisible world, the world of angelic intelligence and divine reality, which is given sensory form by imagination." Stephania Pandolfo [77]

Biblical Character: Angels

Biblical Text: "Then the angel showed me the river of the water of life, bright as crystal, flowing from the throne of God and of the Lamb through the middle of the street of the city. On either side of the river is the tree of life with its twelve kinds of fruit, producing its fruit each month; and the leaves of the trees are for the healing of the nations." (Revelation 22:1-2)

My wife and I have one niece and two nephews. At Christmas, many years ago, when the three were young children, the oldest named my wife, Angel Aunt Cathy. And it stuck. They're adults now, with their own families, and to this day the niece and two nephews and their five children still call her Angel Aunt Cathy. It's especially fun when they send her birthday cards. "Dear Angel Aunt Cathy, Happy Birthday, I love you."

The story is cute, but it's laden with the power of acceptance. For our niece, two nephews, and their spouses and five children represent the depth of diversity in our family. From day one, Cathy has been their guardian angel and the angel of Temperance—the one who can navigate the middle ground. To do so requires an abundance of self-control. In Paul's letter to Titus, he instructs his colleague to "teach what is consistent with sound doctrine." The apostle then outlines the content of his message: first, temperance, followed by self-control, which is the mixture of fire and water (Titus 2:1-8). To blend the opposites of water and fire is the most difficult of all alchemical procedures.

As in the *Sufi Tarot* deck, the *Marseille*, and the *Rider-Waite-Smith*, each depict Temperance as an archetypal angel who is mixing two substances. She is representing the inner experience of alchemy. The angel is intermingling aspects of the unconscious and the conscious that are often regarded as opposites. Symbolically, however, Temperance portrays the unconscious and conscious as being on one spectrum. The angel is holding two cups at odd angles, defying gravity, the water flows from one to the other without spilling a drop. Temperance is negotiating the numinous psychological interplay along the spectrum upon which all opposites interact in the foggy region between the psyche and the material.

As an alchemist, the angel of Temperance creates something new: a third space, that which will arise from the unseen world into the seen world. As I quoted Pandolfo above, in the in-between space, meaning "is given sensory form by imagination." The alchemist's inner work is their imagination, fueled by study, meditation, sweat, and cooking the elements. Their writing and art are the outward, material expressions of the inward brewing (cooking) of their psyche.

The angelic Temperance is the *Soror Mystica*, the alchemical partner, symbolizing the hallowed middle ground between the above and the below. Jewish mystic Reb Schneur Zalman identifies those who traverse in this territory as *beinoni*, inbetweeners. These people are neither saint nor wicked. They're good people who unintentionally get lost on the way. But only by being lost once in a while can the inbetweener become imaginal enough to make their way back onto the trail.[78] In the Abrahamic tradition, the angelic have always walked this middle way: the way of the water between the two cups.

The Bible and the Quran mention angels over 300 times. They are divine messengers to the earthly bound mystics. We find angelic stories in Genesis, Ezekiel, Daniel, the Gospel of Matthew, the Gospel of John, and Revelation (the last book of the New Testament). More often than not, angels appeared in dreams, delivering a direct word from the Divine. In the biblical narrative, interpretation of dreaming belongs to God (Genesis 40:8).

But someone must have the courage to reveal the revelations to those who can't make sense of their dreams. We saw this particularly with Joseph. In some dreams, though, like Jacob's, the angels were actors in the cosmic drama, helping the dreamer with meaning-making (Genesis 28). And in many situations, angels acted as guardians of the dreamer (Psalm 91:11). In other cases, angels hid in the guise of a stranger. "Let mutual love continue. Do not neglect to show hospitality to strangers, for by doing that some have entertained angels without knowing it," it says in Hebrews 13:2. Temperance may appear in our dreams as a messenger, or as a guardian, or an alien in our midst. Our goal is to keep on watch for such possibilities, as the potential always exists for an encounter with the unseen.

In the Tarot, our Divine's messenger is the angel of Temperance. She is Wisdom Sophia's alchemist of the soul. The one who is constantly mixing and blending the opposites of fire (the spirit) and water (the emotions). Her alchemical work inspires our own. She guides us into the imaginal, the third space that we have yet to conceive.

Temperance is the one who opens the door that leads us from the shadows of bias into the light of acceptance. She points to a path that eliminates prejudice and leads to inclusion. Temperance holds the mirror that reflects the other who lives within our self, lowering our walls that block our transmutation from the first half of life to the second. She turns up the heat that melts hate into love. And Temperance is the angel who inspires us to search for yet another way when our first, second, third, fourth, or seventy-seventh experiment has failed. Our angel accepts experiments gone wrong as evidence of progress.

Paracelsus was the consummate experimenter. He was the first to attempt anatomy-based surgery supported by herbal pharmaceuticals. This doctor was a dedicated follower of Christ who also despised the patriarchy of the Church. Paracelsus constantly turned to the angel of his soul to deliver messages to the Lord. He trusted that the angel would bring God's wisdom back to him so that he might carry out his risky craftwork in order to save lives. Paracelsus followed the temperate practice for the sake of his patients.[79]

Temperance is not only a guide, but a role model for spiritual leaders and professional practitioners of all types. The angel of self-control, balance, and alchemy engenders patience that will save lives, relationships, and communities.

REFLECTIONS ON TEMPERANCE AND THE PATH OF WISDOM

- ◊ When have you found yourself playing the role of Temperance and self-control when everyone else was losing their mind?
- ◊ Can you identify practices in your life that you would consider the middle way of Temperance? Why did you include them in your life?
- ◊ What has the path of wisdom taught you?

— CHAPTER 19 —
THE DEVIL

Quick Read: The one who lures us into the places where we entrap ourselves. The Devil is the manifestation of the chaos of duality. The Devil is the trickster, the messenger, and Lucifer the morning star. Holding this card, we have to ask ourselves, *Is there such an entity as The Devil? How do we account for evil in the world?*

Artistic Inspiration: *Rider-Waite-Smith* deck, Pamela Colman Smith. The two humans on this card are similar to the two on the Lover's card. However, with The Devil, they have horns and tails. At the end of the female's appendage is a basket full of apples, while the male's is on fire. Biblically, they represent Eve and Adam. Instead of having free will, they are chained by the neck to The Devil's throne. This reflects the Christian's doctrine of "The Fall;" meaning all humans are born fallen and stained by the so-called "Original Sin" of Adam and Eve. Contrary to The Lover's card, instead of the archangel elevated above the two, it's The Devil, the fallen star, Lucifer. The pentagram of the occult hovers between his horns. The cross marks his right palm, while his left hand is lighting Adam's animal tale on fire.

Illumination: "Thousands of years of tradition have characterized [the] *satan*...as a spirit. Originally [in the Bible] he was one of God's angels, but a fallen one [as with the Essenes and the Gospel of Mark]. Now he stands in open rebellion against God, and in his frustrated rage he mirrors aspects of our own confrontations with otherness." Elaine Pagels[80]

Biblical Character: Lucifer (Satan)

Biblical Text: "Now the day came about and the angels of God came to stand by the Lord, and the Adversary [Lucifer], too, came among them." (Job 1:6)

The Fool has been walking the Path of Wisdom. Our pilgrim has visited Strength (needed for facing one's dragons), The Wheel (a bit of luck), true Justice (standing with the oppressed), The Hanged Man (an inverted perspective), Death (the willingness to die to the old ways), and the angelic alchemical spiritual practice of Temperance (blending the opposites). Now The Fool needs their wisdom in order to be able to climb the steep path of enlightenment.

Few climb the adept's mountain, for it's a switch-back of disorientation at the highest elevation. This journey is much like the progression of spiral dynamics.[81] It is important to remember that as we climb higher, we will not leave behind any of our past. Still, as we make our way into higher consciousness by leaning into our spiritual, psychic, and material natures (in all their variances), our goal is to do so without getting stuck at any one point along the way.

The good days are for remembering, it's the bad days that have made us what we are. My granddad used to tell me, "With age comes freedom." It has taken me years and years to even get a glimpse of what he meant—and I'm still fumbling around "With age comes…" I may not live long enough to figure out what he meant by freedom. But maybe he wanted me to accept those rough days ahead with the attention that they too would be vital for my evolution. I guess he knew I would have to begin this leg of the pilgrimage accepting my self-entrapment of The Devil within.

The book of Job (as well as Numbers) offers a clear picture of the ancient traditions of Lucifer, the Satan as a spirit, a universal energy force, a messenger of the Lord, the Adversary, the spirit that Elaine Pagels wrote about in *The Origin of Satan*. There, she provides us with the mythic evolution of Lucifer from a messenger of the Lord into the agent of rebellion against God. She outlines the technical move of the fallen angel of the Hebrew Bible (Isaiah 14:12-15) into God's binary opposite found in the writing of the Essenes and the post-Jesus Gospel of Mark.

Lucifer's name means "Day Star," or "Light Bearer." Messenger angels, like Lucifer, would deliver the Lord's "obstruction," to prevent some human action; "a reversal of fortune," in Job's situation.[82] In some cases, however, the barrier appeared on the path as protection from a malady. Such was the case of Balaam, who went where the Lord had instructed him not to travel. And "the angel of the Lord standing in the road with a drawn sword in his hand," became the defense against self-destruction (Numbers 22:23-25). In the stories of Job and Balaam, the Lord and Lucifer were playing on the same team—for Lucifer and the other angels were considered "sons of God," Divine beings. In these ancient stories, good and evil were simply different sides of the same coin. The Lord could be the deliverer of good as well as evil; the world and the Divine were not seen as binary nor dualistic.

> I [the Lord] form the light and create darkness: I make peace and create evil. I, the Lord, do all these things. (Isaiah 54:7)

Satan was never the alien being or foreign intruder from somewhere beyond divine reality. Instead, Satan became the "intimate enemy," one's business associate, neighbor, even a relative.[83] The question is, then: how did Satan make the vast leap from God's messenger—the intimate Satan—to the one being at cosmic war with the Lord?

As with all biblical paradigm shifts, this one was slow and subtle. According to Pagels, generations of Jews, either in exile or occupation, had been "pressured to assimilate" into the cultures that ruled over them. While others resisted.

Almost two hundred years before Jesus's appearance on the scene, the Syrian king, anticipating another Jewish revolt, decided to eradicate all forms of Jewish life and religion. Instead of passive resistance, the king's actions incited an insurrection led by Judas Maccabeus. His followers, the Maccabees, fought against their occupiers, as well as the Jews who were supportive of assimilating into the Hellenistic culture. Satan, as an intimate son of God, had transformed into the persona of the enemy itself, both alien in battle and domestic in manifestation. As the Maccabees pressed for political unity among the Jews, the Essenes of Qumran demanded a practice of purity.

The Jewish sect at Qumran attracted over 4,000 men to join them in the caves. Some scholars posit that both John the Baptist and Jesus had emerged from the Essene community. There they lived as monks of poverty, who practiced celibacy and a strict adherence to the laws of Torah. The Essenes considered anyone, including Jews, who had not adhered to their esoteric manner of life, were not allied with the angels of God. These reprobates, the Essenes said, were now in union with Satan, the enemy of the kingdom of YHVH.

For the author of the Gospel of Mark, this cosmic battle with Satan was emblematic of "The Way," the path of those who would truly follow Jesus (Acts 9:2 and Mark 8:34-38). In Mark's gospel, Jesus's story begins almost immediately with forty days of conflict with Satan, the tempter (Mark 1:12). This story was written during the time of the Jewish war against the Roman occupation. And for the author of Mark, Satan personified not only Rome but also Jews who would not accept Jesus as Messiah. Christians quickly identified themselves as being the minority and the oppressed who were in a war against Satan and anyone or any nation who they believed represents the evil one. For many Christians, there must always exist a perpetual "us" versus "them" binary for them to see themselves as "true believers."

The Devil of the medieval Tarot was the embodiment of this dualistic worldview held by the orthodox of the three Abrahamic traditions. The espoused theology of those who embrace dualism envision themselves in a perpetual cosmic war with Satan. Such beliefs have been the causal root of every disturbing action carried out by people of faith for the last 2,000 years: antisemitism, crusades, inquisitions, witch trials, slavery, denial of women's rights, mistreatment of the disabled by passing "Ugly Laws," anti-LGBTQ+ stances, and countless other "sins" that religions have declared war against, including against each other.

Should we burn The Devil card? Remove it from every Tarot deck? No. If we did so, we would avoid our opportunity to remember that The Devil is not our enemy but our intimate angel of the shadows. The Devil is the other side of the coin of humanity. We, as children of God, are like Lucifer carriers of both good and evil. And we, just like the angels, came by this non-duality from our very origins. Then God said, "Let us make humankind in *our* own image, according to *our* likeness" (Genesis 1:26). We can acknowledge our original union with the Divine or we can continue living in the dualistic image into which we have doomed The Devil and ourselves as well. As I quoted Pagels above: Now [The Devil as an enemy] "stands in open rebellion against God, and in his frustrated rage *he mirrors aspects of our own confrontations with otherness.*" (Italics my emphasis.) We can sustain the projection of our devilish shadows all we want onto our enemies and demonize them to death and war. Or instead, we can choose to see both the Divine and the Satan in every other human being and all of creation and love them, neighbor, alien, enemy, and the Divine and The Devil within ourself. (Matthew 5:44).

REFLECTIONS OF THE DEVIL AND THE PATH OF ENLIGHTENMENT

- ◊ Why do you think the first step toward enlightenment begins with The Devil?
- ◊ Have you ever met the intimate Devil? And what was that experience like?
- ◊ What do you think about the presentation of nondualism as presented in this chapter?

— *CHAPTER 20* —

THE TOWER

Quick Read: Restructuring, restoration, renovation, breakdown of beliefs, humility, the way of purification that precedes illumination. This card represents the alchemical chaos that eventually results in transformation. Even with enlightenment we will still be cast into the storm again and again as we continue to spiral into higher consciousness.

Artistic Inspiration: *Alchemical Tarot*, Robert Place. A male and female alchemist are kneeling in prayer before their alchemical vessel. Lightning has struck the *vas.* A white and red tincture is falling into the alchemist's hands.

Illumination: "I declare this tower is my symbol; I declare / This winding, gyring, spiring treadmill of a stair is my ancestral stair;" W. B. Yeats, "Blood and the Moon"

Biblical Character: The Tower of David, *La Maison Dieu*, translated as "The House of God."

Biblical Text: "Your neck is the tower of David, built in courses; on it hang a thousand bucklers, all of them shields of warriors." (Song of Songs 4:4)

"The name of the Lord is a strong tower; the righteous run into it and are safe." (Proverbs 18:10)

There are over 120 ancient towers in Ireland. Two dozen of them are still in excellent condition. My favorites are the Tower of Glendalough and Saint Brigid's Tower at Saint Brigid's Cathedral in Kildare. Both were likely built in the eleventh century. Brigid's Tower is thirty-three meters high and the second tallest in Ireland. Glendalough's tower is just over thirty meters tall. The entrance door of each is six meters off the ground, with windows periodically spiraling toward the top. Brigid's Tower has a base of granite with the elevated section made from local limestone. They made the tower at Glendalough from mica schist. While the original purpose of each tower is unknown, it seems that the verse from Proverbs, quoted above, inspired their builders.

Tourists can no longer enter the Tower of Glendalough, but Brigid's Tower is open to the public. The stairway is not the original, thankfully. Even at that, the path is narrow and winds upward along the interior side of the tower. On a clear day, the view is spectacular and I could imagine standing guard keeping watch over the idyllic village. It was also easy for me "to hear" the sounding of the bell, and to envision the villagers running to the tower for protection. And once inside reciting the Proverb, reminding God of the promise to protect them. Maybe the *Marseille* creators named its Tower, *La Maison Dieu*, "The House of God" after the tower of David, built as part of the city's defense system (Nehemiah 3:1).

Why then is The Tower card as feared as Death? Most Tarot designers have followed the *Rider-Waite-Smith* painting and explanation: danger, misery, crisis, change, destruction. These designs and meanings are based on the Tower of Babel story in Genesis. Some have suggested the two figures falling from the tower are Adam and Eve, who were expelled from Paradise. A few have suggested that The Tower depicts the Christ as the lightning destroying the gates of hell.

Medieval alchemists, however, had a much different view. Robert Place's depiction of The Tower in his *Alchemical Tarot* provides a perfect portrait of meaning. Two alchemists kneeling before the furnace of their work: The Tower. They are praying to God to strike their alchemical vessel, heating its contents of psychic lead, and turning it into their spiritual Philosopher's Stone. The two alchemists, in Place's deck, are not praying for gold or material riches. Instead, they are lifting their prayers so that God might transmute their soul-making into the tincture of healing.

Place's interpretation is based on Belgian philosopher and alchemist Gerhard Dorn (1530-1584), his writings, and the alchemical artistry of Jacobus Sulat, whose pseudonym was Altus. The latter's artwork appears in Alexander Roob's *Alchemy and Mysticism.*[84] The alchemists had built their tower to condense heaven's dew into manna, the food from above (Exodus 16). There were Kabbalists who interpreted the teachings of the *Zohar* in similar terms. "This dew is the manna on which the souls of the just nourish themselves. The chosen hunger for it and collect it with full hands in the fields of heaven."[85] Paracelsus and Dorn read Exodus, and possibly the *Zohar*, as alchemical prescriptions for healing physical and psychological ailments. Carl Jung heavily relied on Dorn's work, as well, to develop his later views. Alchemy was so critical in Jung's personal life that he built his own tower adjacent to his house where he kept his office and did most of his writing. An act of creative magic that Jeffrey Kripal says is "the writing of the real writing us." Kripal goes on later in *Secret Body,* that "writing and reading become, in effect paranormal powers capable of freeing us from our deeply inscripted beliefs and assumptions, be these cultural, religious, or intellectual."[86] To write and read is to live in The Tower with the anticipation that an inspired lightening will strike.

As quoted above, Yeats' series of poems written between 1918 and 1930 reveal a tower as his personal symbol, his talisman, too.[87] At his summer retreat in Thoor Ballylee, near the west coast of Ireland, stands a tower that was built in the fifteenth century. While spending time in that tower he wrote some of his best poetry. You might say The Tower became his muse, the symbol of his soul. The "Tower where a candle gleams," he wrote in his earliest version of the poem by the same name.[88]

We cannot read The Tower as a stand-alone card. If we do, it takes on an ominous meaning. In reading Tarot, we must always look at the entire deck. If I pull three cards, I not only consider the meaning of each separately, but also its correspondence with the other cards in the draw. This theory is based upon the Hermetic "doctrine of correspondence," which is crucial in reading Tarot. A tarotist is always focused toward "building a mental matrix of multidimensional consciousness."[89] This matrix opens onto a portal of consciousness where the reader can see with a "third eye," an eagle's view of the correspondences across multiple layers of mystical gnosis.

This gnosis is a deeper knowledge that goes beyond what we can read in the book that accompanies a pack of Tarot cards. For example, in the previous chapter we spent time with The Devil. This archetype is our intimate provocateur, one who challenges us to confront our shadows, clearing the way for our contemplation of potential transformation. Now, with The Tower we find ourselves in a position of praying to God for that transmutation—for the Divine to strike God's house, us, with lightning in order to energize our soulwork. No risk, no gain.

The alchemists knew better than anyone that their life was at risk. Too much heat, too much lightning, and a soul will be incinerated. But too little heat and nothing will happen.

On the path of enlightenment, The Fool is learning that change is inevitable but also a participatory act, one of co-creation. What you work on, works on you.

To resist transformation is to embrace stagnation. Even Saint Paul got frustrated with his followers' lack of spiritual maturation. Because they weren't ready for the solid food of the "mysteries of God and wisdom," he could only feed them milk (1 Corinthians 2-3). The two alchemists praying before their Tower were practicing the dictum of Paul, "*Work* out your own salvation" (Philippians 2:12). They were praying for transmutation, only accomplished with lightning from above. If The Fool truly desires to know the mysteries and wisdom of the Divine then they must muster the courage of maturity to pray for the energy of God to strike their human house of God, "God's temple," with enough force to transmute them from one stage of the spiral onto the next (1 Corinthians 3:16). To move from fearing The Tower to the imaginal of its innovative force.

REFLECTION ON THE TOWER AND THE PATH OF ENLIGHTENMENT

- ◊ Where has The Tower appeared in your life? What was the outcome?
- ◊ Do you have a partner in your alchemical process? How did they become your partner?
- ◊ What risks have you taken in order for transmutation to take place in your life?

— CHAPTER 21 —
THE STAR

Quick Read: The light comes into the world, knowing intuitively that the truth bearer is the next step on the ascent to higher consciousness. The Star asks us to consider what light we bring into the world and how it shines on the path for others to find their way.

Artistic Inspiration: The *Alchemical Tarot*, Robert Place. A mermaid rises from the waters of the unconscious. She is the light of the moonless night. A seven-pointed star with the third eye shines above her head, surrounded by the seven planets. The Star empties her alchemical elements into the cosmic waters.

Illumination: "Amaliel presented me with a task and I immediately said yes. The expectation was that I would dedicate a year to the task. In the end, it became the greatest work of my life." Hilma af Klint[90]

Biblical Character: The Star of Bethlehem

Biblical Text: "God determined the number of stars; he gives to all of them their names." (Psalms 147:4)

The destruction of The Tower, according to Jungian author Sallie Nichols, has liberated The Fool, and subsequently the five remaining Arcana who will lead our pilgrim into the "vistas of a wider starry sky."[91] The Fool, having traveled through those difficult days of chaos, is now experiencing the rays of en*light*enment, emanating from The Star who shines under the new moon. Our Fool's many nights alone on the desert's sacred path have expanded the imagination. From working with The Star, The Fool will learn how to walk in the moonless night. One aspect of becoming enlightened.

The star that Christians are most familiar with is the one that shines over Bethlehem (Matthew 2:1-12). Magi on pilgrimage from the East compass the stars to find their way to the new king. Modernists have struggled to assign a specific event of astronomy to the wise men's starry guide. Biblical scholar Brent Landau, in his groundbreaking book, *Revelation of the Magi,* translated a third century Syriac book by the same name. The ancient book had been lost in the archives of the Vatican for centuries. In this exquisite little volume, the Syrian author envisioned the star that captured the Magi's curious and devoted imagination as the Christ himself: the eternal Logos moving through space in a timeless manner to share a universal message with the mystics of the East. Both Matthew's version of the story and the tale of the *Revelation of the Magi* provide a mystical potential to the birth narrative. The genius of the latter account, however, is that the star of Bethlehem is also the Christ star.[92]

The Star of the Tarot is no less an intriguing and mystical figure. I chose Place's depiction because the symbol above the woman is the seven-pointed star of Venus. The Star and Venus symbolize the same attributes of beauty, relationship, and empathy. Seven is also a keen number in spiritual circles: seven days of creation, seven planets (of medieval cosmology), seven colors of the rainbow, seven musical notes of the major scale.

As with the *Marseille* and *Rider-Waite-Smith* decks, Place's Star also includes a bird, the *spirit* of fertility, potential, and intuition. While Place's painting does not overtly portray a tree as seen in the other two decks, his Star is herself, the Tree of Life—water and wine, birth and death, the alchemical opposites of red and white flowing directly from her body into the river of the unconscious dream world.[93]

The Star, now liberated from The Devil and The Tower, opens the imaginative portal of possibility which is represented by her nudity. She is humble and vulnerable, yet bold and unrepressed. We hear the bird's spirit message from above that affirms The Star. We taste the life-giving water and wine that flows from her as Tree of Life. In our experience of her sublime beauty, we are free to be birthed into a new imaginaire of our relationship with the Divine and all of creation: the stars, moon, and sun each lighting the way with their own special light. Our soul has opened onto another dimension, one where The Star is simultaneously luminous and dark light.

Swedish artist, the mother of abstract art, and spiritualist, Hilma af Klint (1862–1944), could think, paint, and "see" a dimension rarely accessed by others. Art history scholar Jadranka Ryle wrote of af Klint that she "willingly listen[ed] to the super-physical powers that she [wrote] directly onto the painting."[94] Af Klint created a series of 193 pieces for the *Paintings for the Temple.* The collection included a series of twenty-one paintings titled *The Seven-Pointed Star.* For af Klint, any singular concept, like the Temple, would require a series of images. She illustrated this multi-dimensional world using diagrammatic forms as geometric states of consciousness. Circles as spirals, like the Nautilus, revealing the integration of polarities, which give rise to another state of consciousness.[95] Her *Seven-Pointed Star* series developed into her painting the archetypal fourth dimension of a crucified androgynous Christ.[96] Here we see the quaternity of a cubed cross. Hanging between each section is an x-ray of an androgynous figure. These x-ray figures symbolize the complexity of the union of the seen and the unseen. To the right of the four-dimensional cross is a one-dimensional x-ray figure that is yellow, representing the male. And to the left is a blue figure, representing the female. These two shapes manifest the alchemical work necessary to evolve light into the folds and layers of the unseen—the center that is everywhere, the archetype of the androgynous Christ Star.

Af Klint's connection to the transpersonal space enhanced her varying states of consciousness of the in-between, the dimension where she experienced non-duality. These altered states of awareness were made possible when her conscious self was brought into a direct, unfiltered relationship with the dynamic unconscious.[97] There, she experienced a rare, altered state while being fully alert. Her consciousness interfaced with the collective unconscious, the realm of the archetypes. In her journal, af Klint wrote, "The will power of feeling. The will power of thought."[98] This is a personal testament about the psychic energy needed to engage in the integration of the mind, body, soul, and spirit with the universal Star.

The One (God) created the ever-evolving matrix of cosmic Oneness—the heavens of the sky—the sun, the moon, and the stars (Genesis 1:16). And from the beginning of time, humans have measured time, set the course of their journey across land and sea, and organized their daily lives around the influence of the seven stars (planets) they see with the naked eye: Sun, Moon, Venus, Saturn, Mercury, Mars, and Jupiter.

But The Star has had her detractors. Isaiah, relying on the Canaanite's myth, wrote about the Day Star (Venus) as fallen (14:12). Luke records Stephen's sermon in Acts (7:43), where he quotes the prophet Amos (5:25-27) in his condemnation of idolatry. Amos called to task those Israelites, who in the wilderness with Moses, had made idols of "the star of your god Rephan," Saturn. And while we can point to numerous other biblical texts that appear to warn against dependence upon the influence of the planets, there are others that seem to encourage the practice (Judges 5:20, Job 38:33).

In *The Complete Book of the Dead Sea Scrolls,* Geza Vernes writes, "for if many Jews frowned on astrology, others credited its invention to Abraham."[99] Jewish mystics insist that our lives are not necessarily determined by the astrology of the planets, "but that the arrangement of the planets is determined by our life." The mutuality of the energetic relationship between the material and psychic spins on every dimension. There is a vast difference between worshipping the stars, moon, and sun versus acknowledging that we significantly rely on each of them every day of our lives and that they equally depend upon us. The story of the Tarot is not about following one tradition, one religion, or even one star. A solitary illumination on a moonless night does not cast enough light to walk in the dark. The message of The Star's *spirit* is that there are many lights in the sky. Collectively sparkling, each reliant upon a reflection mirrored back to them from those on pilgrimage.

REFLECTIONS ON THE STAR AND THE PATH OF ENLIGHTENMENT

◊ Where's your favorite spot to watch the stars? What makes that space better than others?

◊ What's your interpretation of the Star of Bethlehem?

◊ How would you describe your star self?

— *CHAPTER 22* —

THE MOON

Quick Read: The Moon's cycle from new to full moon and back again represents the flow of everyday life. Every night, mother moon gathers our memories and dreams and journeys with them into the consciousness of our day. The Moon card asks the question, *"Can you walk in light of the full moon as well the darkness of the new moon?"*

Artistic Inspiration: *Marseille* deck. The midnight sun shines blue, reflected in the water of the unconscious below. Her light casts rays of red, blue, and yellow. The wolf and the dog lap up the manna from heaven, while they guard the way between two towers; one of intellect, the other of intuition. And the scarab represents fertility and rebirth, the one who rises from The Moon's birth water.

Illumination: "Praised be You my Lord with all Your creatures / especially Sir Brother Sun…Sister Moon and the stars, / In the heavens You have made them bright, precious, and fair." Saint Francis of Assisi, from the "Canticle of Brother Sun and Sister Moon"

Biblical Character: The Moon

Biblical Text: "Raise a song, sound the tambourine / the sweet lyre with the harp / Blow the trumpet at the new moon / at the full moon, on our festal day. / For it is a statue of Israel / an ordinance of the God of Jacob." (Psalm 81:2-4)

In the Genesis creation story, the sun is listed first, then the moon, and finally the stars, as in descending in order from the brightest (1:16-17). The three have forever been entwined. Brother Sun and Sister Moon, as Saint Francis imagined. But in the Tarot, the order is reversed: Star, Moon, and Sun. The priority of The Moon could well be connected to the fact that it was established by YHVH as a time to make offerings (Ezekiel 45:17).

The Bible was written by those who lived in the desert. They would often travel at night, under the stars and the moon to avoid the heat of the sun. There is an ancient mythos that far predates Christianity, placing the importance of the moon greater than the sun—a time when the archetypal masculine was the moon and the sun the feminine. Such alternative cosmological deities have been found in the Neolithic and High Bronze Age systems (12,000 years ago to fourth millennium BC), where Luna and Sol were portrayed as sister sun and brother moon.[100] During this same time period, the Egyptians worshipped the sun, whose *goddess deities* were "light that sustains."

The Fool's pilgrimage through the twenty-one Major Arcana is a path of ascension. But they're not climbing a ladder straight to the top. In the Kabbalah, both the descent and the ascent follow a multidimensional serpentine path, much like a labyrinth. Pilgrimage through the Tarot is also neither flat nor one-dimensional. It's a spiral, like following the sheep's path up an Irish mountain. Sheep never walk straight up. Too much energy, too much risk. They take a circuitous route. So too, The Fool ascends from Death's transmutation, The Tower's re-imagination, The Star's alchemy, and now onward to The Moon. The Tarot's pilgrims must travel through the Moon, who rules the night before making their way to the dominating midday Sun.

The paramount importance of The Moon/Sun relationship is that it is inseverable. Neither can stand over the other in their importance to Earth and the human condition. The bond of Moon and Sun represents the indestructible covenant that exists between the Divine lover and the beloved creation. Inseparable, mutually dependent, interchanging who is the lover and who is the beloved. This is the covenant of the biblical story that repeats on almost every page. God is love, and the path toward enlightenment is consummated in an eternal embrace.[101]

The Moon's role in this love affair is celebrated in the Psalm cited above. From new moon, waxing toward the full, and waning to the return. Night after night, the dance of the orbs display themselves on the landscape of the cosmos. And we join them, caught up in the movement between the eclipse of colors—from brilliant yellow, crystal blue, flaming orange, and frightening red. Like a rainbow solstice on seasonal display, we are reminded of our mood swings through sensing, intuition, thinking, and feeling. The Moon is our emotional shadow of The Sun's blinding light. However, The Moon has her own midnight sun of feelings.

The scarab rises out of the water of the unconscious dream world with a message from below. Before acting on our decisions, we must traffic our way past the rival dog and wolf. The domestic and moralistic intellect who is in conflict with the spontaneous intuitions of our wild beast. These warring natures battle between two towers, each guarding the best and worst of our intentions. The dog and wolf, actors in the theater of our dream life. For The Moon is the mother of our dreams, where our emotions find their heat. When we stand between the blood moon and the sun, there will be no difference between the old man and the youth, between the brother and the sister, nor the oppressor and the oppressed. The spirit shall flow freely.

> I will pour out my spirit on all flesh;
> your sons and daughters shall prophesy,
> your old men shall dream dreams,
> and your young men shall see visions.
> The sun shall be turned to darkness,
> And the moon to blood. (Joel 2:28-29)

The alchemist spirit peers over her cauldron, The Moon. The living pour their prophesies, dreams, and visions into the vessel of the sea. Hoping the spirit will coalesce the imaginal blood and water into the scarab's new life. But the dead will not be left out of this cosmic soup.

As The Sun sets, the dead gather as the eastern horizon waiting for The Moon to rise. She is the gatekeeper of things we thought we lost. But The Moon assures us that nothing is lost under her watch, especially not the dead. We gaze and marvel and wonder about her mysteries as we walk in the beauty of her loving light, remembering the souls of those we grieve. The Moon's blood is Eros love, and The Sun's ego of denial is the Logos turned dark. Her mysteries entice and we are pulled like the waves toward her. Some nights are full of The Moon and others, the shadows of the dead cast their dark light against the new orb.

Abraham and Sarah were brother/sister/lovers (Genesis 20:12). The archetypal father and mother of the biblical story were entwined as Logos and Eros, like The Sun's heat and The Moon's blood. The "Abrahamic tradition" might more clearly be known as the mystical tradition of Abraham and Sarah, but our modern sensibilities blanch at the thought of brother/sister marriages. However, mythology, religion, and royal history have long tolerated such unions. In alchemy, their union symbolizes the *hieros gamos*; the mystical marriage of the alchemist to the mystical sister. The symbolic matrimony of the twin siblings represented a return to the original paradise when Adam and Eve were one, the androgynous *Anthropos*: "humans made in our image" (Genesis 1:2). Restoring the day when the moon and the sun were believed to be equal lights in the dome: to be signs for the seasons, and to count the days, and the years (Genesis 1:14). The restoration of the harmony of lights was for the betterment of the world.

My wife gave me the *We'Moon Tarot* deck for Christmas one year. Musawa, founder of We'Moon products, created the deck from the work of female artists around the globe. The art and the accompanying book are from a "feminist perspective…and an earth-based women's spirituality." The art is stunning. And this is one of the most diverse decks I have yet to encounter.

I worked with the deck for weeks. Early on, I had to rely on their book because the suits and some of the names of cards and their meanings differed from traditional Tarot. But this wasn't unusual. I've worked with several other decks that changed the names of suits and identities of the images. Still, after learning this deck, I had an untoward feeling that I couldn't shake. After a couple months, I realized the cards didn't reflect any of my shadows. The cards like Death, The Hanged Man, the Three of

Swords, and the Ten of Swords were portrayed with positive images and meanings. Even in reverse, I struggled to find the shadow of Logos. Then one morning, long before the sun came up, I was reflecting on my six-card pull from the *We'Moon* deck. In that moment, it felt like The Moon had dropped all her weight on my soul. I—a cis, white, straight male—was the shadow of every card in the deck. Aye. The blood-red Moon took priority. The Sun grew dark. I felt extremely humble, and the better for it.

REFLECTIONS ON THE MOON AND THE PATH OF ENLIGHTENMENT

- ◊ Are you a Full Moon person, or a New Moon person? Or are you somewhere on the cycle?
- ◊ The harmony of lights is the restoration of balance between humans, regardless of differences. Do you think this is possible?
- ◊ How might you include The Moon as a part of your spiritual practice?

— CHAPTER 23 —
THE SUN

Quick Read: The Sun is the direct experience of knowledge and ego-consciousness: imaginative words, ideas, and images. The Sun is the "Life Force." This card represents that you are beginning to see things with clarity. Your world appears brighter. However, with expanded consciousness comes the risk of an inflated ego.

Artistic Inspiration: *We'Moon Tarot,* creator of the deck, Musawa. Artist of The Sun, Mosa Baczewska. The subtitle of the card is "Life Force." The stunning image on the card reminds me of the art found in chaos theory.

Illumination: "Only Being can know Being: we 'behold that which we are, and are that which we behold.' Come up then by this pathway, to those higher levels of reality to which, in virtue of the eternal spark in you, you belong.... Trust your deep instincts.... You can only behold that which you are. Only the Real can know Reality." Evelyn Underhill[102]

Biblical Character: The Sun

Biblical Text: "Love your enemies and pray for those who persecute you; so that you may be children of your Father in heaven; for God makes the sun rise on the evil and on the good, and sends rain on the righteous and on the unrighteous." (Matthew 5:43-45)

Tarot cards designed before Copernicus's 1543 theory of a heliocentric universe were developed under Ptolemy's geometric system. Then, in 1662, Galileo published his observations that supported Copernicus's theory. For over a hundred years, the Church's angst against such postulations were based on the Bible's instance that God created the Earth on the first day and the sun and moon followed on the fourth. The battle against a heliocentric universe may have been the Church's resistance to admitting that humans never were at the center of the universe. With a sun-centered universe, humans could no longer be the absolute focus of all things.

But the Tarot never was about a literal story. Its narrative is a metaphor for the mysteries of the cosmos. The Sun is the planet of rational thinking. An archetype who plans and sets high expectations. A light so brilliant that it prevents but a moment's glance, reflecting a larger-than-life ego. Even in reality, The Sun's archetypal symbols never lose their intensity. The Sun's warmth brings life to our gardens and its summer blistering tendencies will wither the heartiest of plants. The sun brings us life, and the sun brings us death. The Sun marks our days on the earth and our nights in the grave.

We'Moon Tarot has a fascinating Sun image. It reminds me of computer pictures produced by chaos theory, the science of surprises. When I worked at a small liberal arts university, I had the privilege of meeting a physicist who was on the leading edge of complexity theory. He brought me into his lab to share a stunning canvas of systems that had been created around "strange attractors." While the images appeared to be art, they resulted from non-linear, complex, unpredictable, chaotic behavior. Much like the magnificent yet strange artistry of a lightning storm.

We might consider the sun to be the most predictable thing in our life. It "rises" every morning and "sets" every evening at seasonally adjusted times. However, solar physicists are quick to point out the grand unpredictability of the sun with its fire-clouds, coronal mass ejections, sunspots, exploding flares, and damaging radiation. It's this generative energy of the unpredictability of the sun that creates the energetic force that sustains our lives.

That two-edged sword makes The Sun a perfect symbol for both the realm of rational thought and the blazing rage of a narcissist's ego. Under its heat, the alchemist's work becomes a living tincture, albeit a volatile one, predictable and unpredictable. Healing life and poisoning life. Providing the balm of Vitamin D, while its burning permutates cells producing skin cancer to a disastrous end.

The alchemical adept must be extremely knowledgeable about the psychological subtleties and paradoxes of achieving an integrated life, yet there is also a child-like imagination necessary to accomplish the goal. We find this conundrum of The Sun on the *Marseille* and *Rider-Waite-Smith* cards. There, children are celebrating under the golden glow of The Sun. They have an imaginal spirit of carefree focus that lifts them into a realm of vast fantasies. Their Sun is a constant reminder that while we might think life is unfair, life is just what it is: predictably unpredictable.

The Sun rises over the good children, and the evil that haunts them. And equally does the rain fall on the just that protects the child and the unjust that wounds them. Weeds grow as tall under the sun as does the wheat. Contradictions and paradoxes, too, are seeds that fall on fertile ground. This is one of the toughest lessons The Fool has had to learn on their pilgrimage under The Sun.

Only when we can walk under the imaginal eclipse of both The Sun and The Moon will we truly begin to see reality as a higher level of consciousness. Cynthia Bourgeault wrote that "Recovering our authentic reconnection to the imaginal is considered by many Wisdom teachers… to be the single most important task of our present era."[103] The imaginal is an engagement with the Divine reality, that which we can see when we have become both the dark and the light ourselves.

"I think you're a mystic," I said to my spiritual director one day. He fingered a book sitting next to his coffee cup. Picking it up, I could see it was Richard Rohr's *The Naked Now.*

"Have you read this?" I nodded that I had. He handed me the book, "Maybe you might want to read it again. Use Ezekiel's method: mark well, look closely, listen intently."

Then he continued: "Everybody's a mystic living their life in a mundane world. That's what makes Christianity a weird religion. The weirdest part, though, is that institutional Christianity doesn't want you to believe that we're all mystics doing the best we can every day, on our way up the mountain."

It seems much easier to operate through life when The Sun is shining on our public life. But it's the monotonous stuff that's so taxing and dangerous. The little things of our ordinary life that can get under our skin. Traffic. Standing in line behind the person in the check-out line who is telling their life story to the teller. Having to go to the DMV; your driver's license has expired. Know it all clergy. Those things can push my buttons in ways that make me worry about the core of myself. Those are the days I feel like a cloud is hovering over me, blocking the sun, and raining on me alone.

Maybe Jesus had trigger points in plain view for others to poke and jab. An overbearing mother. Siblings who thought he was crazy. Religious leaders that questioned his every word, otherwise known as smart-ass priests. Money changers. He was fully human and his reactions mirrored ours: the passion, the anger, and the weird.

Carl Jung said that when we're living the holy normal life, we can truly see ourselves for who we are. It's self-reflection via the painful awareness of embarrassment, regret, even shame. While we hate it, sometimes it's the only thing that keeps our ego in check. Jung said when we're at our "bottommost," our self is signaling us that we are now ready to begin another ascent up the mountain of becoming. He also said that no one but you will know what you're becoming will be like. Weirdly, and thankfully, we can meet our becoming self when we reach the peak of the mountain. The hard part is that after we've embraced our new becoming—our new Sun—we'll have to descend to the bottommost again. A dreary thought, because from there we'll have to climb the next mountain of "an endlessly slow growth" under our predictably unpredictable friend The Sun.

REFLECTIONS ON THE SUN AND THE PATH OF ENLIGHTENMENT

◊ What self-reflection has brought you into another level of consciousness?

◊ What shadows ("bottommosts") in your life have The Sun revealed?

◊ What "becomings" have you met on your ascent of the mountain?

— *CHAPTER 24* —

JUDGMENT

Quick Read: Judgment symbolizes rebirth. It also represents the thin space between the unconscious and the conscious. This increased awareness equals increased responsibility. Judgment reminds us to listen to the lament of the dead. When we draw this card, we are being called to wake up, to become aware.

Artistic Inspiration: *Druidcraft Tarot Deck*, "Rebirth," Philip and Stephanie Carr-Gomm, illustrated by Will Worthington. The angel Gabriel stands at the opening of Ireland's Newgrange. The archangel is calling forth the dead. A naked child steps forth. The hare, who's connected to the underworld, is a symbol of abundance and new potential. This Celtic spirit animal is perched in front of tri-spirals that represent the cycles of life.

Illumination: "Here we must come to a transformed knowledge, and this unknowing must not come from ignorance, but rather from knowing we must get to the unknowing. Then we shall become knowing with divine knowing, and our unknowing will be ennobled and adorned with supernatural knowing." Meister Eckhart[104]

Biblical Character: The Archangel Gabriel

Biblical Text: "A celestial being said, 'Gabriel, help this man understand the vision.' As Gabriel was speaking to me, I fell into a trance…and Gabriel said to me, 'Daniel, I have now come out to give you wisdom and understanding.'" (Daniel 8:16,18, 9:22)

North of Dublin stands the ancient Irish burial mound, Newgrange. The colossus Celtic temple looms from atop a ridge, peering over the rolling green valley of the Boyne River. This unique 5,000-year-old ritual site and its façade of quartz glimmers even on a cloudy day. It's hard to comprehend the imagination of the people who constructed the holy site. To use an Irish word, they must have been "brilliant."

These people built Newgrange around 3,200 BCE, 600 years before the Egyptian Giza Pyramids and 1,000 years before Stonehenge. The ancient Celt's constructed the site without the use of metal tools or mortar to hold the stones together or keep the inner sanctum dry. Yet, the interior has never suffered weather leakage. These people of the New Stone Age carried 200,000 tons of earth—44,000 square feet of dirt—uphill in order to assemble the colossal temple/tomb. The mound's diameter is 320 feet and approximately fifty feet high at its center. The ninety-seven circumference kerbstones that support the mound, each weigh as much as two tons. Most likely, the stones were floated down the Boyne River and transported by sleds up the hill about five miles to the site. These stones contain some of the oldest Neolithic spiral etching in the world. The wall of quartz covering the front of the tomb, where the entrance passage is located, may have been brought from sites south of Newgrange, as far as 100 miles away in the Wicklow Mountains. Archeologists conjecture that the colossal feat of construction took between thirty to fifty years to complete.

The brilliance of Newgrange's architecture is found at its inner sanctum. A passageway to the tomb's center is ninety-seven feet long. There, we find a cruciform space that is twenty-one by seventeen feet wide and twenty feet high. Inside the "cosmic egg" there are three ritual recesses, where evidence of two bodies and three cremains were discovered in the mid-nineteenth century. A few hundred years of looting probably removed other archeological artifacts and human remains prior to the modern archeological work of Michael J. O'Kelly in the 1970s.

Newgrange is unique to Ireland's burial mounds due to its light box that is situated just above the entrance passage. The box provides a perfect stream of seventeen minutes of winter solstice sunrise light that flows down the passageway and into the sacred center.

Entering the tomb, the mystery of the interior temple can be overwhelming. The mystic presence seems reserved for the imaginative. A guide who had been inside at a winter solstice described the experience with misty eyes. "Light sliding up the floor of the burial mound like hot molten lava," he said. "Reaching the pitch-black center, the light would burst alive with a climatic crescendo, illuminating the stones with an iridescent glow. Then, as the sun moved, the light retreated down the tomb's floor, as if to carry souls into the otherworld." For three days, the light of the solstice makes its journey down the path of the light box. It's as if the sun stood still long enough to retrieve the souls of all who were called forth (Joshua 10:13).

In the Tarot packs created prior to the *Rider-Waite-Smith*, Judgment was the only Major Arcana card to include a musical instrument. Judgment is portrayed as an angel calling the dead to rise (Matthew 24:31, 1 Thessalonians 4:16). Christian tradition named Gabriel the archangel of the trumpet who announces the return of Christ even though Gabriel goes unmentioned in the New Testament. But Gabriel is featured in the Daniel text that is cited above, and in the apocryphal text, Enoch, where Gabriel is one of the four ranked angels following Michael (1 Enoch 40).

The story of Judgment has been understood as apocalyptic—the end of the eon in the story of Daniel and the coming of Christ in the New Testament. Based on the Bible's perspective of judgment, this card has carried a heavy air of fear that looms in this life and the next.

I've asked myself too many times why my sister was born with Prader-Willi syndrome. While the cause of PWS is the deformity of Chromosome-15, its appearance is random—one out of every 10,000 births. It's neither genetic nor related to any environmental situation. Complete, total, and undeniable randomness. Yet, my family and I have heard answers to the question, *Why?* that are laced with God's judgment.

◊ The sins of the parents are being punished through the child.
◊ God is trying to teach Dinah's family some valuable lessons that couldn't be learned any other way.

- ◊ If her family were faithful enough, God would prove his existence with a miracle of healing.
- ◊ God has a plan, and while we don't know God's plan, one day we will.
- ◊ We don't know God's plan but we do know one day Dinah will be in heaven where there no longer will be Prader-Willi syndrome.
- ◊ Dinah having PWS is proof that God is not a God of love.
- ◊ Dinah having PWS is proof that God is not an active agent in our world.
- ◊ Dinah having PWS is proof that there is no God.

Despite the diet of judgment that has been fed to our family, I have a different reading of this card. Beyond the apocalyptic prophecies, I'm inclined to follow the Celts interpretation of Gabriel's musical call to be one of celebration and not punishment. I chose the *Druidcraft Tarot Deck* as my artistic inspiration card for that very reason. Gabriel beckons the souls forward to ascend Jacob's ladder from earth into the presence of the Divine (Genesis 28:12).

The story of the Judgment card appears to affirm a positive perspective of the afterlife. In the book of Genesis, there are a few verses that refer to a life beyond death. For instance, "Enoch walked with God; then he was no more, because God took him" (Genesis 5:24). While it is vague as to whether Enoch died or not, it does more than suggest that he disappeared into the bosom of God.

The Bible uses the word Sheol as the abode for the dead, which is more a state of being than a place to go after death. Jacob, upon hearing of Joseph's supposed death, lamented, "I shall go down to Sheol to my son, mourning" (Genesis 37:35). A more definitive Jewish perspective on the afterlife seemed to have evolved over time. Elijah and Elisha, while still living in the flesh, were swept into heaven via God's whirlwind (2 Kings).

The authors of the Dead Sea Scrolls, which apparently included the Essenes, wrote that the afterlife would be a pleasant experience for those who had lived a virtuous life. Both John the Baptizer and Jesus may have been members of the Essenes, possibly influencing their theology of life beyond death. Jesus used the Greek concept of "Gehenna," referring to the abode of the damned. In the Gospel of Luke (16:19-31), he told the parable of the rich man who died and went to Hades (Gehenna), and Lazarus, a poor man, who died and was carried by the angels into the bosom of Abraham. From Hades, the rich man cried out to Abraham, pleading that Lazarus would relieve the rich man's tormented thirst with a drop of water. Upon being refused by Abraham, the rich man continued his lament, begging him to send someone from the dead to warn his brothers and admonish them to repent of their sins. But Abraham, once again rebuffed the rich man saying, "If they do not listen to Moses and the prophets, neither will they be convinced even if someone rises from the dead." The story of Abraham, Lazarus, and the rich man does open up the potential for life after death.[105] It also poises the possibility of listening to the lament of the dead.

We might be more familiar with Rachel's weeping for the dead (Jeremiah 31:15), or "Judah's mourning and lamentations" for the deceased (Lamentations 2:5). In both the Catholic and Episcopal traditions, they affirm mourning as well as praying for the dead. But while listening and praying to the dead might be foreign to many, these parables have much for us to ponder.

Christian theology of the afterlife varies. In most denominations, the belief persists that, at death, the soul separates from the body. Where the soul goes after death has more than one answer. And what about the body? For many Christians, at the second coming of Christ, the body will be restored and reunited with the soul. Of course, that creates another list of questions about what the body will look like. And then where will the resurrected person reside? Heaven or hell? And where are these places?

There are other theories about life after death. Interestingly, some of these suggestions come from the scientific community. Physicist Harald Atmanspacher suggests that the mind and body survive death in a "psychophysically neutral ground."[106] Atmanspacher, Christopher Fuchs, Dean Rickles, and Wolfgang Fach are among some of the leading researchers on the Jung-Pauli conjecture. Their idea suggests that we are more than a brain in a body. Instead, we are the mind and the body as something more. We each are a singularity, a personal psychic matrix that survives death within the cosmic web of synchronicity.

Atmanspacher and Fuchs' *The Pauli-Jung Conjecture and Its Impact Today* is most insightful regarding the intersection of philosophy and science in researching this mind-body problem. The Jung-Pauli conjecture was originally based on philosopher Baruch Spinoza's (1632–1677) work. Then Jung brought his ideas of the collective unconscious, synchronicity, absolute knowledge, and the archetypes into conversation with Pauli's theories of quantum physics.

The Jung-Pauli conjecture posits that the mind (consciousness) and body (which includes the brain) are complimentary aspects of one "underlying reality." Jung and Pauli considered quantum theory as a viable means of addressing the mind-body as more than a physical entity, but an integrated one within its own self. Quantum mechanics suggests that whatever has been observed as two aspects, was, before observation, a part of an "inseparable whole." Put another way, our consciousness is the product of our inseparable mind-body, which is living in the background reality, a psychophysical neutral reality.

Using alchemical terms, Jung described the background reality as the *unus mundus,* the one world (The World card of Tarot). Jung wrote in a letter to Pauli:

> In reality, however, there is no dissected world: for a unified individual there is one 'unus mundus.' He must discriminate this one world in order to be capable of conceiving it, but he must not forget that what he discriminates is always the one world, and discrimination is a presupposition of consciousness.[107]

Later, he would name this one world "acausal synchronicity." These conjectures provide plausible theories for how we might consider life after death, and they do not run contrary to the biblical narrative. In Genesis, when Abram (15:15), Ismael (25:8), and Jacob (49:13) died, they were gathered together with their tribal ancestors. With Jung and

Pauli as support let me suggest that the personal psychic matrix of the dead will be brought together in something like a unified web of synchronicity, that which maintains a sustained relationship between the living and the dead.

In his book, *The Gospel According to Judas: Is There a Limit to God's Forgiveness,* author and former Fuller Seminary professor, Ray S. Anderson (1925-2009), tested the imagination of the phrase in the Apostles Creed, "He (Jesus) descended into hell." Anderson's writing flows between non-fiction exploration and fictional imagination. His subtitle prepares us to see how far we might think God's unconditional love could be stretched. In Anderson's story, after Jesus is placed in the tomb, he goes into Hades where he meets Judas, his betrayer, and offers him forgiveness. Anderson based his perspective on the biblical narrative of the Christ descending into hell and proclaiming the Gospel, "Even to the dead, so that, though they had been judged in the flesh as everyone is judged, they might live in the spirit as God does" (1 Peter 4:16). Saint Paul took that notion further saying that "neither death, nor life, nor angels, nor rulers, nor things present, nor things to come, nor powers, nor height, nor depth, not anything else in all creation, will be able to separate us from the love of God in Christ Jesus our Lord" (Romans 8:38).

For me, the Tarot's Judgment card is proclaiming the good news that nothing can separate anyone from the love of the Divine. No matter where we are in life or death, the angel of the Lord has a message for us…we are the Lover's Beloved. And the Lover will go into the depths of whatever hell we are experiencing to bring us hope.

REFLECTIONS ON JUDGMENT AND THE PATH OF ENLIGHTENMENT

◊ What do you imagine an individual psychic matrix might be for an individual in the afterlife?

◊ Can you play with the idea of the web of synchronicity? What might that be?

◊ Have you heard the lament of the dead? Talked to the dead?

— CHAPTER 25 —
THE WORLD

Quick Read: The World represents completion, androgyne, enchantment, illumination, and enlightenment. The World points to the end of our pilgrimage, another step of individuation, and into a higher level of consciousness. We have spiraled into another layer of the rose.

Artistic Inspiration: *The Wildwood Tarot*, artist, Will Worthington. His depiction of The World is an ancient tree. Its root structure is so massive that it is visible above ground. At the base of the tree is a wooden door. On a green field just outside the door is a labyrinth that begins and ends at The World Tree's entrance.

Illumination: "If one attempts to deal with terms like 'Great Mother,' 'Totem Animal,' [or] 'Tree of Life,' in a purely theoretical way, without having experienced their numinosity, they will lose their meaning in relationship to the human soul." Marie-Louise von Franz[108]

Biblical Character: The Cedar of Lebanon

Biblical Text: "I [God] made [the Cedar of Lebanon] beautiful with its mass of branches, the envy of all the trees of Eden that were in the garden of God.... Its top is above the clouds and its roots deep into the waters below.... The birds made their nests in the boughs; and under its branches all the animals gave birth to their young; and in its shade, all great nations lived." (Ezekiel 31)

The symbols on *The Wildwood Tarot's* World Tree reveal a strong correspondence with Ezekiel's Tree of Life. The figure at the center of Worthington's image is similar to a massive cedar whose top we cannot see and whose roots are extended out of sight. To reach the base of the tree, the pilgrim must walk the labyrinth's path. At the base of the artist's tree is a closed wooden door which leads into the treasure-house of enlightenment. The Fool began their pilgrimage stepping through a portal and now they will end this leg of the journey by stepping through the holy door of The World Tree.

On Pamela Colman Smith's World card, the opening leads into an enlightened consciousness. The Fool's pilgrimage has been given the force of Ezekiel's vision: the winds of the four directions, the four living creatures, with four wings, and the four faces (the human, the lion, the ox, and the eagle). These are symbols of the integration of the human intellect, the lion's courage, ox's strength, and the eagle's perspective from on high. Collectively, these archetypes lift The Fool higher into The World Tree at another level of being and wisdom.

The World card is a symbol of the pilgrim who has become the sage and the crone. We don't need a merit badge to wear on our sash proclaiming our proficiency. "Do not be wise in your own eyes" (Proverbs 3:7). Still, we have walked hand-in-hand with Wisdom while traveling with The Fool. We have gained experience and have now been initiated into the way of desert's sacred path. For "Whoever walks with the wise becomes wise" (Proverbs 13:20).

On every one of my walking pilgrimages, I've had deep respect for folks who wear well-worn boots and a tattered backpack. I feel more comfortable with pilgrims who are not afraid to pull out a map, and when they do, it's in a waterproof bag. I'm more willing to trust the pilgrim who knows the goal is not to win a one-hundred-yard dash, but to finish the marathon healthy, and in one piece. The wise pilgrim takes regular breaks, drinks plenty of water, carries a healthy snack of nuts and fruit, and is always prepared with a blister kit. A wise pilgrim is one who steps through the door of The World Tree while leading others from the back of the line.

The World is akin to the New Jerusalem, the metaphoric city that shall be named, "The Lord is there" (Ezekiel 48:35). Under the great cedar's shade, every other city will be built. For the City of God shall be the Lover's Beloved. "The home of God is among mortals. He will dwell with them as their God; they will be his people, and God himself will be with them" (Revelation 21:2-3, Ezekiel 37:27). The World becomes the new home, the place to which all pilgrims can return and find rest and peace, while they prepare for their next adventure. The penultimate pilgrimage that will take them higher on the rose's spiral into yet another state of enlightenment.

We cannot fully understand The Fool's pilgrimage along the three paths of the Tarot without the amalgamation of all seventy-eight cards into our personal matrix. The archetype of completeness, however, does not require the physical presence of every card for the whole to be one. Rabbi Arthur Green, author of *A Guide to the Zohar*, wrote that "the way to clarity is to discover the mysterious."[109] The Tarot's reality is laced with riddles and the conundrum of mystery but it's also the gateway to deeper levels of understanding our self.

On my many pilgrimages across Ireland, I always carried a Tarot deck in my backpack. On the Wicklow Way there stands an ancient tree, hundreds of years old. She is the Mother Tree and rests just a mile south of the Knockree Hostel along the bank of a gently flowing stream. The base measures ten feet in diameter, big enough to hold a reddish rectangular stone that's two feet high and five feet long. The tree created a portal large enough for a person six feet tall to disappear into it while standing on the stone. I've been to visit this tree on multiple occasions, each time learning from her ancient wisdom. Taking out the Tarot deck and spreading the cards across the top of the stone altar, I've asked Mother Tree several questions. On one visit, she told me to "break the deck." Surely, that's not what I heard? A broken deck is when one or more of the cards are missing from the pack. Most Tarot readers consider a broken deck to be worthless. I mean, what good is a deck without a High Priestess? In this case, I would be giving away twelve cards—a mysterious riddle and a true conundrum.

The Mother Tree is like The World card to me. She always has much to teach me, and I do my best to listen. That night, at dinner with our twelve pilgrims, I passed the deck around and told my colleagues they could flip through and choose one card of their liking or they could draw one blind. After they made their choices, I asked them if they would mind sharing what card they had drawn and what they saw in it. After they all had a turn, I told them they could keep their cards. My fellow pilgrims had watched me do readings with the deck all week, and they had observed my ritual at the Mother Tree. As far as they knew, that was the only deck I was traveling with, which was the case. I'd had that deck for years; it was well worn and had a thousand stories to tell.

Truthfully, it was hard to break that beloved deck, and to part with those twelve cards. But now those stories were in the hearts of my friends who carried each card to different homes. A deck of Tarot cards is like a mighty cedar tree; it has lived for centuries and has scattered many seeds. Whether the cards live as one tree or are seeds that have been planted in twelve different places, neither the tree nor the deck is ever broken. They are in the hands of more than one person, each walking their own labyrinthine path.

The World is the final mile-marker of The Fool's sojourn. The Fool has completed their last leg of a soul-making pilgrimage. The World is the representation of a successful adventure, a job well done, but one that is never finished. Reportedly, Jung said it would take him ten lives to reach complete individuation. I have to imagine that if it would take him ten, it would take me, well, I don't know, too many to count. The point is, we have journeyed with The Fool toward integrating mind, body, and soul; to uncover the collective of the mind-body as the soul. And in that unity, we experience Reality as being one with the One.

The wise Fool is now ready to step out onto the next elevation of the great spiral, to begin another pilgrimage. Every pilgrimage ends with an odd cocktail of the glorious sensation of an afterglow shaken with the awful feeling of being hungover. The unbridled emotion of successfully completing a goal that, at one point, might have felt impossible, juxtaposed against a wave of exhaustion and depleted adrenaline. And The Fool knows that true alchemical soul-making not only requires the support of all four of Ezekiel's living creatures, but also two of The World's magical wands. There's a bit of madness involved in such an adventure, and simultaneously, a hunger to begin again.

The next pilgrimage is born of a "longing for enlightenment"[110] that travels deeper into the center of the rose. "Wisdom [Rose] is radiant and unfading, and she is easily discerned by those who love her and is found by those who seek her. I will tell what wisdom is and how she came to be, and I will hide no secrets from you...The multitude of the wise is the salvation of the world" (Wisdom of Solomon 6:12, 22, 24). Still, we know through experience that every pilgrimage begins again with chaos, but we go because each familiar step takes the pilgrim higher into the spiraled rose at the foot of The World Tree. It's time to begin again, to step through the portal. "Come and see" (John 1:39).

Before we leave The Fool and their pilgrimage through the Major Arcana, I want to add a note to my suggestion in chapter 4, about creating your own Rose Bible, the book of the mystics. The idea first appeared in my conversation with my pastor in chapter 2. Then in chapter 3, I poised the possibility that you can create your own Tarot deck, which could be a component of your Rose Bible. In the final chapter, I will outline ways to gather notes about your Tarot deck, all which can be included in your book. Along the way, I've offered my interpretation or commentary on Bible verses. I encourage you to do the same. I'm not suggesting that anyone re-write the Bible. I'm simply entertaining the idea that we can dive deep into the biblical story and there find ourselves in union with the Divine. "Show that you are a letter of Christ, prepared by us, written not with ink but with the Spirit of the living God, not on tablets of stone but on tablets of human hearts," it says in 2 Corinthians 3:3. Or, as the authors of the *Zohar* wrote, study and meditate on the Torah in order to discover an "innovated word of wisdom."[111] I've taken that to heart in my rendition of Isaiah 35, which is at the front of my own Rose Bible:

> A path shall appear in the desert,
> Which shall be called the Sacred Way.
> The arid desert shall be glad,

The wilderness shall rejoice
And shall blossom like a rose.

The Way shall be a pilgrimage for those who seek the soul.
While the Gate is narrow,
And the Way is steep and rocky,
The pilgrims will sing.
And though the Night's Moon shall be New,
And the Day's Sun eclipsed,
The pilgrims shall behold the glory of Sophia Wisdom,
For She shall be the Key to the Gate
And the Light of the Sacred Way.
For the traveler, not even fools, shall go astray.

Sophia shall lead the pilgrims
To discover the Blue Tincture of healing, which will
Strengthen the hands of the poor;
Making firm the tottering knees!
Saying to the anxious of heart,
"Be strong, fear not;
Behold the Presence of Sophia is among us.

She will open the eyes of the blind,
And the deaf shall hear.
The lame shall leap like a deer,
And every tongue shall sing.
For the gentle rain shall nourish the desert,
And the streams of wilderness, shall become a healing pool;
The inhabitation of the dragons, shall bloom marigolds;
The abode of the ravens shall be the mighty cedar.
For Wisdom Sophia shall crown every pilgrim with Wisdom everlasting.

— CHAPTER 26 —

MINOR ARCANA: THE PIPS

In order to grasp the Tarot, like the Bible, we need an understanding of the arc of its narrative. Single cards read outside of the context of the whole can be misleading, or misunderstood, or worse, made meaningless. The Major Arcana on a whole, point to the big picture, the narrative frames and archetypes of life. Similarly, the Minor Arcana, the pips and the court cards, have a collective story. The pips symbolize the subtleties and intricacies of our daily lives. The court cards (discussed in the following chapter) are representative of people who effect how we "live, move, and have our being" (Acts 17:28).

The term "pip cards" was most likely derived from an Old French word, *pepin*, meaning seed. Pips refer to the value of the number on the card. You might think of it like the number of seeds being cast on the ground (Matthew 13:1-23). These numbered cards are extremely helpful in processing our way through daily problems. Those sticky situations that can manifest within relationships, family, or with friends, colleagues, our boss, our spiritual leader, or in our religious places; some seeds fell on the path, some on rocky ground, some among thorns, and some on good soil.

Minor Arcana, both pips and court cards, are divided into four suits. The Swords, Wands, Pentacles, and Cups each carry a particular distinction and set of symbols that differentiate them from one another. The history of the suits is uncertain about its origination. One theory is based on Plato's cardinal virtues that were amalgamated by Thomas Aquinas into Christianity in the thirteenth century. Prudence (wisdom), justice, temperance (restraint), and fortitude (strength) would become correspondingly, Coins, Swords, Cups, and Wands.[112] As we saw in chapter 3, the fifteenth-century *Mamluk* deck, created by Sufis, also used these four suits. While each card and suit of the Minor Arcana are unique unto itself, there are similarities that exist among the suits of the pip and court cards, significantly within the numerology of the Tarot.

BIBLICAL AND TAROT NUMEROLOGY

Marie-Louise von Franz wrote in *Number and Time,* "The Western mathematician seeks quantitative, structural connections in number theory. While the [Eastern mathematician has historically] looked for qualitative and feeling-toned relationships."[113] In other words, numbers, like symbols, are archetypes that carry a universal symbolic meaning aside from their quantitative value. Numerology from ancient times is essential for comprehending the biblical narrative. The qualitative significance of each number spans the narrative from Genesis to Revelation. For example, what was most likely the meaning of seven in Genesis has the similar intent in Revelation.

The Israelites used numbers like most of us: for counting (Jeremiah 33:13), as a rhetorical devise (Job 5:19), symbolically (Isaiah 30:26), and mystically (Isaiah 11:2-3). In Hebrew, each number corresponds to a specific letter of the language. There are twenty-two letters in the Hebrew alphabet. The first ten letters represent one through ten correspondingly. Subsequently, the next nine numbers designate the values of twenty, thirty, and up to 100. The final three letters, numerically, are 200, 300, and 400. This is important information when considering numbers in the Bible.

For our purposes, the symbolic numbers one through ten—as you'll encounter them in the pip cards and their general meanings as corresponded with the Bible—*may* be described as follows.

ONE

One is about beginnings (Genesis 1:1). Creation began with the conception of a holy idea. One represents the monotheistic God found in the three Abrahamic traditions (Genesis 1:1, Isaiah 57:15, John 1:1, Qur'an 1:1). One equates with ten, [10=(1+0)=1]. "But many who are first will be last, and the last will be first" (Mark 10:31). This means that the direction of the pip story typically begins with the Ace. However, there may be times when you will want to start your narrative with the Ten [10=(1+0)=1]. The ending may be the beginning of the journey that has yet to start. You may have decided (Ace) to end a relationship (Ten). But you haven't gotten to the place of actually ending it (Ten) in order to begin again (Ace).

TWO

Two encompasses our relationships and the dual aspects we observe in our world (Genesis 1:1-27). Two also represents the potential for every opposite to unite with its pair. For two polar identities to maintain the tension of the union effectively, a covenant is imperative. A give-give relationship of mutuality, as in the covenant between God and creation (Genesis 9:8-17).

THREE

Three symbolizes the past, present, and future. The triangle is the symbol of the creation of energy (Genesis 1:1-27, air, water, fire) of which earth is the container. It was the third day of creation when the "trees of every kind bore fruit with the seed in it" (Genesis 1:12). To pray three times a day (Psalm 55:17 and Daniel 6:10) is to engage with the energetic force of the Divine and the cosmos. There are three physical places within the worship sanctuary (1 Kings 6). Yet "three things are wonderful for me; four things I do not understand" (Proverbs 30:18). Meaning the triangle produces a mysterious fourth.

FOUR

Four acknowledges stability, the square, the foundation: the four directions, the four winds (Genesis 1:14-19). The four rivers are crossroads (Genesis 2:10-14). There are four living creatures who surround the throne of God, providing protection (Ezekiel 1:10). Every process begins with forty years in the wilderness (Numbers 14:20, Revelation 4:6-7). And a person metaphorically reaches the second-half of life at forty (Exodus 2:11, Acts 7:23).

FIVE

Five represents contractions and disturbances that bring uncomfortable change. On the fifth day, God created the great sea monsters (Genesis 1:21). Human frailty (we don't live forever) is represented by the five senses. And five is the halfway mark to Ten (or One). We can see five as half-full or half-empty.

SIX

Six is represented by the Star of David and the union of opposites—the symbols of fire (above) and water (below). Community was established on the sixth day after God created animals, trees, plants, and humans (Genesis 1:24-31). The blessing of the community's work represents communication and problem solving (Leviticus 25:21).

SEVEN

Seven is the number of mystery. Seven is the time for assessment, reflection, and rest (Genesis 2:1-3). Seven is also the number of plenty: seven festivals (Leviticus 23:34), seven planets (known in the time of the Bible), and seven good years (Genesis 41:1-36). It's the number of the purifying process (Psalm 12:6). The seven gifts of the Spirit: wisdom, understanding, counsel, fortitude, knowledge, piety, and fear of the Lord (Isaiah 11:2 and 5). And seven symbolizes forgiveness (Matthew 18:21).

EIGHT

Eight symbolizes eternity (8 on its side is the lemniscate), which signals the potential for completeness (Leviticus 23:39, Numbers 29:35). It's also a sign of thresholds and transitions. A doorway has four-sided frames, which from the perspective of either going in or out is eight-sided (1 Kings 7:5).

NINE

Nine is the number of readiness: The Day of Atonement, *Yom Kippur* (Leviticus 23:32). Nine signals a preparation is necessary for a movement to the next level: Abram was ninety-nine and Sari was ninety when God changed his name to Abraham and her name to Sarah (Genesis 17).

TEN

Ten stands for completeness: the Ten Commandments (Exodus 20), and the ten plagues (Exodus 7). The work has finished and we are ready to step onto the next level of consciousness. Ten also symbolizes the ourob-oros of endings and beginnings, both of which require a ritual (Malachi 3:10).

Having a comfortable knowledge of numerology is important in reading Tarot. The early pip cards, like the *Marseille* deck, are absent pictures. Their meanings are determined based on the number and the suit. With decks whose pips have pictures, it's still the suit and number that provide the most significant meaning.

We all journey through each of the numbered cards of each suit many times throughout life. Each card presents the subtleties to our personality. For we all have thinking, feeling, sensing, and intuition within us, just some to more degree than another. For example, if we blend our aspects of being a thinker (Swords) with those of our feelings (Cups), we have an expanded potential for many unique encounters with the Divine. Multiply those thoughts and feelings by their numerical value, and the experience intensifies.

SUITS AND TYPES

Having covered the numerology of the pips, we can now delve into the specifics of each suit. There are four suits in each deck, similar to playing cards: Swords (Spades), Wands (Diamonds), Cups (Hearts), and Pentacles (Clubs). Some Tarot designers have used different images for certain suits. For example: Staffs instead of Wands and Coins instead of Pentacles. The symbolism and its meaning remain the same behind the alternative images. For our purposes, we will stay with Swords, Wands, Cups, and Pentacles.

We'll consider the suits according to their element and Jungian personality type correlation of thinking, feeling, sensing, and intuition. One point to remember is that we can use the suit to help us make meaning of a specific situation in our life or to work with a dream. In this case we would select the cards based on the association between them and the people and circumstance of the issue or our dream. The final chapter will cover in more detail how to use the cards in this case.

SWORDS—AIR

The Swords represent thinking and the element of air. This suit is focused on the rational and systematic process of decision-making. The ego is front and center. The images are confrontational, honest, and filled with shadows. Reading the cards from Ace to Ten can feel defeating as the story travels from bad to worse. From a Jungian perspective, "every gain for the self, is a defeat for the ego." Another interpretation is to follow the story from the Ten of Swords toward the Ace of Swords. This pilgrimage presents the alchemical process from chaos to the phoenix. The suit of Swords reminds us not to over think our day-to-day issues. The Swords in the *Marseille* are bent, suggesting that it might be time to bend our thinking a bit. That said, there's no need to over-analyze which direction any suit ascends or descends. Trust yourself to take the pilgrimage in the direction that works best for you at the moment.

The Bible's account of the sword is two-edged (Hebrews 4:12). One side is for protection, and the other for punishment. God is "the shield of your help, and the sword of your triumph" (Deuteronomy 33:29). The other edge is equally sharp, "You have feared the sword, and I [God] will bring the sword upon you.... You shall fall by the sword" (Exodus 11:9-10). The New Testament wields the sword equally heavy as the Tanakh. Jesus spoke of the two-edged sword: "Do not think that I have come to bring peace to the earth; I have not come to bring peace, but a sword" (Matthew 10:34). And he says later in the same Gospel, "For all who take the sword will perish by the sword" (26:52). The same can apply to the Tarot's Swords. There are always two sides to every thought, idea, or plan. Think through them carefully.

The *Rider-Waite-Smith* deck portrays the Ten of Swords with ten weapons plunged into the character's back. The person is lying face down on the ground. The image challenges us to think anything but negative thoughts about drawing this card. It doesn't take much imagination to see that this poor soul is dead. This card represents the alchemist's first stage of transmutation—chaos. Every opportunity for innovation begins with an insurmountable problem. The Swords are trying to teach us not to give up, but to stay the course. This suit is like a horror novel—it starts off bad, then things get worse before they solve the riddle and all is well. No one knew this story better than Job, who we explored earlier in this book.

The next card in the series, Nine, depicts despair, cruelty, and entrapment. It's hard not to think that Chicken Little's story is true: the sky is falling; the world is going to end; and the Apocalypse is upon us. The simple thing to do is to throw in the towel, tap out, and give up. The problem is that the problem won't go away. No matter how far we run from it, deny or suppress it, the dark cloud continues to hover over our head (Job 27:21). As the Irish say, "Wherever you go, there you will be."

Then comes the Eight of Swords. Within the center of the storm, there is a moment of quiet in which we experience a strange sense of stability. We know the storm isn't over, yet we've seen the sun skirting around the edges of the clouds of chaos. Our thinking is telling us not to trust our intuition. The temptation is to double down on the details of our difficulty, but that only repeats the cycle that got us where we were in the first place. The Eight of Swords reminds us that "Indeed over all the glory there will be a canopy. It will serve as a pavilion, a shade by day from the heat, and a refuge and a shelter from the storm and rain" (Isaiah 4:5-6). In Julian of Norwich's words, "All will be well."

With the Seven comes the reminder that the stakes are high. We're engaged in the risky work of soul-retrieval. We're desperately trying to "work out our own salvation with fear and trembling" (Philippians 2:12). By now, you have a plan; work that plan. And amid your work, blind spots may arise, shadows of the fear of failure will emerge. Confront your blind spots, work with them. Now is the time to lean into your strategy and believe in yourself (Isaiah 4:1).

With the Six of Swords, help is on its way. You've come to realize you are not alone; "we are surrounded by so great a cloud of witnesses… so that you may not grow weary and lose heart" (Hebrews 12:1, 3). Many have walked the same pilgrimage before and their footprints may be faint, but they have paved the way. Our spiritual allies and angels are speaking their truth into our soul.

You're halfway through this trial. But the doubts close in with the Five of Swords. Something fails. It feels like a self-fulfilling prophecy. You thought it couldn't get worse, but it did. Yet, if you step back, you'll recognize that this was only a setback, and it can be overcome. People have died by the sword, and families have sat on the ground in lament. But "On that day the branch of the Lord shall be glorious…for the survivors of Israel" (Isaiah 3:25-4:2). As my grandmother used to say, "It's time to put on your big girl boots."

At some point, we all need to drop our backpack and take a break. The Four of Swords encourages us to reserve some significant time for reflection. Now is the moment to get on the balcony and scan the bigger picture. Journal and contemplate on what you see. "Be still in the Lord and wait patiently" (Psalm 37:7). Get in touch with the other edge of your sword—balance the opposite side of our thinking and lean into our feelings.

During our reflection, the thoughts we had buried deep within ourselves may pierce our heart like the Three of Swords. The ancient adage says, "The tears of the soul water the rose." Even for the rational thinker, the emotions can rise to the surface when we quiet our mind. Three times in the Bible we are told that Jesus wept: in grief over the death of his friend, Lazarus (John 11:35); over the city of Jerusalem (Luke 19:41); and as the great high priest, he shed tears on behalf of his flock (Hebrews 5:7). Jesus modeled for his followers that thinking about our feelings and feeling about our thoughts is an honorable path forward.

The Two of Swords signals the need for decisions. Every day is consumed by a multitude of choices, some of them quite significant. I had a friend tell me, "If God would only tell me his plan, I would do it." Growing up, my church leaders told me that God had a specific path for my life. They intimated that knowing God's will was only a perfect prayer away. And they also stated—quite plainly—that God's will meant being faithful to the tenants of the church. Discernment, however, is a process that can lead us to making wise decisions that others may not understand.

The author of the New Testament letter of James offers a path for this process: "The wisdom from above is first pure, then peaceable, gentle, willing to yield, full of mercy and good fruits, without a trace of partiality or hypocrisy. And a harvest of righteousness is sown in peace for those who make peace" (James 3:17-18). And the psalmist provides us with a four-step exercise for discernment. The process is about the work of being at one with the One, which has nothing to do with knowing God's will in regard to making a specific decision. The spiritual work entails trust, delight, commitment, and stillness (Psalms 37:2-7). Jeremiah encouraged us with God's words: "When you search for me, you will find me; if you seek me with all your heart, I will let you find me" (Jeremiah 29:13-14). I find all these texts comforting, in that nothing here has anything to do with the dogma of the church. Nor do they say anything about God having one specific plan for our life. These readings, however, have everything to do with the work of our spiritual unity with God, which is most likely the Divine's singular desire for our life.

The Ace of Swords represents the experience of Oneness. Peace has settled within our soul. We have the knowledge of an inspired intellect, clarity, and originality. Our process has yielded the gold of soul-making. "Faith without works is dead" (James 3:14-26). We have made our way through the path of the Swords, thankfully in one piece. The fruit of our labors will reveal a new and unique insight, an innovation that can bring significant change.

CUPS—WATER

The Cups are the suit of feelings, which are at the root of our emotions. Cups symbolize water, the unconscious, which includes dreams and the imagination. These images can provide a language for emotions that rise to the surface. Emotions that are not processed will overwhelm us and, at times, display as irrational actions. The Cups are the cauldron for the heat of our emotions. And sometimes we feel blue (the symbol of feelings). Depression may set in. True, the psalmist said that "[God] heals the brokenhearted and binds up their wounds" (Psalm 147:3). But the world of the unconscious and its shadows are no easier to deal with than the thoughts of the Swords. We do not have to manage our emotions and our feelings on our own. My therapist listened to me for twelve years and gently showed me how to find my way out of the dark. Please ask for help when you need it.

With the Ace of Cups, we acknowledge that we were born from water. Born from the emotions of childbirth. The image of the beginning of life is at the heart of baptism as new birth in the Christian tradition, as well as other religions who incorporate a ritual of water. In many ancient traditions, they also ritualized the act of the dead returning to water. Buried in the vast sea, it completed the circle of life (Revelation 22:1-2). All things arise from the watery unconscious and return to the ocean of the unconscious. Hermes Trismegistus said, "As above, so below, as within, so without, as with the universe, so the soul." The Ace of Cups is a picture of what was before there was an above and below. That which is before your beginning, when you *were,* but not yet material in this universe. You were a feeling before you were a thought.

The dream world is the portal of the unconscious often depicted as water and the gateway into our consciousness. The Two of Cups is the experience of making love in a dream. If Jung is correct, our dream love-making is the inner imagination of our Ego mating with our Self—two becoming one. Being uncomfortable with that image is a sign that it's time for some self-reflection. From the Gospel of Thomas we hear Jesus say, "When you know yourselves, you will be known and you will understand that you are children of the living Father. But if you do not know yourselves, then you live in poverty." To know oneself is to experience one's self intimately—the totality of one's true self—one's inner being and one's outer being.

Traditionally, the image on the Three of Cups is known as the Three Sisters. "My child, keep my words and store up my commandments with you.... Say to wisdom, 'You are my sister,' and call insight your intimate friend" (Proverbs 7:8). The Three Sisters—the human, the wisdom, and the insight—represent the elements of earth (human), air (wisdom), and fire (insight). Yet the three are incomplete without water. Three is the formation of the triangle, the generator of energy and the potential for the creation of the fourth, that which is the integrated being. Maria the Jewish prophetess, possibly the first alchemist of the Western world, said, "One becomes two, two becomes three, and out of the third comes the one as the fourth."[114] Three is unstable as a creative force; not to be feared but tended with care. Too little heat, nothing happens, too much heat and a disaster erupts. Too little emotion, passionless; too much emotion, a shit show.

With the Four of Cups comes the understanding that stability can be deceptive. All things are good. Everything is going along just fine. Similarly, the biblical prophet Samuel established the Ebenezer stone, a symbol that "Thus far the Lord has helped us" (1 Samuel 7:12), but Samuel wasn't near the end of his work. Truth was, rough waters were just ahead. He was about to retire. He had returned home, built an altar, and prepared his sons to take over his work, but his plan turned sour. His sons failed to lead successfully, and in response the people of Israel demanded a king. Institutional and personal stability is an illusion. The Four of Cups can be like building The Tower. We can erect a standing stone and sit back and admire it while we wait for it to fall on us. Or we can build The Tower and pray for God to strike it with lightning, giving enough emotional charge to complete our pilgrimage. Weird on either account, but the latter is proactive, while the former is fatalistic.

The Five of Cups reminds us that we always need to be working toward complete integration. There will be days when some of the Cups will be knocked over and their contents spilt. The temptation is to sit on the ground and wail about our losses. But the work is 1) to acknowledge that some Cups are still standing, and 2) in most cases, the others can be set upright and refilled. It's all a matter of perspective.

After the turbulent work we've encountered in the Five of Cups, some emotional healing is needed. The Six of Cups is about the process of emotional recovery. One that requires community support—our family, a mentor, coach, spiritual director, pastor, therapist, or small group. We do not need to walk our pilgrimage alone. The Lord said, "I will satisfy the weary, and all who are faint I will replenish." And the prophet Jeremiah responded, "I awoke and looked, and my sleep was pleasant to me" (Jeremiah 31:25-26). For the Cups to be replenished we must rest and then we will be able to wake up to our purpose and calculate our next steps.

As our emotional wounds heal, we're often faced with choices about how to move forward. More often than not, all the options could turn out to be good ones. The Seven of Cups is a warning to take our time. Don't move too quickly, be patient. Jesus tells the parable of the person who swept and organized their house, clearing out one demon [shadow]. Surprisingly, then, seven other demons appeared (Luke 11:24-26). Maybe it's better to make friends with the demons we have. Let them join our circle and listen to them. Once they feel heard, they might quiet down a bit. As Jesus taught, the demons will never go away. Before we decide how to move forward, evaluate the options carefully.

Emotional soul work requires a significant amount of craftwork and that's what the Eight of Cups is about. Our goal is to construct a reliable boat that can float on the sea of unconsciousness, a vessel that can withstand the emotional storms that could drown our soul. Craftwork of the soul demands attention to detail. Our best spiritual practices are often the simplest, but we must be consistent with them for their benefit to be affectual. Check your ship for leaks before you shove out onto the dark sea (Ezekiel 27:1-6).

With the Nine of Cups, we've come to feel that we don't have to live our life entirely on the unconscious waters. There must be a safe harbor, a home of security, where we can spend valuable time with those we love. "Then they were glad because they had quiet, and he brought them to their desired haven" (Psalm 107:30). Here, in this place of safety, we can acknowledge the strenuous work of integrating our feelings and our thinking. And we can accept the praise of, "Well done thou good and faithful servant" (Matthew 25:23).

The Ten of Cups acknowledges that our humbling process of integration is over for now; our capacity for love has expanded. We hear God's words singing in our ears. "I have set my bow in the clouds, and it shall be a sign of the covenant between me [God] and the earth" (Genesis 9:13-17). Now is the time to celebrate, dance, and look at the rainbow of promise; emotional stability is something we all can have.

PENTACLES—EARTH

The Pentacles (sometimes called Disks or Coins) are the cards with which we explore with our five senses. Through them, we perceive what the majority of the world considers to be material reality. Physicalists say that if I can't see, touch, smell, taste, or hear it, then whatever we might be imagining doesn't exist. It is therefore not real. Modernity brought us physicalism (materialism) and the supposed disenchantment of the world. My guess is that if you're reading this book, you probably don't buy into this myth. You might not accept the notion of ghosts, angels, demons, and spirits, but I imagine that God or the Divine or the Higher Power, captures your attention somehow.

Still, in the world of the Pentacles, nothing is enchanted. That doesn't mean the archetypes behind the cards are atheists, but they might be very thoughtful agnostics. And while these cards are about material security, they also include the necessity of self-care as well as care of the Earth, our island home. The first chapter of Genesis stresses human responsibility for the care of all of creation (Genesis 1:28-30). Admittedly, those verses and the misinterpretation of the word "dominion" have been one of the reasons some religious folks have turned a blind eye to much of humanity's abuse of the environment and have been unwilling to acknowledge responsibility for climate change. Okay, sermon over. Back to the Pentacles.

With the Ace of Pentacles, good ideas yield good plans that take shape with hard work. Every successful endeavor begins with a well-thought-out plan (Swords), *and* an excellent budget (Pentacles). "For which of you, intending to build a tower, does not first sit down and estimate the cost, to see whether he has enough to complete it?" (Luke14:28) The Ace of Pentacles is a reminder to begin at the beginning. And don't get ahead of yourself. You can dream all you want, but without a good plan and the resources to back it, you'll never be able to finish the project. And of course, your plan, along with a healthy line of credit to support your brilliant ideas, will never come to fruition without the physical work necessary to build the tower.

With the Two of Pentacles, we see that once you have a plan, you need to consider all the things you don't know that you need to consider. The old adage that two heads are better than one is the Two of Pentacles' motto. Every book needs an excellent editor, and every contractor needs a skilled crew. For twenty years, I was a college baseball coach. Over time, I realized that coaches never won games; they could only lose them. The coach is only as good as the players on the field who are playing the game. But even with talented players, magic only happens when the chemistry among the players is brewing, and for that magic to be affectual it must extend to the relationship between team and coach. The Two of Pentacles is pressing us to find partners for whatever endeavor we're planning, co-creators that can build a healthy and powerful chemistry. The Acts of the Apostles, the fourth book of the New Testament, opens in an upper room. Together, the disciples of Jesus, his mother and brothers, and other women, "were constantly devoting themselves to prayer" (Acts 1:12-14). Soul to soul, committed to the plan of Jesus who said: "Peace be with you. And as God has sent me, so I send you" (John 20:19-21). A simple plan that would cost many of them their material lives, but *together* they would change the world.

The Three of Pentacles reminds us that the temples and cathedrals that have endured for centuries are stone structures with a solid foundation. Each with a cornerstone that has bonded the individual building blocks into a collective strength for generations (Isaiah 28:16). The Bible doesn't mention the pyramids, but they were most likely built 1,000 years before Moses. For whatever reason, the writers of Genesis ignored them. However, their architectural marvel is worth recognizing as a model for the Three of Pentacles. The materiality of the triangle had been spiritualized by the Egyptians, particularly in Aleister Crowley's *Thoth* deck. Mystic Manly P. Hall writes in *The Secret Teachings of All Ages*, that the "Great Pyramids [are] a standing sermon," a testimony to the union of the material and the spiritual.

With the Four of Pentacles in hand, we are reminded that in order to maintain our material stability we must set aside some time for self-care of the body. Jesus made it very clear that his disciples needed time to get away and renew their mind and body, to eat and to rest (Mark 6:31-32). Sometimes our daily tasks feel overwhelming, and many times they are. But we can't solve all the world's problems, must less ours, if our collective mind-body-soul is not healthy.

By the time the Five of Pentacles arrive, you're halfway through your project. You might feel like you're walking in two worlds. There appears to be only two options: press forward, or let go of what you've been working on in the material world. Discernment is critical at this crossroad. "The wise mind[body] will discern both the time and way" (Ecclesiastes 8:5). Patience breeds endurance.

With the Six of Pentacles, your project is producing positive results. The balance sheet is leaning toward the better side of the ledger. The team is winning at least half of its games. Your painting looks like the model. Now is the time to let the world in on your secret. You don't want to boast but you do want to share; to give back. "Generous and ready to share" (1 Timothy 6:18).

The Seven of Pentacles warns of the fear of failure and its ability to prematurely shut down some otherwise great projects, innovations that had so much promise. You have planted the garden, now you must see it through. Our best investment is in our potential. We must believe in ourselves, trust in our work in such a way that others can see our vision and will want to join us in our endeavors. "Write the vision; make it plain, so that others may read it" (Habakkuk 2:2).

Here's an Eight of Pentacles. You are finally feeling like you know what you're doing. You've moved from apprentice to a respected person of your craft. Others recognize your well-developed skills and are seeking your advice. "An intelligent mind acquires knowledge, and the ear of the wise seeks knowledge" (Proverbs 18:15). You are experiencing the stability that comes with a great plan well-executed.

You're holding the Nine of Pentacles. Yeats envisioned the Tree of Life as twenty-one cones. Each cone leads to the next higher level of consciousness. Collectively, the cones are a series of advanced stages that lead us to a holistic perspective. There isn't a destination of achievement, simply a perpetual process of evolution. The Apostle Paul complained that his students never seemed to be able to graduate from Spiritual Practice 101 to Spiritual Practice 201, much less to a graduate level class. The Nine is encouraging us to look ahead to what's next. We've accomplished what we've set out to achieve, but we know the master of the craft is always trying to improve.

With the Ten of Pentacles, you've arrived at a point where you can see that the material and the spiritual are one. What you've created has a life of its own. The ceramic bowl you took out of the kiln has come alive with colors you never could have imagined. The students you taught five years ago have graduated and are coming back to say that you were their inspiration. The business you almost gave up on is now taking on interns who stand in line to soak up your knowledge. You have graduated into the material/spirituality of nondualism. Craftwork is soulwork and soulwork is craftwork—indistinguishable, one and the same.

WANDS—FIRE

The Wands represent our intuition—our spirit. This suit mirrors our spiritual alchemical process. Simply put, in every stage of our maturation, we must tend the fire; as stated before, too little heat, nothing happens, too much heat, and brace yourself for a bonfire.

Spiritual alchemical phases move on a serpentine path from chaos, to cracking the egg, to the weird raven with the peacock tail, and finally to the phoenix rising from the ashes. This labyrinthine path is the best image of the alchemist's spiritual (or psychological) pilgrimage. Like clay on a wheel, the spiraled process forms a cauldron in which each pilgrim must be about the art of making a cosmic soup. The strange concoction will become a salve that is used for the sake of healing a spiritually wounded creation and those that inhabit it.

Wands correspond with the spiritual practices learned while on the pilgrimage, like healing touch, Reiki, and laying on of hands. In each of these alchemical techniques, the adept is a conduit of spiritual energy between the Divine spirit and those in need. The Wands from Ace to Ten symbolizes the healing process.

The salamander frequently appears on the Ace of Wands card. In alchemy, these amphibians represent new beginnings. The brilliant colors of the salamander resemble the peacock and its connection to rebirth. Energy generated under the eye of the Ace of Wands is filled with mystery and magic. These are the inspirations of our soul's interpretive narrative, often a story infused with fantastical images. "I will pour out my spirit on all flesh; your sons and daughters shall prophesy, your old [people] shall dream dreams, and your young [people] shall see visions," said the prophet Joel (2:28). Now is the time when our intuition will fuel our spiritual imagination. Taking on a new spiritual practice can invigorate the soul.

As our mind-body-soul pours forth its creative energy it becomes incumbent upon the alchemist to engage with their spiritual partner. In this case our ally may reside in the spiritual world: an angel, an ancient one, a biblical character. Or maybe they are an *anam cara.* Courage and intuitive boldness are necessary to bring together two souls, who working in tandem, transmute the fantastical ideas into a spiritual manifestation. Dangerous work that is often misunderstood and typically misinterpreted. In the Second Letter of John, the author writes to "the elder, the elect lady." He commends her spiritual work within the community as "from the beginning." The author and this female elder have been partners in spreading the message of "loving one another" (2 John 4-6). The Two of Wands assures us we are not alone in the work of the Spirit. The work done during the phase of the Two of Wands has engendered potential for the adept to become a master of fire. Brigid the Firekeeper, the Patron Saint of Ireland, was the bridge between Druids and Christians. She was a healer, midwife, an abbess, and advocate for the poor.

The Three of Wands represents the triangle of our ego, unprocessed blind spots, and unrefined precious treasures. We prepare to light our spiritual fire by forming these three branches into a triangle. Underneath them we place the kindling of the spiritual practices we have acquired on pilgrimage. The Spirit will spark the flame from the gifts we have been given and nurtured. We will become like the glassblower who tends "the refiner's fire" (Malachi 3:2).

The Four of Wands reveals that we are at a spiritual crossroads. Our intuition might be challenging us to consider things we never thought were possible. There's an oddity about the fourth day of a walking pilgrimage—it's the day your body accepts your backpack as part of itself. After three grueling days, on the fourth day, instead of feeling relief whenever I took my pack off, I felt lightheaded and a bit dizzy. I had to sit down to re-orient myself. My son, who is a psychologist, told me about the brain's adaption based on inverted images. Each of the participants in a study would wear a pair of glasses that inverted what they saw. On the fourth day, their brain adapted and inverted to make everything look right side up. Again, on the fourth day of this experiment, participants were told the take the glasses off, and almost every person then saw everything inverted. It took another three-plus days for their brains to re-invert back to normal. Such is the experience of day four of fire work. In deciding which road to travel, we have to acknowledge that walking the spiritual path has turned upside down how we think, feel, sense, and intuit life. And in doing so, we may have to summon the strength to travel the dizzy way with a spiritual partner that no one may see.

You're halfway to creating your spiritual tincture, but now a messy, creative chaos has settled in. The Five of Wands is an experience that can be more distracting than troublesome. Like stubbing the toe of your boot, but not losing your balance. Reminding us to pick up our feet; even the best of hikers have had a spill. Still, we maintain our confidence that comes from our experience. Our reliance on the Divine fire has proved itself worthy. "I lift up my eyes to the hills—the Lord will keep your going out and your coming in" (Psalm 121). You've started a new spiritual practice. Don't give up.

With the Six of Wands, you're experiencing a breakthrough. You've tended the heat. The elements in the cauldron are beginning to blend; the soup smells wonderful, but it's not quite ready. Maybe a little more salt? Less heat? Taste it again. Oh, it needs a bit more basil. Time to cover the pot. Set a timer and don't walk away too far; success is close at hand. The story of Gideon is a perfect example of the details required in preparation of a meal fit for the angels (Judges 6:19).

The Seven of Wands tells us not to let our spiritual ego get the best of us. I love to cook, but I've made too many mistakes when I became sure of myself. I didn't double-check my recipe because I'd made the dish several times, and so instead of baking soda I used baking powder. Or two tablespoons instead of two teaspoons of salt. It doesn't take much to ruin a cake when the chemistry is off. We can say the same when building a leadership team. Too many extraverts, too many introverts, too many of any type can skew the chemistry. Not that every group has to be completely balanced, but someone needs to be attentive to how the individuals on your team work best together. This is when our intuitive Wand serves us the best.

I've done hours and hours of pre-marital counseling. Occasionally, it was appropriate to administer the Myers-Brigg Type Indicator. On rare occasions, the couple's personality types were identical. Sounds good, right? They share a lot in common so they should be happy ever-after. The problem is they also share the same shadows and projections—which would be the equivalent of a cup of salt instead of two teaspoons. Moses was afraid to speak, so Aaron became his mouthpiece. Two opposites worked well together to lead the Israelites out of Egypt (Exodus 4). There are times when our intuition will be counter to the norm.

An Eight of Wands card reminds us of when things are getting too hot. No time to delay, you must double down on your intuition. The time to gather more data has passed. The team is looking to you for a decision. Sometimes doing nothing is the best option, but this is not one of them. You have experience, rely on it. In Exodus, God told Moses to go to Egypt, but he made every excuse possible not to act. God, on the other hand, needed an immediate response. The Israelites were suffering; no time for delay, get moving (Exodus 3). Light a fire under it.

There comes a time when we must prepare ourselves for a transformative re-centering. Welcome the Nine of Wands. The work is difficult and dangerous. Moses had to stare down Pharaoh. Multiple plagues later, the Israelites were making a run for the Red Sea. Survival seemed impossible. No way they could get all those people across the water. They were all going to die, and then the sea parted. Their adversary was extinguished. Then the Israelites found themselves walking in the wrong direction; for forty years, no less. Don't give up, they were told, there is a promised land. "Every place the sole of your foot will tread upon I have given to you, as I promised to Moses" (Joshua 1:3). The Nine of Wands is calling us to trust in the *spirit,* the unknown, unseen, small voice that beckons us forward.

With the Ten of Wands, now is the time to re-evaluate. Some things need to be burned off. If we're going to make it through the desert pilgrimage we have to unload unneeded items. It is never easy to give up a cherished heirloom, or long-time friend, or a calming habit, or a sacred tradition. All options are good, some even insidiously so that they overwhelm our daily functions. The Ten of Wands instructs us that the flames will consume the phoenix, but *then* it will rise from the ashes. What we burned off will be transmuted. Spiritual flames—the alchemical process—is the proving of metals. For the fire strengthens them. "The crucible is for silver and the furnace for gold" (Proverbs 17:3 and 27:21).

As you may have intuited by this point, the pips of the Minor Arcana are some of the most important cards in the Tarot. They are our map for everyday life because the pips are reliable. Images on the pip cards provide clues for interpretation, but more importantly, they open our imagination to unique possibilities, specifically built upon our individual nature. In working with the pips, remember, they apply best to circumstances, situations, and the issues of our daily life. The cards will reflect back to us what's happening underneath the surface of these events. In the final chapter I'll give you some specific examples of how to read the cards in concert with one another, assisting us in times of complex discernment.

And now as we move to the court cards, and the people in our life, the ride can get pretty turbulent.

— *CHAPTER 27* —

THE COURT OF CARDS

A close friend of mine, a Tarot master, starts his classes with the pips. Following his delightful stories about how the numbered cards can shine a light on our little secrets, he instructs his students to pull out all the court cards and separate them from the deck. With flair, he says, "Throw those cards over your shoulder and never look back. They're of no use and we're better off without them." His suggestion is worth considering, but I won't go that far. Like our families and friends, royalty can either be romanticized or demonized.

Written somewhere near the seventh century BCE, the author of Deuteronomy knew all too well the pitfalls of a king. The king should be humble, resist empire-building, and follow the Book of Law (Deuteronomy 17:15-20). God seems to have thought that these were reasonable guidelines for any leader. But in ancient days, they were often ignored until King Josiah (621 BCE), the reformer, appeared on the scene. He set the rule of the monarchy back on its original intent, with some favorable results (2 Kings 22, Matthew 1). But few of the latter kings would follow in his footsteps.

The Tarot has built within its system a reminder of how the royal court should operate. But those early Tarot designers and artists also understood the monarchy and their human tendencies all too well. And for those of us who don't live under the rule of a royalty, the archetype of family dynamics will emerge within the court cards. We all seem to have people interacting with us every day who act like kings, queens, knights, and pages.

FEATURES OF COURT CARDS

Most Tarot decks follow the *Rider-Waite-Smith* configuration of the court cards: King, Queen, Knight, and Page. Crowley and Harris's *Thoth* deck deviated from this, incorporating the Queen, Knight, Prince, and Princess, while eliminating the King. Crowley's deck is based on the Egyptian god, Thoth, who was ruler of the moon and inventor of writing. *Thoth*, as champion of the moon, follows the linage of the matriarchal royalty, one in which the heir of the ruling person follows not from the king but from the queen. In this tradition, the order of succession is determined by the offspring of the queen and the knight. It's the knight who has come from outside the realm and has slain the king in an epic battle. In the hero's mythic tale, the king must sacrifice his life as the ultimate act of a servant leader. In the matriarchal kingdom, the queen is the true ruler, whether she is sitting on the throne of authority or not. The Bible, at times, seems to understand this line of authority: "Say to the king and the queen mother: 'Take a lowly seat, for your beautiful crown has come down from your head'" (Jeremiah 13:18; see also 2 Kings 10:13 and 11:1).

As I wrote in chapters on The Moon and The Sun, during the European Neolithic and the high Bronze Ages, the social and spiritual systems were matriarchal (from 12,000 years ago to the fourth millennium BC). Creation myths of these peoples told the story of the moon being created first. It was the light of her night star that sustained the Earth. As time went on and the story evolved, the sun was included in the mythos. And *she* (the sun) reigned over the day and the masculine darkness of the moon ruled the night.[115] In this latter story, the feminine Sol (sun) and masculine Luna (moon) were portrayed as sister sun and brother moon.[116] The two orbs represented the eyes of the greater divine. The mutuality of the light of day and the darkness of night—two perspectives, one cosmos, the opposites of the sun and the moon, united—gave the divine perfect third-eye vision. These spiritual constructs were evident as early as the fourteenth century BCE in the Egyptian's worship of the sun as multiple goddesses.

In the modern era, Mexican artist Frida Kahlo (1907–1954) provided insight into the matriarchal system, and the third eye. Her "Portrait of Neferunico, Founder of Lokura" is a unique display of the artist's pain fueled mysticism as well as the ruling Egyptian Queen, Nefertiti. Neferuncio was the love child of the pharaoh, Akhenaten (ca.

1353-1336 BCE), and Nefertiti. Akhenaten was known as a heretic for his attempt to transform Egypt's polytheism into monotheism—the worship of the Sun of Akhet.[117] Kahlo's portrayal of Neferuncio reveals his third eye. For Kahlo, the mystic's eye "indicates the power of her intuitive insight."[118] Professor of Spanish, Mimi Yang, suggests that the painting is a process of "making self," a journey that carries the painter "from self-consciousness, self-awareness, self-knowledge, self-representation, to self-enlightenment."[119] Queen Nefertiti evidently made such a sojourn. She was a beauty among the fairest, and a woman of wisdom and chief counsel to her husband. After his death, some scholars have suggested that Queen Nefertiti served as pharaoh, turning a patriarchal system on its head.

Is the King card necessary in Tarot? No. Consider what life may have been like if the Israelites would have demanded of the prophet Samuel a queen instead of a king (Samuel 8). Even after Samuel outlined the potential ills of living under a king, the people pressed forward for a male ruler. Few of Israel's kings ever lived up the servant leader model. Still, the majority of Tarot decks today maintain the archetype of a king.

The court cards have more of a tendency to reveal the shadow side of our personality than other cards. Among Tarot readers, there's always a question of whether to read reversals, cards that are drawn upside down. My opinion is that every card has both light and a shadow, and whether the card is upright or upside down, we need to take a serious look at both the chaos and light. Our shadows follow us everywhere.

The shadows of some cards are obvious: Death, The Devil, The Hanged Man, The Tower. And the pips have their own dreaded cards, like the Three of Swords and Ten of Swords. But even the most glorious of positive cards, like the Ten of Cups, still have a shadow side. In my own Fool's pilgrimage, I've found identifying the court cards with their shadows helpful, especially when I have faced the pervasive underbelly of institutions, religions, and political leaders.

Whether you chose to eliminate the royalty from your deck, or toss out the King, or rearrange their order of hierarchy, or have your Tarot characters sit in a circle, the archetypes of light and shadow are forever present in our lives. That said, before engaging with the specific court cards of each suit, here are some general similarities among these characters.

PAGE (PRINCESS OR PRINCE)

In general, Page cards are more often than not androgynous in appearance. References to the royal court in the Bible include servants, slaves, and eunuchs, without regard to sexuality. A page might fall into these categories. Psalm 22:9 could have been the plea of any page, "Do not turn your servant away in anger; you who have been my help." The psalmist was making their plea to God, but the king represented the Holy One, so we can easily imagine the Page making such an entreaty to the throne. The Bible does mention princesses seven times, once as being an honored guest and another as being wise (Psalm 45:9 and Judges 5:29). In the stories of King Saul his son Jonathan, the prince, was an heir but did not become king. Though David was not Saul's son, he would be chosen the king. As the ruler, David's son, Solomon (a prince), did ascend to the throne. In the story of Esther, the seven princes had prowess in battle (Esther 1:14). They were the chief of their particular family but were not necessarily the son of the king.

As mentioned above, aside from the *Thoth* deck, the prince and princess are typically considered a potential heir to the throne.

KNIGHT

Often a figure riding a horse, slaying a dragon, or defending the castle. The Tarot Knight is the King's trusted advisor, and/or general. The Bible doesn't use the term "knight," instead, a captain fills this role. Abner was Saul's captain (1 Samuel 13:2, 17:55), and so was Joab when serving as David's right hand (2 Samuel 8:18, 15:19-22). As we saw earlier in the book of Judges, Barak was the leader (captain) of the Israelite military under Deborah's direction. In this case, the knight was loyal to the judge, the queen of the land, and would fit the scenario presented in the *Thoth* deck.

KING AND QUEEN

In chapter 8, we visited the role of the king in more detail as the Emperor. We've seen, how the Bible addressed the selection, authority, and responsibilities of the king in several books of the Hebrew Bible. The most influential queen in the Bible may have been Esther, whose story we encountered as Strength. Bathsheba—who became the queen mother of King Solomon—had sway over King David in choosing her son as his replacement (1 Kings 2:19). And Athaliah, who was a vengeful and ruthless queen mother, reigned for six years after the death of her son (2 Kings 8:26, 11:1-4).

The importance of the Queen card should be placed in the historical and political context of the Bible and medieval Christianity. The sheer inner will and outer force a woman had to summon within herself to reign effectively is probably beyond our imagination. Their stories are often clouded with bias and cultural prejudices. The most prominent queen in the Bible was the Queen of Sheba, which we discussed in the chapter on The Lovers.

When a culture's god was portrayed as male, there was an attempt to balance the father/mother archetypes. The "queen of heaven" was often an acceptable answer. In the Celtic tradition, Maeve was the mythical warrior queen. Her tribe buried her in Connacht, under a stone mound. All future Druid kings would then be required to enter into a mystical marriage with the heavenly Queen Maeve. A similar heavenly goddess appeared in the biblical book of Jeremiah. Most scholars consider Jeremiah's queen of heaven to be the Canaanite goddess of fertility and love, Astarte or Ashtoreth. Jeremiah admonished the Israelites to desist in their worship of her (Jeremiah 7:18, 44:7-19, 44:25). The reign of the Tarot's Queen is a stark reminder of the power of the feminine spirit in The High Priestess, The Empress, Strength, and Temperance, traits we find needed in every leadership role.

Maybe you're like my friend and ready to toss the court cards in the trash. Or, possibly you have already identified someone you know personally, or a politician or institutional leader that looks a whole lot like one the court's royalty. So let's turn specifically to the court cards of each of the four suits.

COURT OF SWORDS

While keeping in mind their similarities, the Swords, Cups, Pentacles, and Wands do have their own peculiarities that set them apart when it comes to the court cards. The Sword's court—the Princess, Knight, Queen, and King—act as warnings against the dark side of The Moon. Symbolically, shadows appear in the Bible as scorpions, dragons, or serpents. In the Swords, we typically find these dangerous figures wrapped around the feet of the character or hanging about nearby. In the final chapter, I have outlined a daily Tarot practice, one that provides a step-by-step method intended to reduce the sense of being overwhelmed by a flood of The Emperor's and Sun's intellectual information. In other words, too many Swords and their shadowy images can lead to a Tarot migraine.

The Princess (Prince/Page) of Swords is the mood fighter who won't allow herself to become entangled in other people's problems. She speaks truth to power. The problem is that she embarks on her chosen lifestyle by withdrawing from her circle of friends. She makes her way through life on her own. If she continues on this path, she'll become the serpent of higher consciousness. Her truth can either cure you or kill you, but no one is ever sure which it will be, least of all the Princess herself. Both Moses, as a young man and Prince, and his sister Miriam are good examples of the intellectual volatility represented by this character (Numbers 21:6-9).

The Knight of Swords is a passionate thinker who questions the logic of everything. He is definitely on a mission to slay the dragon (the ego), but he's in an awful hurry to complete the task. The Knight has become an unpredictable wild card. Similarly, in 2 Samuel 3:26-39 we hear the bloody story of David's commander, Joab, killing Saul's commander, Abner. David had made a pact of peace with Abner but Joab wanted revenge, and so without the king's knowledge or permission he stabbed Abner to death. David's wrathful grief was clear. May "The Lord pay back the one who does wickedly in accordance with his wickedness."

While the Bible has pointed out a few good kings, it has given a lot of attention to a specific character as a terrible example of the King of Swords. Nebuchadnezzar reigned from 605 BCE to 562 BCE. He ruled with a heavy hand over his kingdom and particularly the Israelites who were in exile. King Nebuchadnezzar's story is spread over seven books of the Bible: Daniel, 1 and 2 Kings, Ezekiel, Jeremiah, Ezra, and Nehemiah. "He killed those he wanted to kill…and degraded those he wanted to degrade…he acted proudly," says Daniel (5:19-20). In one word, he was a narcissist. This is the shadow of the King of Swords. Behind that beautiful mind is the dangerous person who has the well-being of only one person in mind—his own.

The Queen of Swords is the ultimate mask-cutter, the keeper of boundaries. She is the mother counselor while simultaneously possessing a child-like curiosity. She appears in the Bible as the Queen of Sheba, who, when hearing of the fame of Solomon "came to test him with hard questions." After being satisfied with Solomon's answers, the king gave her "every desire that she expressed, well beyond what she had brought to the king." There are always two sides to every sword. Solomon's generosity may not have been purely gracious. And later we find out that he did have other motives (1 Kings 10 and 11).

You might have decided by now to *cut* all of the Swords, from Ace to King, out of your deck. Or at least you hope to never draw a card with any kind of sword in the picture. If that's so, you have fallen into the lure of the Swords—they're two edges to every blade. And you can't have one sharp edge without the other. You can't think your way through life without an equal dose of feelings. And you can't feel your way through life without the balanced side of thinking.

COURT OF CUPS

Feelings and emotions are often used interchangeably, but they are not the same. Feelings are how our mind articulates the physical experiences of emotions, like joy, elation, sadness, and grief. When we fall in love, how do we express what's flowing through our body? When we held our lover for the first time, can we tell someone what those emotions made us feel? When a loved one dies, can we express the grief? Emotions can flow to the surface in the terms of tears, celebration, anger, and frustration. Our feelings, then, interpret what those emotions mean to us. Trouble is, we can learn to bury those feelings deep within us, and that can damage the essence of our being. The court of Cups reflect the wide range of our emotions, the joy and loss, in the same image. We must respect and pay attention to the spectrum of emotions and feelings that each card throws our way. Without dutiful reflection, we can become emotionally overwhelmed.

With the Princess (Prince or Page) of Cups, once again, the royal court exposes our shadows that have been hiding in our blind spots. They typically appear—not in meditation—but in awkward moments while we're on the world's stage. We often find the Princess lost in the intimacy of her artistic endeavor. She has intense emotional swings. She can be the wild child who can tame water and fire. The problem is, she may not be able to interpret these emotions. "If the snake bites before it is charmed; there is no advantage in a charmer" (Ecclesiastes 10:11). But love her or hate her, you can't live without the Princess because she might be the next Queen.

The Knight of Cups is the warrior who has been to battle and returned home with the wisdom of a sage. No matter his age, we must respect his well-earned metals of honor as well as his wisdom, which may have come from traditions different than our own. This warrior can speak multiple languages, has experienced the ways of other religions, and has made friends with various ethnic groups. While his friendships come with rich feelings, he does not look through rose-colored glasses. With him comes the unfettered emotional wounds of war: loss of innocence, dismemberment and disability, and the grief of dead comrades. As with the biblical Samson, a warrior's emotions are raw and he feels alone and misunderstood. His home has become the battlefield (Judges 13-16), and now he feels like an alien in a world that may celebrate him but doesn't understand him.

The King of Cups has dreamed of being a leader with material wealth and along the way he sacrificed his capacity for emotions. He feels lost when confronted by the sea of the unconscious, so he masks his feelings. Then he erupts in violence followed by long bouts of brooding, sincere emotional confessions, and tearful apologies. Unfortunately, without outside help like therapy or spiritual guidance, the cycle repeats.

The Queen of Cups is the ever-giving mother, the helper and sustainer who is sensitive and compassionate. The biblical Bathsheba gave everything for her children, her grandchildren, her nieces, her nephews, her students, the neighborhood children, the orphan. Every child was her child, and she wanted to save them all. In return, she needed their love and devotion. And if they don't willingly give her what she needs, manipulation becomes her best weapon (1 Kings 1).

I have found it helpful to pull out the Cup cards when I'm focusing on a life issue that requires more than thinking than feeling. I'll do the inverse when faced with emotional decisions, asking some of the Swords to be my companions. The suits can remind us of our need for balance throughout our life processes. The real beauty of working with the Tarot is not necessarily in the blind draw, but in asking selected archetypes to walk alongside us in situations with sharp edges or turbulent waters.

COURT OF PENTACLES

We are now moving from thinking (Swords) and feeling (Cups) to sensing (Pentacles), and intuition (Wands), a path that will hopefully bring Jung's four interior functions into a state of integration.

The Pentacles represent the sensing function, the exterior world experienced by our sight, smell, hearing, touch, and taste. This suit also symbolizes the material world. That's why some decks refer to this suit as Coins. How we make our money usually gets rolled into the Pentacles. Some people consider their occupation their vocation, and therefore beyond the money they're paid for doing the work. Nevertheless, we live in the twenty-first century, and even if we live off the grid, rarely can anyone survive without material goods. There's nothing evil about the material aspect of our lives.

The Princess (Prince/Page) of Pentacles is the best athlete and dancer in her class. She can make her body do the impossible. She's courageous and focused. Her fearlessness gives her a sense of invincible confidence. Unfortunately, that attitude leads her to take enormous risks with her body. She goes rock climbing without a partner. She dismisses the use of a helmet when she straddles her bike. Her motto is "no one ever died riding a bull." But Saint Paul says, "do you not know that your body is a temple of the Holy Spirit with you?" (1 Corinthians 6:19)

The Knight of Pentacles is a warrior at heart but was assigned to the Army Corp of Engineers. She knows her work of rebuilding infrastructure is vital to the military project, but she longs to be on the battlefront with her comrades. She wants to fulfill her call of duty. If denied an opportunity to live out her dream, frustration can turn to resentment. I think the story of Rahab is emblematic of a unique Knight of Pentacles. She was an outsider yet risked her life to save the two spies sent by Joshua to Jericho (Joshua 2 and 6).

The Earth elements are the King of Pentacles' domain: gold and silver are his politics. He is a materialist. His relationships are most often transactional. He's a master of the physical, willing to push the limits of strength and endurance training, which at his age may not end well. While Naaman wasn't a king, he was the commander of a great army. He had the wealth of a great warrior, but he also had leprosy. However, when given the opportunity for healing, he felt dismissed by God's agent for not receiving what he considered to be an appropriate material remedy. He had to be humbled by his servants in order to see that materialism (Pentacles) often needs a spiritual touch (Wands) (2 Kings 5:1-19).

The Queen of Pentacles is the mother of caretakers. She is an herbalist and a midwife. She is intimate with physical pain and sacrifice. Her connection with nature allows her to physically carry the burden of others, which is often displayed in a dark melancholy. Her shadows can strike out in an attempt to control her environment. The Egyptian midwives, Shiphrah and Puah, who spared baby Moses' life fit the Queen of Pentacles well (Exodus 1).

Working with the Pentacles correspond to ascending the adept's mountain (moving Ace to Ten) or descending (Ten to Ace). The pattern following the cycle of life: ascending from birth to midlife; descending from midlife to death. This model accommodates Jung's perspectives of the two-halves of life. Our first half incorporates learning the rules and practical lessons of life. The second half of life, we become masters of our craft and eventually in our latter days we become a mentor for others. As an elder sage/crone, it is as if we live in a house perched on the highest edge of a grand redwood. From our vantage point we can see the world, and others will ascend the tree to seek our wise counsel.

COURT OF WANDS

The Wands represent fire and intuition, the spiritual aspect of the personality that balances the material. I often hear people talk about their sixth sense as something that should be added to the original five senses, which all engage the material. That "spidey sense," the things we can't see but intuit their presence, belong to the Wands. Dreams roam in this realm, as well as the paranormal like telepathy. Synchronistic events and prophetic knowledge are also aspects of the Wands.

The Princess (Prince/Page) of Wands carries the wand of spiritual liberation. She is open to new possibilities. She is independent and spiritually fearless. However, she may imagine that she has control of the powerful tiger; too much conviction can lead to a flaming disaster. In the New Testament, Ananias and his wife Sapphira thought they were spiritually above the rules of the community. Selling a piece of property, they held back some of the proceeds, while telling the Apostle Peter that they had given the entire sum to the collective. Upon admitting their deceit, they both died (Acts 5:1-11). Considering ourselves in control of the spiritual is a dangerous illusion.

Knight of Wands is the symbol of spiritual evolution. He's also a renegade priest. The Knight represents double fire. He believes that no flame burns too bright and that a few more logs won't hurt anything. But suddenly the house is aflame. The story of John the Baptist is a good example. He was a firebrand: "I am the voice of one crying in the wilderness" (John 1:23). He called out Herod for his illicit relationship with his brother's wife, Herodias. His straight talk cost him his head (Matthew 14:1-12).

The King of Wands must slay his own dragon. The King will always need to negotiate the seemingly difficult path between simultaneously being strong and compassionate. King Solomon prayed for wisdom and understanding and it was granted to him by God (2 Chronicles 1:10). Still, he struggled with weighty demands of being genuinely human. Spiritual authenticity always leaves a visible mark, usually delivered by those faithful to their brand of orthodoxy.

The Queen of Wands, or Queen of Fire and Intuition, is a mystic. Mystical women have been feared by every generation of men. Countless numbers of women have been imprisoned, tortured, and burned because they were misunderstood. Thirteenth-century French Christian mystic Marguerite Porete was burned at the stake for her belief that the laity could be at one with God through the free movement of the Spirit. In the fifteenth century, Joan of Arc was burned at the stake for political reasons masked as heresy, the blasphemy of wearing men's clothing, and having visions. Other women who are now revered were threatened with heresy and other "crimes" during their lifetimes: Brigid of Kildare, Hildegard of Bingen, Julian of Norwich, and Margery Kempe.

Women mystics of the Bible have suffered no less under the scrutiny of the orthodox. The medium of Endor, for example, has either been ignored, explained away, or swept up into King Saul's dubious story as a way of decrying women with mystical gifts (1 Samuel 28). Mystics see the spiritual world through a unique lens; a perspective that brings them unusually close to the thin veil. They may listen to the lament of dead, as did the medium of Endor. She heard the ghostly words of the prophet Samuel and simply repeated his message to the fear riddled king. We need to learn that there is no need to fear the Queen of Wands—lean in, she has the mystic's voice and knows the secrets of desert's sacred path.

WHAT'S NEXT?

Wisdom integrates the intellect, emotions, senses, and our intuition into a mature mind-body-soul. But a person who is spiritually inspired by air, water, earth, and fire is rarely understood by institutional religion. The mystics among us push at the boundaries of tradition, hoping to explore the intimate invitation of the Divine. They rely on experience over dogma. Their rituals evoke the imaginal. They are never afraid to venture into the realm of the spiritually unknown, the thin place. As Mordecai whispered to Esther, "Who knows, maybe you were called for such a time as this." This is the heart's desire of the mystic. Remember, Richard Rohr said we're all mystics. So "Take delight in the Lord and he will give you the desire of your heart," as it says in Psalm 37:4. In fact, that entire psalm could be considered the mystic's path of instruction, wisdom, and enlightenment.

In the final chapter, we're going put into practice what we've learned on our pilgrimage. Collectively, these exercises encompass the range of the Bible and Tarot experience. If you don't have a Tarot deck, now's the time to have one close at hand.

— CHAPTER 28 —

THE PRACTICE OF READING THE BIBLE AND THE TAROT

I the Lord make myself known to them in visions;
I speak to them in dreams.
Numbers 12:6

My dreams have always been a source of inspiration, prodding and provoking me to reflect and reimagine. Some of those dreams have been long and complex. Others were simple and to the point. I dreamt I was tearing pages out of a book and eating them. I've spent a lifetime reading, studying, and writing about the Bible. That doesn't mean I've swallowed everything handed out to me as the only truth. But the Bible has tattooed some lessons on my soul.

A beloved professor at Grand Canyon University, Dr. J. Niles Puckett, was also my Sunday school teacher when my family attended a local Baptist church. Dr. Puckett was the founding professor of Christian studies at the university and had been teaching his undergraduate classes for fifty years. I had the privilege of taking "The Life and Teaching of Jesus" from him.

He began every class with a brief extemporaneous prayer. Then he took off his watch and set it on the podium alongside his Greek New Testament, from which he taught. "I'll take five minutes of questions," he would say in his soft and gentle Southern accent. I remember there were four "preacher boys" who sat at the back of the room. Each and every class they would dominate the five minutes, not with questions, but instead "correcting" Dr. Puckett's interpretations of Jesus's teachings. He listened politely. Then he would pick up his watch signaling the end of the Q&A. Without fail, he would say, "Boys, you may believe whatever you like. And now on to today's lesson." Puckett's words are as fresh today as they were four decades ago.

The Tarot is like a series of seventy-eight stained-glass windows, each telling a story of the soul. As I have discussed, the biblical characters reflect the archetypes of the Tarot. Or, if you like, you can invert that sentence and the point is the same. The biblical stories are about humans and their relationship with the Divine. The Tarot is a collection of stories about humans and their relationships with their archetypal self. It all points to the same conclusion. Life is a pilgrimage on the path of wisdom's way, and the techniques and practices that intersect the Bible and the Tarot can shine a bright light on our daily walk.

No one has cornered the market on Tarot because the narrative is imaginal. In other words, the important thing is what you bring to the images and what meaning you derive from them. Reading Tarot is much like jazz. Improvise, just make sure you're in the same key as the other players. To improvise well, you will need to know how to play an instrument. There is an art to playing jazz, as well as reading Tarot. And as with music and art, mistakes can at times lead to something unexpected, inspirational, and beautiful.

There is no Tarot bible, no one standard manual for studying the meaning of these cards. Archetypes span ages and cultures because their meaning flow and evolve with people and their environment. There are hundreds of Tarot decks and multiple dozens of books on the subject today, including reprints of books written in the early twentieth century. I've been fortunate to study under some excellent teachers who offer classes online and in person. Each brings their own perspective to the psychology and the spirituality of Tarot. None of them have offered their way as the only one.

My recommendation is that if this is your introduction into Tarot, go slow. Too many decks, too many books, and too many teachers lead to paralysis. It's much better to have one deck and one journal that are both well-worn and filled with your thoughts and ruminations. That said, here are some additional considerations for your Bible and Tarot practice.

A SIMPLE DAILY PRACTICE—EXERCISE 1

Not to be a prophet of the obvious, but life in the twenty-first century has the lights on 24/7. There's little time to squeeze something else into our already over-scheduled routine. So, start with a practice that only takes five-minutes a day. All you need is a deck of cards and a stack of 3x3 sticky notes.

On the first day, choose a card anyway you like, random or flip through the cards and pick one that captures your imagination. On the top sticky note, write the name of your card for the day. Next, write your first reaction to what you see on the card. (Please, do not pull out the "Little White Book" that comes with every deck to see what the card means. Or look back through this book. There's time for that later. Besides, you'll ruin this exercise.) Take the sticky note off the stack and put it on the face of the card. Put the card in your backpack, or bag, or your pocket, whatever you carry around with you. If anything in the day makes you think of the card, pull it out and write that spark of an idea on the sticky note.

The next day, put the card with its sticky note on the bottom of the Tarot deck. Choose another card and a fresh sticky note. Repeat this process for seventy-eight days until you've made your way through the entire deck. Then, on a fresh sticky note, write about your experience through the cards. Keep your sticky notes in a separate pile so that you can refer to them later. If you're still interested and intrigued by the Tarot and the Bible, try the next exercise.

EXERCISE 2

Remember what Dr. Puckett said, "You may believe whatever you like." Let's take the previous exercise and add one thought to it. Using the same technique of one card and one sticky note per day—write the name of the card on top of the sticky note and then write whatever connections you can see relating to the Bible, good or bad or nothing. Whatever it is that brings a correspondence between the Bible and the Tarot, write it on the sticky note and then place it on the card and carry it around with you the remainder of the day. Repeat this process through the entire deck. Again, when you've made your way through the deck, use one sticky note to capture what you thought of the experience. Take the sticky notes off the cards and place them in a separate pile. If you're still interested, let's move on to something else.

EXERCISE 3

Using the sticky notes that you've created in the previous two exercises, match the notes from exercises one and two with the Tarot card. Now you have seventy-eight cards with two sticky notes on each. Again, only using one card a day with its two sticky notes—add a fresh sticky note and look for any correspondences between your first and second sticky note. I'm sure what you've already realized is that you're building a relationship with the cards. You're establishing your own meaning with the archetypal images and what you know about the Bible.

EXERCISE 4

This daily exercise will take about fifteen minutes. To get started, it will take about thirty minutes for this one-time setup. You will need a journal with at least seventy-eight pages. Write the name of one card on the top of each page. Start with The Fool followed by the twenty-one Major Arcana. Then take the cards from each suit: Ace through Ten and the four court cards arranging them in the order you choose. Take the three sticky notes for each card that you created in the above exercises and place them on the appropriate page. Beautiful, you have now organized your Tarot journal. Each day, shuffle your cards and draw one card randomly. You can use the information from this book (or any other) to make a few notes about the card you've drawn on its corresponding page. Put a blank sticky note on your card and carry it around for the day. Journal about what has happened during the day that has been reflected back to you from the Tarot card. Take note of any biblical character representations or archetypal symbols that appear in the day. Transfer your sticky note into your Tarot journal.

Work with the exercise for at least a month. Most likely, you will draw a card you have already worked with before you have drawn every card in the deck. When you do, work with the card again. We are constantly learning new things about the cards, the archetypes, the images and their biblical correspondences.

EXERCISE 5

This daily three card draw can take ten to twenty minutes, depending on how deep you dive into data gathering. All the information you'll need is in your Tarot journal and this book.

Shuffle your deck and randomly chose three cards. Lay them face up, horizontally, in front of you. The card to your left reflects what's been happening the last few days, weeks, or months. The card in the middle is a mirror of how you're feeling at this very moment. The card to your right is suggesting what you might lean into for the coming day. This card is not forecasting your future. It's like the dream you had last night being interpreted for you and now you can put what you've learned into action. The three cards are to be interpreted as a whole. Ask yourself, *How does the card to the left influence the card in the middle? And when we look at all three cards together, how does that perspective influence what the card on the right is asking me to consider?*

For example: I drew three cards this morning; Nine of Cups, Ace of Pentacles, and Strength. This is how I read this draw.

- ◊ Nine of Cups: My wife and I just signed off on the proofs of our recent book. We've been basking in the elated feeling of holding the proof copy in our hands. That feeling is very satisfying.
- ◊ Ace of Pentacles: At the same time, I am writing this book; what Annie Lamott calls the "shitty first draft." It's free flowing and creative—putting ideas to paper without editing.

◊ Strength: My wife and I both have aging parents. My sister is developmentally disabled and I am her guardian. We're constantly facing tough decisions. Every day brings a new challenge. The card is suggesting I lean into two of the meanings for the card: 1) stay strong, and 2) I'm not alone. Our family is a source of courage and they are very willing to help if I will simply ask them.

This draw was helpful for me. The three cards in correspondence reflected to me that I rarely allow myself time enough to enjoy an accomplishment. I'm always looking ahead to what's next.

While my wife and I were in the details of editing our co-authored book, I was working on this one. I have not given myself time to celebrate, and I should. It's okay to "make a joyful noise" (Psalm 100). As others have said, I write to save my soul. While I'm not totally sure what that means, I know writing keeps me sane. As an introvert and a writer, I can travel deep into myself easily (Isaiah 35). And then a problem arises. I can stay in that mindset. I can easily lean into Proverbs 31:8; "Speak out for those who cannot speak," while also forgetting to ask my wife and our adult children for assistance (Psalm 128:3). Sometimes it takes more courage to ask for help than it does to simply "get the job done."

The best thing about this process is—*There is no right way!* All that matters is how you relate the images on the cards to your life. If this is helpful—by all means keep working with it. If this process does not work for you—then don't spend another minute trying to make it work for you. If you're still curious, what follows are some "going deeper" exercises.

STEPS TO GOING DEEPER

Some people know more about Tarot than others. So what? Everyone is the Tarot master of their own life when you're reading the cards for yourself. If, however, you decide you want to read Tarot for others, here are some items to consider.

1. Start by taking some classes from a reputable teacher—do your

research about the person offering the instruction. If you're interested in online courses, check out The Tarosophy Tarot Association at Tarotassociation.net or Tarot Professionals on Facebook. Each is an excellent resource for finding reputable instructors.

2. Study several approaches to reading Tarot. Below, I offer a few standard "spreads." These are the manners in which you display or arrange the cards for a reading. We've already covered two of these: a one-card draw, and a three-card pull. There's no difference between a draw and a pull, it's simply a name that readers use for how you select the cards. You can, however, do a blind draw, typical for a reading. Or you can do "a sort," meaning you look at the cards face up and pick the ones you want to work with.
3. Practice with a trusted friend and move very slowly. Don't take money even if someone offers it to you. If you want to make money reading Tarot, find a full-time mentor.

DISCERNMENT: MAKING TOUGH DECISIONS

Life brings us opportunities and challenges. How we process them may be more important than the decision itself. I will be upfront: I do not believe God has one perfect will for your life other than "to love God; to love your neighbor as yourself; and to love your enemy" (Deuteronomy 6:5, Leviticus 19:18, Luke 10:25, Matthew 5:44). And while you're working on that list of the most difficult commandments of all time, consider how Jesus said that in order to exercise his commandment of love, we must give water to the thirsty, feed the hungry, clothe the naked, visit the sick and those in prison, and welcome the stranger (Matthew 25:35). God doesn't usually "call" us to a specific job or situation, but to a "holy life" (1 Timothy 1:10). Everything else is pretty much left to your own best judgment, including—what kind of career you want, do you want a life partner, who that partner might be, having children or not, where you live, who you work for, or are you your own boss, or any other decision you consider life affecting.

God gave you a mind-body, which collectively is your soul. You have been given the opportunity to expand your wisdom that you can use in the practice of discernment. That's a fancy way of saying, you're facing a life altering decision and you need a process in order to make a wise choice.

Here's where the Bible and the Tarot can really work together. By combining biblical characters with the Tarot archetypal images, you can create a storyboard. Let's start by discerning whether to move? Please remember, I'm not working from the premise that God's will has a chosen place for you to live. That being the case, it is good to gather some biblical background to assist in your decision-making process. The people in the Bible were nomadic, especially in the Genesis story. Others lived an agrarian lifestyle. There were cities, but we could consider only a few a metropolis. In Jesus's time, about 100,000 people lived in Jerusalem whereas nearly a million live there now. The other places referenced in the Bible were small villages. Even though Bethlehem, six miles south of Jerusalem, was considered the City of David, its population was probably no more than 600 people.

Your first question might be, "Why am I considering a move?" The answers could be many, but let's use the top three cited in a recent survey. Our answer can also help us choose a biblical character and a Tarot card to aid us in our process.

1. *To be closer to loved ones.* Jacob moved his entire family to Egypt in order to be closer to his son, Joseph (Genesis 46). As Jacob was on his way, he stopped in Beer-sheba to pray; there, God assured Jacob that he would not travel alone. A corresponding card could be The Chariot. Wisdom Sophia is the charioteer. She is the presence of the Divine on our journey through the desert that is inhabited by dragons (Isaiah 35).
2. *Job opportunity.* The Apostle Paul was constantly on the move. Of course, you say, he was a missionary. But he was also on the run. Either way, he moved a lot. With that in mind, he wrote to the people of Philippi, "Finally beloved, whatever is true,

whatever is honorable, what is just, whatever is pure, whatever is pleasing, whatever is commendable, if there is any excellence and if there is anything worthy of praise, think about these things. Keep on doing the things that you have learned and received and heard and received and seen in me, and the God of peace will be with you" (Philippians 4:8-9). The Fool would be a good option for the discernment of moving for a job opportunity. The Fool would be in sync with Saint Paul's encouragement. Let's think on the positive.

3. *Livability.* Psalm 34:1-2 makes it pretty clear that wherever you go, God will be there. "The earth is the Lord's and all that is in it, the world and all who live in it; for he has founded it on the seas and established it on the rivers." You want to live in the city, God is there. You want to live in the countryside, God is there. You want to live by water, God is there. The World card is a perfect companion for discerning your options of livability.

Using what we've learned, let's focus on reason two: considering moving for a job opportunity. Saint Paul is our companion and The Fool our archetypal image. Here's where the imaginal comes into play; "play" being the operative word. Yes, I know you have to make a serious decision, but without some play, your mind will simply spin, and spin, and spin. If you don't play, at least be honest with yourself.

Okay, here we go. We're going to play like Paul and The Fool are having a conversation about a decision I had to make a few years ago.

Paul said, "So, Gil is thinking about moving to Seattle for a new job."

The Fool, "The weather's better than living in the desert."

"I guess, but that depends. Maybe living without seeing the sun for weeks on end could be depressing?"

"True. But you lived your entire life in the desert."

"Israel has mountains and forests."

"Hmm. Okay. Back to Gil's new job opportunity," The Fool said.

"What kind of job is it?"

"Church something, I think."

"Not too well in touch with Gil, are you?" Paul quipped.

"I saw him yesterday. I was the third card in his draw. I was suggesting he trust his feelings. Besides, his daughter lives there."

"A double down; daughter and career. Are his feelings positive about the job?"

"Yes, I'm pretty sure they are. He was reading what you wrote. I thought that was helpful."

"Thanks," Paul smiled. "Is there something holding him back?"

"His daughter-in-law is pregnant with their first grandchild. And they live in the same city as Gil and wife do. Moving to Seattle would put them a long way away and they would only see the grandchild sporadically."

Paul asked, "How does that make Gil feel?"

"Sad."

Paul asked, "What do you think he's going to do?"

"Tough choice. Bigger church, more money, living in a place he really likes, living close to his daughter. I'm going with the grandchild." The Fool said.

"Probably so," Paul chuckled.

The point of the exercise is to move the thoughts out of our head and onto a piece of paper. When we can see our thoughts on paper, in front of us, it's easier to sort out the issues, apply a little humor, and face what we're really thinking and feeling about the options before us. In my situation, both options were good. I can easily imagine that either choice would have had a positive outcome.

You can use this technique for pretty much every decision you need to make, even if the options are to act or to do nothing. Your biblical ally and your Tarot ally can talk it out. If you like, the three of you could entertain a three-way conversation. The only limits are what Jung called your active imagination.

DREAM INTERPRETATIONS

The following dream process has five steps and may take several days. I've had dreams that have taken months to work out. Jung thought dreams appeared in a series and formed a fluid narrative, and that's the goal of the following technique. Take as much time as needed for each step. The "bigger" the dream, the more complex the process and the longer the interpretative narrative.

Step One. Jung encouraged his patients to use a technique he coined as "dream amplification," which is simple. Write your dream in a journal or on a piece of paper or open a Word document. Make sure you have enough space between the lines to make notes (double or triple space). After you've written the dream, using colored pencils, underline words that stand out to you. Make a note under the word you underlined regarding why that word stood out to you and why you choose the color you used.

Step Two. Using the Tarot, choose cards that represent everything except the people in the dream. Make notes under those images about what they represent in your dream. It only matters what you think they mean, not what some book tells you. On a separate journal page, make note of why you choose the Tarot card for the dream image. Did the color pencil you used to underline the words have any correspondence to the images on the cards you selected?

Step Three. For every person in the dream select a biblical character and make note of them under the person in the journal. Again, in your journal make note of why you choose these characters to represent those in your dream.

Step Four. Being mindful of the Tarot as archetypes, choose cards that symbolize the archetype of each person in the dream. For example, the Emperor (or a King) for a father figure and Empress (or a Queen) for a mother. Make note of them in your journal and why you selected these archetypes.

Step Five. Let the dream settle for a few days, then come back to it. Have you changed your mind about any of the cards or characters you've selected for the dream? Make any changes you feel necessary. Now begin re-writing the dream using the biblical characters with their archetypal Tarot card for each person and the symbol of the Tarot card to express the meaning of the objects. You are now in the process of writing an interpretative narrative for your dream. When I've assisted people with their dream interpretation, I'm always amazed at how this process creates space in the dreamer's imagination and what brilliant meaning they make of the dream. More often than not, the dreamer tells me either the biblical character, or the Tarot image, or both, spoke to them and helped them make sense of the dream.

SPREADS

There are multiple spreads to use in reading the Tarot. Each one has a unique twist. The most important consideration is to find one or two spreads that you're comfortable working with and stay with it until you feel like it is time to move on to another spread.

We've already covered a one-card draw and a three-card spread. There are two others I like to use. The five directions spread and the Enneagram spread. The first is fairly simple, the latter not so much. Both involve a circle.

For the five directions spread, draw a large circle on a piece of paper. Mark the top of the paper as north, placing the east to the right, south to the bottom of the circle, and west to the left. The fifth direction is the center of the circle. Draw a card for each of the five directions. In this draw, we will read the cards from east, to south, to west, to north, and finally the center. As with all spreads, I read the cards as a collective narrative. The directions tell the following stories:

> East—represents spring, the rising sun, a new day, a new project, birth and rebirth.
> South—represents summer, harvest, family, children.
> West—represents the season of fall, established career, accomplished at a trade, skill, craft, master teacher.
> North—represents winter, retirement, the season of the sage or crone, approaching the final chapter of life.
> Center—represents the collective mind-body, that which is the soul.

Draw a card for each direction, starting at the east and finishing at the center. Place the five cards face up. Again, starting in the east: *What do you see on that card? What is it telling you?* Make notes on your piece of paper. After going through the five directions, return to the east. How does the direction's story influence how you read the story of each Tarot card? Make notes at each direction. Once you've jotted down what the card and each direction has expressed to you, it's time to read the story of the draw. *What story are you hearing from the collective? What Bible story expresses this narrative?* The key is not to over-think it. Go with the flow, the first thing that comes to mind. Trust yourself. Remember, being able to read the story of the circle takes practice.

The Enneagram spread requires some knowledge about the personality types of this nine-pointed star. If you know nothing about the Enneagram, or very little, but are interested, The Enneagram Institute is an excellent online tool. In *Walking with the Spiritual but Not Religious,* my wife Catherine and I wrote two chapters about the Enneagram that can be helpful in getting started. However, if you have some knowledge of this personality typing tool, here's a technique I used to bring the Enneagram, the Tarot, and the Bible together in a 3-D spiral.

Start by drawing a circle on a piece of paper. Place the nine Enneagram numbers in their corresponding place on the circle. If you have a diagram that already has the numbers and connecting lines that can be helpful in the Tarot read. Decide whether you will use the connecting lines based on your comfort with the Enneagram. I suggest that on your first few attempts of this spread, not to concern yourself with the interior connecting lines between the types and that you only use the Major Arcana. After some practice, you can add in the rest of cards and work with each type's wing and other personality components.

Next, draw nine cards and place them on the Enneagram circle, beginning at one, then two, and on to nine. Once the cards are in place, look for the connections between the personality type of the Enneagram number and that of the Tarot card. An important concept of the Enneagram is that each of us, at some level, has all nine types within us.

Some types are more dominant, while other numbers carry our shadows. With that in mind, every archetype of each Tarot card has all nine types within its character. By using the Tarot characters as identifiers, you can begin to discover yourself in every card and every Enneagram type. Some parts of yourself will be easier to see in the Tarot and the Enneagram type, others will be more difficult. The tougher it is to see your persona in the pair, the more likely that a shadow or blind spot is hiding in the combo. Take your time with this reading. When I have shared this process with my spiritual companions, it usually takes them months to process the full experience.

Here's a brief example that doesn't go into too much detail about the Enneagram types, but is helpful enough in these exercises. I have included a one-word descriptor for each type, which can be found in *The Wisdom of the Enneagram*, by Richard Riso and Russ Hudson.

Using only the Major Arcana, I made a blind draw of cards for each of the Enneagram types. I have included notes for each Tarot card, which came from the notes in the previous chapters.

> One (Reformer)—Justice: impartial, speaks truth to power, balance.
> Two (Helper)—The Moon: life cycle, mother, gatherer of memories and dreams.
> Three (Achiever)—The Star: the light, intuitive, truth bearer.
> Four (Individualist)—The World: completion, androgynous, illuminated.
> Five (Investigator)—Judgement: rising to self-awareness, increased awareness.
> Six (Loyalist)—The Sun: unity, direct experience, pure knowledge.
> Seven (Enthusiast)—Hierophant: teacher, sage, priest.
> Eight (Challenger)—The Emperor: architect, builder, protector.
> Nine (Peacemaker)—The Tower: restructuring, restoration, renovation.

For this exercise, I'm only going to focus on my Enneagram type and my preferred wing (which is one of two adjacent cards to my type). My preferred type is four. My most preferred wing is five.

As a four, I am an individualist. Fours are always imagining what could be. Jacob is one of several candidates as a biblical character for a type four. He was a dreamer. So much so, he limped away from one of them. For me, as I'm completing this book, I've already started another. Therein lies the shadow of the four, the romantic, the day dreamer can find himself sleeping on stone and waking up with a wounded hip. In this draw, The World card is reflecting back to me that the book your reading was nearly complete at the time I wrote this example. The shadow lurking about is my ego telling me how illuminating this book is and that it will be read by many people. That last sentence drives me into my five wing, going back to my notes, feeling the need to ensure that the book is well written and absent of errors. The Judgement card is jumping into my shadows, telling me this book will be dead on arrival and it will never be published and no one would dare read such trash. Good thing I have an encouraging editor. Revise, revise, revise, and revise some more.

While using the Enneagram, the Tarot, and the Bible requires a bit of knowledge for each, I have found that working with the trio has been an excellent tool. One that refuses to let me deny and ignore my shadows. Once I see the blind spot, I can begin to integrate the wholeness of my mind-body-soul.

Reading the Bible and the Tarot in tandem is a practice that can expand your understanding of both. Each is complimentary of the other. In reading the Bible alongside the Tarot, here are a few final things to remember:

1. As Dr. Puckett said, "You may believe whatever you like."
2. Reading the Tarot (and the Bible, for that matter) should be fun.
3. There is no right way to integrate the Bible and the Tarot. Only your way.

4. Go slow. Don't eat the entire seventy-eight course meal in one setting.
5. And, going back to chapter one in this book, not everyone will think that reading the Bible and the Tarot are cool. But that's okay because, going back to number one on this list, *you may believe whatever you like.*

FREQUENTLY QUOTED BOOKS

KABBALAH

Perle Epstein, *Kabbalah: The Way of the Jewish Mystic* (Boston: Shambhala, 1988).

Arthur Green, *A Guide to the Zohar* (Stanford, CA: Stanford University Press, 2004).

Dovid Krafchow, *Kabbalistic Tarot: Hebraic Wisdom in the Major and Minor Arcana* (Rochester, VT: Inner Traditions, 2005).

Heather Mendel, *The Syzygy Oracle—Transformational Tarot and the Tree of Life: Ego, Essence and the Evolution of Consciousness* (London: John Hunt Publishing, 2012).

CHRISTIAN

Valentin Tomberg, *Meditations on the Tarot: A Journey into Christian Hermeticism* (New York: Jeremy P. Tarcher, 1985).

Sallie Nichols, *Jung and Tarot: An Archetypal Journey* (York Beach, MA: Samuel Weiser, 1980).

Williams, Charles, *The Greater Trumps: A Novel* (Grand Rapids, MI: Eerdmans, 1987).

SUFISM

Ayeda Husain, *The Sufi Tarot* (Carlsbad, CA: Hay House, 2022).

Stephania Pandolfo, *Impasse of the Angels: Scenes from Moroccan Space and Memory* (Chicago: University of Chicago Press, 1997).

Stephania Pandolfo, *Knot of the Soul: Madness, Psychoanalysis, Islam* (Chicago: University of Chicago Press, 2018).

GENERAL TAROT RESOURCES

Angeles Arrien, *The Tarot Handbook: Practical Applications of Ancient Visual Symbols* (New York: Tarcher/Putnam, 1997).

Paul Huson, *Mystical Origins of the Tarot: From Ancient Roots to Modern Usage,* (Rochester, VT: Destiny Books, 2004).

Alejandro Jodorowsky & Marianne Costa, *The Way of the Tarot: The Spiritual Teacher of the Cards* (Rochester, VT: Destiny Books, 2009).

Stuart R. Kaplan with Mary K. Greer, Elizabeth Foley O'Connor, Melinda Boyd Parsons, *Pamela Colman Smith: The Untold Story* (Stamford, CT: US Games Systems, 2018).

Stuart R. Kaplan, *Encyclopedia of Tarot* (Stamford, CT: US Games Systems, 1978).

Robert Place, *The Tarot, Magic, Alchemy, Hermeticism, and Neoplatonism* (Saugerties, NY: Hermes Publications, 2017).

Papus, *The Tarot of the Bohemians* (Hollywood: Wilshire Books, 1978 edition).

Rachel Pollack, *Seventy-Eight Degrees of Wisdom: A Tarot Journey to Self-Awareness*, (Newburyport, MA: Red Wheel/Weiser, 1980/2019).

NOTES

1 Anonymous (Valentin Tomberg), *Meditations on the Tarot: A Journey into Christian Hermeticism* (New York: Jeremy P. Tarcher/Putnam, 2002), 605.

2 C. G. Jung, *The Structure and Dynamics of the Psyche,* Collected Works Volume 8 (Princeton: Princeton University Press, 1981), 289-90.

3 C. G. Jung, *The Red Book, Liver Novus* (New York: W.W. Norton, 2009), 324.

4 Stuart R. Kaplan, *Encyclopedia of Tarot* (Stamford, CT: U.S. Games Systems, 1978), 1.

5 Paul Huson, *Mystical Origins of the Tarot: From Ancient Roots to Modern Usage* (Rochester, VT: Destiny Books, 2004), 28.

6 https://biblicalstudies.org.uk/pdf/churchman/016-166_542.pdf, "Bibliomancy," Article VII, 542ff.

7 Dovid Krafchow, *Kabbalistic Tarot: Hebraic Wisdom in the Major and Minor Arcana* (Rochester, VT: Inner Traditions, 2005), 1.

8 https://www.wopc.co.uk/history/earlyrefs

9 https://www.wopc.co.uk/egypt/mamluk

10 Ayeda Husain, *The Sufi Tarot Guidebook* (Carlsbad, CA: Hay House, 2022), vii.

11 Huson, *Mystical Origins of the Tarot*, 39.

12 Robert Place, *The Tarot, Magic, Alchemy, Hermeticism, and Neoplatonism* (Saugerties, NY: Hermes Publications, 2017), 274.

13 Ramon Llull, *Blanquerna,* trans. E. A. Peters, ed. Robert Irwin (New York: Hippocrene Books, 1990).

14 Kaplan, 352.

15 Place, 137.

16 Stuart R. Kaplan, with Mary K. Greer, Elizabeth Foley O'Connor, Melinda Boyd Parsons, *Pamela Colman Smith: The Untold Story,* (Stamford, CT: U.S. Games Systems, 2013), 11.

17 Ibid, 12.

18 Ibid, 76.

19 Christine Payne-Towler, *Foundations of the Esoteric Tradition: Tarot of the Holy Light, Vol. 2* (Noreah: Brownfield Press, 2017), 76).

20 Stuart, 84.

21 Angeles Arrien, *The Tarot Handbook: Practical Applications of Ancient Visual Symbols* (New York: Tarcher/Putnam, 1997), 13.

22 Ibid, 13.

23 Bill Plotkin, *Soulcraft: Crossing into the Mysteries of Nature and Psyche,* (Navato, CA: New World Library, 2003), 248.

24 Sallie Nichols, *Jung and Tarot: An Archetypal Journey,* (York Beach, MA: Samuel Weiser, 1980), 26.

25 Thomas Merton, *Seeds of Contemplation*, (Norfolk, CT: New Directions Books, 1949), 22ff. Also, Thomas Merton, *The Inner Experience: Notes on Contemplation,* editor William H. Shannon, (San Francisco, CA: Harper Collins, 2003), 6ff.

26 Richard Rohr, *Immortal Diamond: The Search for the True Self,* (San Francisco, CA: Jossey-Bass, 2013).

27 C. G. Jung, *The Black Books 1913–1932: Notes of Transformation, Volume 4,* ed. Sonu Shamdasani, trans. Marting Liebscher, John Peck, and Sonu Shamsasani (New York: W.W. Norton, 2020), 220.

28 Jacob Boehme, *The Way to Christ* (New York: Paulist Press, 1978), 218ff.

29 Jung, *The Red Book*, 229.

30 Ibid, 163.

31 C. G. Jung, *Symbols of Transformation,* Collective Word Vol. 5, (Princeton: Princeton Press, 1912/1976) 236.

32 Jean-Yves LaLoup, *The Gospel of Mary Magdalene* (Rochester, VT: Inner Traditions, 2002), 29.

33 Aleister Crowley, *The Book of Thoth* (San Francisco: Weiser Books, 1944/2021), 54.

34 Pierre Teilhard de Chardin, *Hymn of the Universe*, (New York: Harper & Row, 1965), 14.

35 Pierre Teilhard de Chardin; *Writings Selected with an Introduction by Ursula King,* "Science and Christ," (Maryknoll, NY: Orbis Books, 1999), 92ff.

36 Pierre Teilhard de Chardin, *The Divine Milieu* (New York: Harper & Row, 1960), 62.

37 Tomberg, 604

38 *The Gnostic Bible: Gnostic Texts of Mystical Wisdom from the Ancient and Medieval Worlds,* eds. Willis Barnstone and Marvin Meyer (Boston: Shambhala, 2009), 371ff.

39 Charles Williams, *The Greater Trumps* (Grand Rapids, MI: Eerdmans, 1987), 94-5.

40 Ibid, 194.

41 Piers Anthony, *God of Tarot,* (New York: Ace Books, 1980), 17.

42 Corinne Heline, *The Bible and the Tarot,* (Marina del Rey, CA: De Vorss, 1986), 134ff.

43 See John Matthews, *The Grail Tarot: A Templar's Vision* (New York: St. Martin's Press, 2007), 19. And *The Zohar: Pritzker Edition* (Stanford: Stanford University Press, 2004), 2.

44 *The Gnostic Bible,* 497ff.

45 Cynthia Bourgeault, *The Meaning of Mary Magdalene: Discovering the Woman at the Heart of Christianity* (Boston: Shambhala, 2010), 167.

46 Sallie Nichols, *Jung and Tarot*, 92.

47 *Tanya, the Masterpiece of Hasidic Wisdom*, Rami Shapiro, translator and annotator, (Nashville, TN: Jewish Lights Publishing, 2014), 142-5.

48 Stephen Hoeller, A. *The Fool's Pilgrimage: Kabbalistic Meditations on the Tarot* (Wheaton, IL: Quest Books, 2004), 104.

49 Walter Brueggemann, *Theology of the Old Testament: Testimony, Dispute, Advocacy* (Minneapolis, Fortress Press, 1997), 731.

50 William Lindsay Gresham, *Nightmare Alley* (New York: New York Review Books, 2010), 138.

51 Papus, (Gerard Encausse) *The Tarot of the Bohemians: The Absolute Key to the Occult Sciences* (Hollywood, CA: Wilshire Books, 1978), 125.

52 Judith Margolis, "Spiritual Androgyne in the Art of Michael Sgan-Cohen and Carole Berman," *Nashim: A Journal of Jewish Women's Studies and Gender Issues*, (Indiana University Press, Number 10, Fall 5766/2005), 226-242. I borrowed the term from this article in which the author describes how both artists "used gender-ambiguous sexual imagery to explore issues of Jewish mysticism."

53 *The New Oxford Annotated Bible* (New York: Oxford University Press: 2018), 31.

54 *The Complete Dead Seas Scrolls in English*, trans. Geza Vermes (New York: Penguin Books, 2004), 532-4.

55 Christopher Moore, *Lamb: The According to Biff, Christ's Childhood Pal* (New York: Harper Collins, 2002), 29.

56 Arthur Green, *A Guide to the Zohar* (Stanford, CA: Stanford University Press, 2004), 98.

57 *The Zohar: Pritzker Edition,* Daniel Matt, translation and commentary (Stanford, CA: Stanford Univeristy Press, 2004), xxix.

58 Mary McDermott Shidler, *The Theology of Romantic Theology: A Study in the Writings of Charles Williams* (Grand Rapids: MI, Eerdmans, 1962), 3.

59 Lew Wallace, *Ben Hur* (New York: Bantam, 1956/1965), 166.

60 Cynthia Bourgeault, *A Short Course on Wisdom* (Telephone, TX: Praxis, 2002), 30.

61 Barbara Brown Taylor, *The Luminous Web: Essays in Science and Religion* (Lanham, MD: Cowley Publication, 2000), 74.

62 Maggie Nelson, *The Argonauts* (Minneapolis: Greywolf Press, 2015), 122.

63 Jung, *The Red Book,* 226.

64 L. S. Miles, "Queer Touch Between Holy Women: Julian of Norwich, Margery Kempe, Brigitta of Sweden, and the Visitation, *Touching, Devotional Practices, and Visionary Experiences in the Late Middle Ages,* ed. D. Carrillo-Rangel.

65 Ibid, 231.

66 Ibid, 231.

67 Bourgeault, *Wisdom,* 62.

68 Michel de Certeau, *The Mystic Fable: Volume One, The Sixteenth and Seventeenth Centuries* (Chicago: The University of Chicago Press, 1992), 163-67.

69 Jodorowsky, Alejandro & Costa, Marianne, *The Way of the Tarot: The Spiritual Teacher of the Cards* (Rochester, VT: Destiny Books, 2009), 185.

70 *Tanya,* xxxvi.

71 Kelly Brown Douglas, *The Black Christ* (Maryknoll, NY: Orbis Books, 2001), 105.

72 Jacob Boehme, *The Way of Christ,* Peter Erb, trans. (New York: Paulist Press, 1978), 46.

73 *The Other Bible,* Willis Barnstone, editor (New York: HarperCollins, 1984), 433.

74 C. G. Jung, *Alchemical Studies,* Collective Works Vol. 13 (Princeton: Princeton Press, 1983), 46.

75 Morton Kelsey, *The Other Side of Silence: Meditations for the Twenty-First Century* (New York: Paulist Press, 1995), 128.

76 C. G. Jung, *Mysterium Coniunctionis,* Collective Works Vol 14 (Princeton: Princeton Press, 1976), 546.

77 Stephania Pandolfo, *Knot of the Soul: Madness, Psychoanalysis, Islam* (Chicago: University of Chicago Press, 2018), 189.

78 *Tanya,* ix.

79 *Paracelsus: Selected Writings,* Jolande Jacobi, editor (Princeton: Princeton University Press, 1979), 164.

80 Elaine Pagels, *The Origin of Satan* (New York: Random House, 1995), xvii.

81 Ken Wilber, *Integral Spirituality: A Startling New Rule for Religion in the Modern and Postmodern World* (Boston: Integral Books, 2006).

82 Pagels, *The Origin of Satan*, 39.

83 Ibid, 49.

84 Alexander Roob, *Alchemy and Mysticism* (Los Angeles: Taschen, 2006), 304ff.

85 Ibid, 303.

86 Jeffrey Kripal, *Secret Body: Erotic and Esoteric Currents in the History of Religion,* (Chicago: University of Chicago Press, 2017), 1, 15.

87 Susan J. Graf, *W.B. Yeats—Twentieth Century Magus* (York Beach, ME: Samuel Weiser, 2000), 189.

88 Ibid, 189. Graf provides ten lines that had been edited out of "The Tower" in a revised version of the poem.

89 Christine Payne_Towler, *Foundations of the Esoteric Tradition: Tarot of the Holy Light, Vol.2* (Noreah: Brownfield Press, 2017), 21.

90 Hilma af Klint, *Notes and Messages* (Chicago: University of Chicago Press, 2018), 16.

91 Nichols, *Jung and Tarot*, 296.

92 Brent Landau, *Revelation of the Magi: The Lost Tale of the Wise Men's Journey to Bethlehem* (New York: HarperOne, 2010), 93.

93 Place, 469ff.

94 Jadranka Ryle, "Feminine Androgyne and Diagrammatic Abstraction: Science, Myth and Gender in Hilma af Klint's Paintings," *The Ideas of North: Making and Identities* (Helsinki: The Birth and the Star, 2019), 76.

95 Ibid, 155.

96 Hilma af Klint, *Visionary,* ed. Kurt Almqvist and Louise Belfrage (Stockholm: Stolpe, 2020), 82.

97 Marybeth Carter, "Crystalizing the Universe in Geometrical Figures: Diagrammatic Abstraction in the Creative Work of Hilma af Klint and C.G. Jung, *Jung Journal: Culture Psyche, The San Francisco Jung Institute Library Journal*, Summer 2020, Vol. 14, Number 3. 147-167.

98 Af Klint, *Notes and Methods,* 238.

99 *The Complete Dead Sea Scrolls in English,* Geza Vermes, 370ff.

100 Joseph Campbell, *Goddesses: Mysteries of the Feminine Divine* (Novato, CA: New World Library, 2013), 44ff.

101 Llewellyn Vaughn-Lee, *The Lover and the Serpent* (Longmead, UK: Element Books, 1990), xv.

102 Evelyn Underhill, *Mysticism* (New York: Penguin, 1955/1974), 34ff.

103 Cynthia Bourgeault, *The Holy Trinity and the Law of Three: Discovering the Radical Truth at the Heart of Christianity* (Boston: Shambhala, 2013), 173.

104 Meister Eckhart, *The Complete Works of Meister Eckhart,* "Sermon 2" (New York: Crossroads, 2009), 43.

105 James Hillman and Sonu Shamdasani, *Lament of the Dead: Psychology after Jung's Red Book* (New York: W.W. Norton, 2013).

106 *Beyond Physicalism: Toward Reconciliation of Science and Spirituality*, eds. Edward F. Kelly, Adam Crabtree, Paul Marshall (Lanham, MD: Rowman and Littlefield, 2015), 198.

107 *The Pauli-Jung Conjecture and Its Impact Today,* H. Atmanspacher and C. Fuchs, eds. (La Vergne, TN: Ingram Books, 2014), 205.

108 Marie-Louise von Franz, *C.G. Jung: His Myth in Our Time* (Toronto: Inner City Books, 1972/1998), 130.

109 Green, *A Guide to the Zohar*, 18.

110 Ibid, 83.

111 *Zohar,* Matt, 25.

112 Huson, *Mystical Origins of the Tarot*, 25.

113 Marie-Louise von Franz, *Number and Time:* Reflections Leading Toward a Unification of Depth Psychology and Physics (Evanston, IL: Northwestern University Press, 1986), 39.

114 C. G. Jung, *Psychology and Alchemy,* Collected Works Volume 12, (Princeton: Princeton University Press, 1977), 23, 160. See also, *Aurora Consurgens: A document attribured to Thomas Aquinas on the problem of opposites in alchemy,* ed. Marie-Louise von Franz (Toronto, Canada: Inner City Books, 2000), 158.

115 Robert Wang, *The Jungian Tarot and Its Archetypal Imagery* (Stamford, CT: US Games Systems, 2017), 45.

116 Joseph Campbell, *Goddesses,* 44ff.

117 *Ancient Egypt,* David P. Silverman, ed. (New York: Oxford University Press, 1997), 128ff.

118 Frida Kahlo, *The Diary of Frida Kahlo: An Intimate Self-Portrait* (New York: Abrams, 2005), 221.

119 Mimi Y. Yang, "Articulate Image, Painted Diary: Frida Kahol's Autobiographical Interface," *Interfaces: Women, Autobiographies, Image, Performance,* eds. Sidonie Smith and Julia Watson, (Ann Arbor: University of Michigan Press, 2002), 325.

Printed in the USA
CPSIA information can be obtained
at www.ICGtesting.com
LVHW091807250724
786322LV00001B/76

9 781958 972458